p38. chief
p63 The sooth sayer "It is alive"
p75 Chimaria
p78. pirate dolphins
p84 nikosthenes amphora. oranges black brown yellow
p102 satyrs cup.
p114 The goddess of Caldevigo
p119 statue showing dress
p122. The Minotaur
p136. Benvenuto situlae. poem of 7 Venetians
p143 Bronze worshipers
p144 goddess
p171 Kylix - Penthesilea painter.
p224 Egyptian influ
p222. Etruscan - corinthian pitcher
p232 - Human? figures
p847. female head. lotus flower.
p248. gorgon
p865 gold pendant - acorns

The Etruscans Outside Etruria

Paolo Bernardini
Angelo Bottini
Paolo Bruschetti
Giovannangelo Camporeale
Loredana Capuis

Bruno D'Agostino
Ettore M. De Juliis
Luigi Donati
Luciana Aigner Foresti
Maurizio Landolfi

Adriano Maggiani
Alessandro Naso
Rosa Maria Albanese Procelli
Claudio Sabbione
Giuseppe Sassatelli

Edited by Giovannangelo Camporeale

Translated by Thomas Michael Hartmann

THE J. PAUL GETTY MUSEUM
LOS ANGELES

© 2001 Arsenale-EBS
Arsenale Editrice
A division of EBS
Via Monte Comun, 40
I-37057 San Giovanni Lupatoto (Verona)
www.arsenale.it

Original layout: Leda Psallidi

English translation © 2004 J. Paul Getty Trust

First published in the United States of America in 2004 by
Getty Publications
1200 Getty Center Drive, Suite 500
Los Angeles, California 90049-1682
www.getty.edu

Christopher Hudson, *Publisher*
Mark Greenberg, *Editor in Chief*

Ann Lucke, *Managing Editor*
Mollie Holtman, *Editor*
Robin H. Ray, *Manuscript Editor*
Pamela Heath, *Production Coordinator*
Hespenheide Design, *Compositor and Designer*
Thomas Michael Hartmann, *Translator*

Library of Congress Cataloging-in-Publication Data

Etruschi fuori d'Etruria. English
 The Etruscans outside Etruria / Paolo Bernardini ...
[et al.] ; edited by Giovannangelo Camporeale,
translated by Thomas Michael Hartmann.
    p. cm.
 Includes bibliographical references.
 ISBN 0-89236-767-9 (hardcover)
 1. Etruscans. 2. Europe—Civilization—Etruscan
influences. 3. Italy—Civilization—Etruscan influences.
4. Europe—Antiquities. 5. Italy—Antiquities.
I. Bernardini, Paolo, 1963–II. Camporeale,
Giovannangelo. III. Title
 DG223.3E88613 2004
 930'.049994—dc22

                    2004003228

Printed and bound in Italy

Contents

Preface

| GIOVANNANGELO CAMPOREALE

The rich natural resources of Etruria's soil and subsoil were a determining factor in the birth and development of the Etruscan civilization, which was undoubtedly the greatest on the western Mediterranean Sea in pre-Roman antiquity. Having access to valuable primary resources such as agricultural products, wood, wool, salt, minerals, and metals, Etruria had participated in a wide-ranging trade circuit since the eighth century B.C., and it soon became a destination for refined works from the Near East, Greece, and central Europe. Master artisans from the Near East, the Aegean world, and central Europe were also attracted there by opportunities to work for an affluent local clientele, a process that some of the ancient writers explicitly describe. Demaratos, a rich merchant from Corinth, deserted his native city for political reasons toward the middle of the seventh century and moved to Tarquinia, in Etruria. A company of artists followed him, and we even know some of their (artistic) names: Ecphantus (Cornelius Nepos in Pliny *Naturalis Historia* 35.16), Eucheir, Eugrammus, and Diopus (Pliny *Naturalis Historia* 35.152). Despite the fact that we have no specific precedents in the representational art record of seventh-century Etruria, this account is supported after a fashion by the large number of vases from Corinthian workshops that reached Etruria during that century. At other times we can hypothesize the arrival of foreign masters with a high degree of probability. Such is the case with ivory-working in Etruria, which, at least during an early period (from the end of the eighth to the beginning of the seventh centuries), must have been confined to masters with professional experience and the appropriate tools: These masters had arrived in Etruria from their native countries in the Near East together with raw materials from their homelands. But the Etruscan world was not solely on the receiving end. It also exported both raw materials and finished products. Whatever form these exchanges or commerce took, they were rich with cultural implications. As we will see in the following pages, some of these merchants or masters may well have emigrated.

On the facing page, Janus-faced, red-figured *kantharos* with the faces of a satyr and a maenad, second half of the fourth century B.C., attributed to the Clusium Group, from a tomb in Peschiera in Todi (Perugia). Rome, Museo di Villa Giulia

The contributions of Near Eastern and Greek cultures to Etruscan culture have been studied extensively, but the Etruscan contribution to other cultures has not received as much attention. The goal of this volume is to provide a survey of the movement of Etruscan culture into the various regions of ancient Italy, the Mediterranean, and continental Europe: to follow—as its title states—the Etruscans outside Etruria. Chapters have been delegated to specialists on specific subjects, allowing attention to be focused on specific questions that vary from area to area. Naturally, given the inevitable limits of space and the vagaries of evidence, we make no claim to have exhausted the subject. Each chapter is accompanied by an essential bibliography (located at the end of the book), which allows the interested reader to delve further into specific subjects.

Each region posed its own set of problems. The Etruscan presence in Emilia was massive and defining, to such an extent that until the Gauls' descent in the fourth century B.C., the region could be considered an appendage of Etruria itself. In Campania the situation was largely the same. Cultural evidence at Pontecagnano and Capua beginning in the ninth century and at Fratte, Suessola, Nola, Herculaneum, Pompeii, Nocera, and Sorrento from the end of the seventh century indicates that these areas were significantly Etruscanized and remained so until the second half of the fifth century, when the Samnites arrived in the region. In Rome the Etruscans took a leading role between the end of the seventh and the end of the sixth centuries, the period of the Etruscan kings L. Tarquinius Priscus, Servius Tullius, L. Tarquinius Superbus, and L. Porsenna. Then, although a fair number remained, Etruscans in Rome were marginalized from political life and confined to the Etruscan quarter (*vicus Tuscus*). Finally, there are few Etruscan objects in Apulia or

Calabria; they give evidence of trade but do not imply the presence of (substantial) groups of Etruscans.

The situation in the eastern basin of the Mediterranean was different from that of the western. In the former, where civilizations more ancient and advanced than the Etruscans had developed, only a few valuable Etruscan works (generally bronzes) have been found in the great sanctuaries, such as Olympia, Delphi, the Heraion of Samos, or the Athenian Acropolis. In the western basin, where civilizations less ancient and advanced than the Etruscans had developed, massive amounts of less valuable Etruscan works (generally pottery) were found in houses or tombs. Transport toward each of these regions took place by sea.

Etruscan works had been exported to central and northern Europe since the eighth century B.C., but this exchange was elitist and mostly involved the wealthy class. It took place overland, via the great Alpine passes and routes running along river valleys.

The Etruscan products outside Etruria are not as numerous as the Greek vases found in Etruria, but they are not few. What is obvious is that the more abundant the available material is, the broader the cultural horizon it represents, and the more complex and consequently accurate answers it gives to our questions.

The nature and condition of the surviving objects can tell us a great deal: their quantity, dates, methods of diffusion, places of departure and arrival, brokerage, places and methods of trade, the tastes and affluence of their buyers, and the acculturation process of Etruscan customs at various places and times. Local replicas of Etruscan works are also interesting and are a tangible sign of the acculturation process. In addition, the exportation of other

Bronze boat of Sardinian make, middle of the seventh century B.C., from the Tomb of the Leader in Vetulonia. Florence, Museo Archeologico

more perishable or consumable products can be traced from the presence of certain
works, as can the spread of customs. The great quantity of transport amphorae, bucchero vases, and pottery from wine services that were found in various European
areas leads one to deduce the exportation of wine and the spread of the custom of the
symposium—a ceremony centered on wine-drinking—along with its related ideology.
Valuable works can be explained as gifts between high-ranking individuals, although in
all probability they also indicate widespread trade activity. The Homeric poems supply
interesting facts in this regard. The *Iliad* (7.464ff.) describes the Greeks' nocturnal meal
as they camped beneath the walls of Troy. The soldiers drank wine that Euneos, king of
the island of Lemnos, had sold to the army, and their leaders were supplied free of charge.
In the *Odyssey,* Odysseus meets with the cyclops Polyphemus in order to trade wine for
cheese and wool.

The picture of Etruscan exports widens and becomes even clearer by utilizing data
from the historiographical tradition that refers to perishable consumer goods. The
ancient sources tell how Rome turned to Etruria for its grain supply a number of times
during the course of the fifth century B.C. (492, 441, 440, 433, and 411 B.C.). This fact
sheds light on the relationship between Etruria and Rome regarding this specific product, but it also leads one to think that the episode in which Porsenna reached Rome at
the end of the sixth century from Chiusi or Volsinii—inland cities of Etruria whose
economies were largely agricultural—was probably connected to trade in products of the
soil. Wood also played a major part in trade. Livy (37.45.18) recalls how three Etruscan
cities (Perugia, Chiusi, and Roselle) contributed fir timbers to the expedition that
P. Cornelius Scipio prepared in 205 B.C. against Hannibal, to be used in shipbuilding.
Strabo (5.2.5) enthuses over the quality and quantity of Etruria's wood, which fetched
good prices on the markets. The role of salt in the greater economy must not be overlooked, though its traces are mostly hypothetical. Salt would explain the arrival of a
substantial quantity of Euboean pottery in Veii and Rome during the eighth century:
sources date the wars between these two cities over the possession of saltworks at the
mouth of the Tiber to this same period.

In order to evaluate exports correctly, every find must be investigated as to type as well
as date, findspot, and the context of its discovery. The significance of an object can differ
depending on whether it comes from a tomb, an inhabited area, or a sacred district. In
addition, decisive factors emerge on a case-by-case basis and must not be overlooked. For
example, when Etruscan weapons from the eighth and seventh centuries B.C. were found
among the ex-votos discovered at the sanctuary in Olympia, they could have been interpreted as offerings from warriors after a victorious military expedition. When it was
revealed that these were parade weapons, however, they came instead to be interpreted
as offerings from high-class figures, who used them to display their status.

But were the offering bearers Greeks or Etruscans? Sometimes literary or epigraphic
evidence can clear up such questions. Once again taking the example of the sanctuary at
Olympia, a number of Etruscan-made helmets came to light. Each bore a dedicatory
inscription from Hieron of Syracuse identifying them as the spoils of war from the naval

battle of Cumae (474 B.C.), in which the Syracusans beat the Etruscans. These, however, are rare cases, and in general the objects remain open to either interpretation, at least for now. The ethnicity of the transporters in this trade is just as uncertain.

Large amounts of Greek material flowed into Etruria, as we know from both ancient sources and the archaeological record. On the literary side, we have Pliny's story of Demaratos, mentioned above, and also information in Herodotus that the Phokaians "were the earliest of the Greeks to make long sea-voyages: it was they who discovered the Adriatic Sea, and Tyrrhenia, and Iberia, and Tartessus" (1.163.1). On the archaeological side, we have, for instance, an anchor from the end of the sixth century B.C., which was discovered in the Gravisca port area, bearing a Greek dedication from a rich Aiginetan merchant named Sostratos to Apollo. Etruscan materials flowed along similar lines back into Greece. Most of all, tradition tells us the Etruscans were a major presence in maritime traffic, first as a legitimate sea power and then as notorious pirates.

If, as is commonly held, ancient navigation clung primarily to the coastline, ships most likely bought and sold at every port where they moored. The shipwreck from the island of Giglio (late seventh to early sixth centuries B.C.)—with its mixed cargo of Corinthian ointment jars, Greek musical instruments, Etruscan works in bucchero, Etruscan metal ingots, and so forth—gives us some idea of this commerce during that period. In such cases it is folly to propose an ethnicity for the traders. The issue of brokerage is another problem. The provenance of Etruscan objects from places other than the strip of coastline or inland regions suggests a distribution network, which could have been mediated by Etruscans or by other local peoples. Moreover, exchanges or commerce, whether direct or mediated, were the beginning of a more involved process, that of acculturation.

The solutions proposed for these questions, in light of the available data, often appear to conflict with one another, inasmuch as the goods vary according to their historical period, their destination, and their nature. A solution that is valid for one case may represent a model; but it may not be extended to other cases without further verification.

Obviously the line of reasoning followed for maritime routes applies for those on land. If individuals such as merchants, artists, artisans, and political figures arrived along with the raw materials, works of art, or manufactured goods, the effects on the receiving culture were more intense and broader. Rome showed a significant openness toward the Etruscan world and culture during the period of the Etruscan kings, for example, and Vulca, a sixth-century sculptor from Veii who was also active in Rome, exerted considerable influence on artistic production in Rome itself during that era (Varro in Pliny *Naturalis Historia* 35.157). Customs, experiences, and ideas traveled along with these individuals. After all, even the everyday activity of exchanging or trading is essentially a relationship between people; in antiquity such interactions were carried out in accordance with the customs of the time and the sociopolitical organization of a domestic (a palace, for instance) or public (a square, sanctuary, or port) environment. It is no accident that the great sanctuaries—places where people of different ethnic groups commingled—were active centers of this cultural exchange.

Etruscan Civilization

| GIOVANNANGELO CAMPOREALE

Above, the foundations of seventh-century B.C. houses in San Giovenale (Viterbo). These structures are made of ashlar blocks of nenfro, the tufaceous rock of volcanic origin that is common throughout southern Etruria.

Sources of Information

Our picture of Etruscan civilization is pieced together from various sources, both direct and indirect. Direct sources include epigraphic, archaeological, anthropological, naturalistic, onomastic, and place-name evidence; indirect ones include the historiographic, literary, comparative, and folkloric sources. Each source, regardless of which category it belongs to, needs to be placed in context within the period and the environment in which it was produced. The facts gleaned from these sources have contingent rather than general value, value that is transient rather than definitive. They can also represent models—models, however, that may not be applied rigidly but must be checked each time for relevance. In order to clarify these statements, let us briefly set out some of the problems regarding sources of various types, or at least those that are widely in use.

The direct sources, precisely because they provide firsthand information, have a higher level of reliability than others. Among these, epigraphic sources—when they are comprehensible, that is—are undoubtedly the most significant and trustworthy, since they objectively establish a historical event. It suffices to think of the many funerary inscriptions, which give us information about a precise fact—an individual's death—through a standardized language and a (usually) brief text. Nevertheless, in

using epigraphic sources, the location and age of the written objects need to be examined carefully, as do collateral elements such as their type, content, and number. For example, the presence of the Etruscans outside of Etruria has been unequivocally proven by Etruscan epigraphs found outside the geographic borders of Etruria. But this supposedly incontestable presence can also be explained away by collateral evidence. For example, the dedication epigraphs on a number of bucchero cups of Caeretan made from the end of the seventh century B.C., found in the sanctuary of Mater Matuta in Satricum (ancient Lazio), imply only that Etruscans who came from Caere frequented the sanctuary. The Etruscan epigraph on a funerary stela from Busca (Cuneo) that dates to the sixth and fifth centuries, the only evidence of Etruscans in that location, simply points to the presence of one or more Etruscans there at the time the monument was made. An Etruscan text of a commercial nature on a lead panel from Pech Maho, Languedoc, dating to the fifth century, gave rise to the theory that Etruscan merchants were living on the coast of the Gulf of Lion; but in fact they could have been there on a temporary basis. Finally, a religious calendar from the second and first centuries, written

upon a band of linen wrapped around the mummy of a young girl discovered in Egypt, only implies the presence of an Etruscan community at the site where the text originated, not the site where it was found.

Archaeology undoubtedly provides the most numerous and the most remarkable sources. Consequently, they form the richest, and often the only, records for our reconstructions. New discoveries, which especially in recent times have rolled in at regular intervals, yield many new pieces of evidence that can abruptly alter interpretations that had once seemed definite. The case of the Villanovan facies in Volsinii (Orvieto) is a worthy example. Up until the 1960s, there was no cultural evidence that the Etruscans had been there before the seventh century B.C. Then a moderate quantity of clay fragments from the ninth and eighth centuries was discovered in necropoleis from the Archaic period (Cannicella and Crocifisso del Tufo), which were quite close to the cliff where the settlement itself stood. This allowed the birth of the Etruscan city to be backdated by a couple of centuries and, in addition, for the settlement and its related necropolis from the ninth and eighth centuries to be situated on the cliff.

In literary and historiographic sources, information about the Etruscans is spotty and was inserted within contexts of diverse content. Information is often accompanied by value judgments that can be either positive or negative, depending on the writer's pro- or anti-Etruscan stance. These elements need to be critically evaluated through deduction. At the same time, one needs to ascertain whether the information came from the author's personal experience or derived from someone else's. In the latter case, a historical framework is critical.

Above, cenotaph in the form
of a monumental tumulus,
seventh century B.C. At its
center is a trench that was
used for ritualistic purposes
and later filled in with
earth. Inside, an iron trident and an altar were
found. Via San Jacopo, Pisa

On the facing page, Etruria
proper with the principal
cities marked (the Etruscan
and Latin names of the
cities, if known, are in
parentheses)

In the best-case scenario, a fact crops up
in a number of sources so we can make
comparisons and draw more trustworthy
inferences. Sometimes facts from different
sources concur. For example, archaeological
evidence at Volsinii (Orvieto) strongly
decreases during the years around the middle of the third century B.C. This agrees
with information, handed down by ancient
historiography, that the Roman consul M.
Fulvius Flaccus destroyed the city in 264 B.C.,
and that in the process the inhabitants were
moved elsewhere. At other times, the facts
do not agree, at least on the surface. For
example, the dedicatory epigraphs in
Etruscan at the sanctuary of Pyrgi give
proof of the cults of Uni, Tina/Tinia,
Thesan, and Farthan, while a Phoenician-
Punic epigraph mentions only that of
Astarte, and Greek writers noted those
of Ilithyia (Strabo 5.2.8) and Leucothea
(Pseudo-Aristotle *Oeconomica* 2.1349b;
Aelianus *Varia Historia* 1.20; Polyaenus
Strategemata 5.2.21). Here, clearly, Ilithyia
or Leucothea are a Greek interpretation and
Astarte is the Phoenician version of the
Etruscan god Uni, the great goddess who

was the equal of Tinia (Zeus). Sometimes
pieces of information actually contradict
one another. For example, the Villanovan
necropoleis, which are the oldest cultural
evidence of Etruscan civilization, have
produced various finds that point to an
Etruscan connection with the areas of central and eastern Europe. Meanwhile, the
ancient writers speak only of Etruscans
originating in the Aegean basin, more precisely in northern Greece (among the
Pelasgians) or in Lydia. In such cases, the
historiographic sources can be neither
accepted nor rejected, but in either case
must be subjected to criticism and
explained.

Finally, many sources that have been lost
are nonetheless attested. These include
works of literature, epics, theater, mythology, history, and religion in the Etruscan
language that ancient writers have communicated to us through brief abstracts, titles,
or the names of authors. Aulus Caecina,
Publius Nigidius Figulus, and Tarquitius
Priscus made Latin translations of a number of these works in the first century B.C.
There were also works, now lost, written
by Greek and Latin authors about the
Etruscans, such as Aristotle's *Customs of
the Etruscans,* Verrius Flaccus's *Rerum
Etruscarum Libri,* or Emperor Claudius's
Tyrrheniká. The loss of these works
significantly limits our knowledge about
the Etruscan world.

Names

The ancients had various names for the
region where the Etruscan civilization
flourished. The Greeks called it Tyrrhenía
or Tyrsenía, while the Latini called it
Etruria ("Aetruria" in some inscriptions) or
Tuscia. The latter endured the longest.

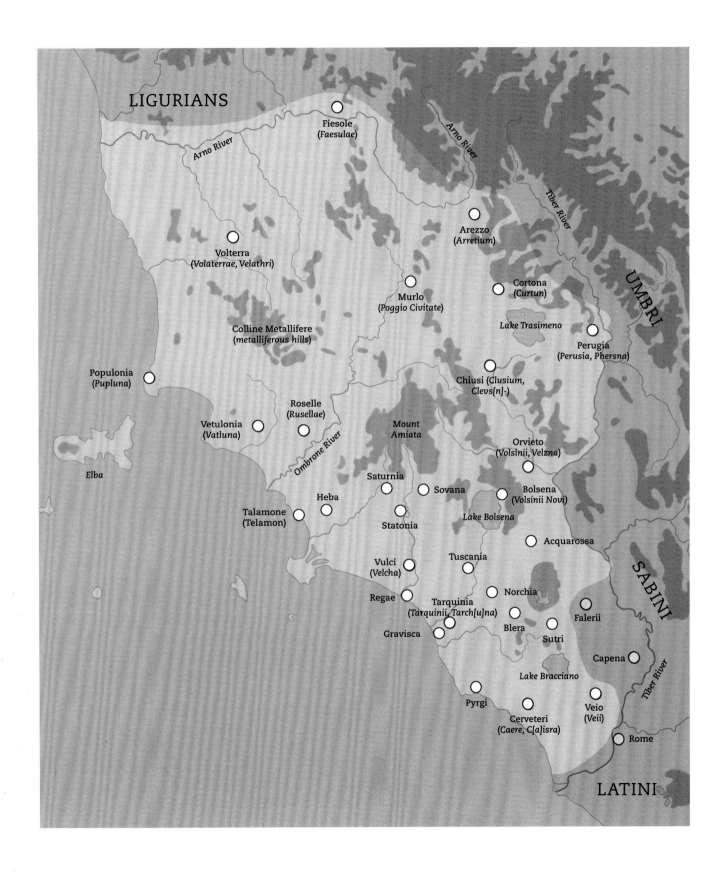

LIGURIANS

Arno River

Arno River

Tiber River

UMBRI

Fiesole
(Faesulae)

Arezzo
(Arretium)

Volterra
(Volaterrae, Velathri)

Murlo
(Poggio Civitate)

Cortona
(Curtun)

Lake Trasimeno

Perugia
(Perusia, Phersna)

Colline Metallifere
(metalliferous hills)

Chiusi (Clusium,
Clevs[n]-)

Populonia
(Pupluna)

Roselle
(Rusellae)

Vetulonia
(Vatluna)

Mount
Amiata

Orvieto
(Volsinii, Velzna)

Ombrone River

Elba

Saturnia

Sovana

Bolsena
(Volsinii Novi)

Heba

Statonia

Lake Bolsena

Acquarossa

Talamone
(Telamon)

SABINI

Tuscania

Vulci
(Velcha)

Norchia

Falerii

Regae

Tarquinia
(Tarquinii, Tarch[u]na)

Blera

Gravisca

Sutri

Capena

Lake Bracciano

Pyrgi

Veio
(Veii)

Cerveteri
(Caere, C[a]isra)

Tiber River

Rome

LATINI

During the Middle Ages, the names Tuscia Longobarda and Tuscia Romana were bequeathed to two regions that correspond to present-day Tuscany and northwest Lazio, both part of ancient Etruria. In late medieval times Tuscia became Tuscany, a name that has survived to this day.

The Etruscan ethnic group bore a similar variety of names among the ancients. The Greeks called them Tyrrhenoí or Tyrsenoí; the Latini Etrusci, Tusci, or even Lydii (recalling the tradition of their Lydian origins); and the Umbri called them Turskus. Their own name for their ethnic group must have been Rasna (Rasenna in its Greek form), which according to Dionysios of Halikarnassos was derived from the name of a leader (1.30.3).

Territorial Range

Strabo (5.2.1–9) and Pliny the Elder (*Naturalis Historia* 3.50–55) left behind quite precise geographic descriptions of Etruria, indicating that its border to the north was the Tuscan-Emilian Apennines, to the west the Tyrrhenian Sea, and to the south and east the Tiber River. These descriptions actually refer to Roman Etruria in the Augustan period, although in all probability the borders were not much different during the Etruscan era.

Two fundamental points, however, should be kept in mind for this period. First, if, as we believe, Etruscan civilization unfolded between the ninth and first centuries B.C., the borders cannot have remained static during this entire period. Second, if, as commonly held, the political structure in Etruria consisted of autonomous cities rather than a unified state, what we call Etruscan territory was more culturally than physically defined, corresponding

to the aggregate margins of the areas controlled by individual cities.

There is no shortage of controversial questions regarding this subject, and some are worth mentioning here.

More than thirty miles north of Rome, west of the Tiber in Etruscan territory, lived the Faliscans and the Capenati. Culturally these peoples could have been considered Etruscan, although linguistically they were Latini. Conversely, less than ten miles north of Rome, east of the Tiber in Latin territory, was Fidenae, a city that was traditionally Etruscan and was always allied with Veii in wars against Rome (Livy 1.15.1; Strabo 5.2.9).

The area west of the middle and lower regions of the Arno River, which stretches to the spurs of the Apennines, was considered Etruscan in the geographical sources mentioned above, as well as in epigraphic sources that date back to the seventh century B.C. Yet Polybius (2.16.2), Pompeius Trogus (Justinus *Epitome* 20.1.11), and the unknown author of *De Mirabilibus auscultationibus* (92) mention the presence of Ligurians in the same region, which would have extended, as Polybius specified, to the gates of Arezzo. A passage from Livy (41.13.4) regarding Luni could clear up these questions: The city was a Roman colony founded in 177 B.C. at the mouth of the Magra in Ligurian territory, which was once Etruscan. In other words, both peoples were present in the region, but in chronological succession. The Ligurians, who originally settled in the Apuan Alps, may have been forced to push south by pressure from the Gauls, who began to assert themselves on the Po Plain beginning in the fourth century and attempted to penetrate further into peninsular territory. In fact the people who lived in the region

west of the Arno, and who beginning in the third century repeatedly fought against the Romans until they were subjugated, were Ligurians.

The Etruscans sited their cities in locations that were naturally defendable. In northern Etruria, this meant the tops of hills; in southern Etruria, we find them situated on plateaus bordered by ditches or watercourses that connected to other areas by land bridges. These natural defenses were often augmented by artificial ones, namely enclosure walls. Tradition speaks of twelve chief Etruscan cities (or *populi*), without providing a corresponding list. The trouble is that when one attempts to make a list, the number comes out greater than twelve. It is therefore thought that there was a sort of rotation, or a set of conditions for admission to the canonical number on the part of new cities, which supplanted others that had disappeared. This may have been the fate of Veii after 396 B.C., when the Romans destroyed it and absorbed its territory. Each city controlled a certain *agger*, or territory, including a number of lesser cities

Porta Marzia, Perugia, third to second centuries B.C. The monument was salvaged and inserted within the city walls by Antonio da Sangallo the Younger, whom Pope Paul II (1534–49) charged with building the Fortezza.

Above, a road, wall, and gate from the Hellenistic and Roman periods in Saturnia (Grosseto)

At *right*, the ruins of a Roman theater in Volterra (Pisa) from the Augustan period. The portico and the thermal baths are from the Imperial period.

arrayed along the longest lines of communication or in areas of substantial production. A number of great Etruscan cities were situated along the Tyrrhenian belt—Caere, Tarquinia, Vulci, Roselle, Vetulonia, Populonia, and Pisa—yet all of these were miles from the coast where their ports were located. Other great cities—Veii, Capena, Falerii, Volsinii, Perugia, Arezzo, Fiesole— were situated along the valleys of the two great rivers of the region, the Tiber and the Arno, or their tributaries, such as the Chiani (Chiusi and Cortona). Other cities worth mentioning were found along the valleys of lesser rivers: Tuscania was in the valley of the Marta, Sovana in that of the Fiora, Saturnia the Albegna, and Volterra the Cecina.

The great Etruscan cities have been identified at their respective sites. Unfortunately, in most cases, the urban framework and the extent of the residential areas are not known. There are various reasons for

The remains of the fourth-century B.C. walls in Saturnia (Grosseto)

this. In cities where life continued throughout the Middle Ages and into the modern era—places such as Caere, Chiusi, Volterra, or Fiesole—archaeological operations are impossible. In cities where life was interrupted in antiquity or during the Middle Ages, such as in Veii or Vulci, archaeological projects can be pursued but must contend

with the high costs of excavation. In addition, it has for centuries been primarily the necropoleis of Etruria that have been explored, since they are easier to recognize and they immediately yield gratifying results. Only in recent times have excavation programs turned toward urban or urbanized areas.

Quite a few minor cities are known, generally through their respective necropoleis and, in some lucky cases, from their inhabited areas. Many of their ancient names remain unknown, as do their histories. Such is the case with Acquarossa near Viterbo and Accesa near Massa Marittima.

Expansion

Beyond Etruria as it is conventionally known, there was also an Etruria of the Po Valley and a Campanian Etruria. Attracted by the fertility of the land (Polybius 2.17.1; Strabo 5.4.3; Plutarch *Camillus* 16), the Etruscans eventually settled on both the Po Plain and in Campania, and sources say that the two regions were organized into twelve cities, modeling themselves after Etruria proper (Livy 5.33.7–10; Dionysios of Halikarnassos 14.113.1; Strabo 5.4.3). Plutarch (*Camillus* 16), on the other hand, assigns eighteen cities to the Po Plain. Once again, compiling a list of these cities is anything but easy, and indeed the situation in each of the two regions was not homogeneous.

Cultural expressions in the Po Valley at Felsina (Bologna) can be defined as Etruscan beginning in the ninth century B.C., and linguistic evidence in Etruscan begins in the seventh century. Two sepulchral *cippi* from Rubiera (Reggio nell'Emilia) that date to the end of the seventh or the beginning of the sixth centuries bear animalistic friezes from the more genuine figurative repertory of the Etruscan Orientalizing period, as well as inscriptions in Etruscan. By contrast, the great Etruscan cities of the Po Valley—Marzabotto, Spina, Adria, and Mantua—date back to the period between the sixth and the early fifth centuries and coincide with the urban restructuring in Felsina.

According to current theory, the region's impetus toward Etruscanization originated in the cities of northern Etruria. The arrival of the Gauls in the early years of the fourth century marked the end of the Etruscan period there.

In Campania, too, cities such as Pontecagnano (Salerno) and Capua, which today is Santa Maria Capua Vetere (Caserta), show cultural signs of the Etruscans as far back as the ninth century B.C. and linguistic evidence beginning in the sixth century. In other cities—Suessola, Nola, Pompeii, Herculaneum, Pozzuoli, Norchia, Sorrento, Marcina, and Fratte di Salerno—an Etruscan facies appears in archaeological and epigraphic data or in statements by ancient writers. Among other evidence from Capua is a terra-cotta plaque with a long Etruscan inscription dating to the fifth century; it is a religious calendar, a text written for a community. It is quite probable that the movement toward Etruscanization in the region began in southern Etrurian cities. In Campania, too, the Etruscan period ended with the arrival of a new ethnic group, the Samnites, during the second half of the fifth century.

Another region with a strong Etruscan element was ancient Lazio. In Rome, in particular, between the end of the seventh and the end of the sixth centuries B.C., political power lay in the hands of the Etruscan kings L. Tarquinius Priscus, Servius Tullius, L. Tarquinius Superbus, and L. Porsenna. Etruscans created or commissioned great works of art and craftsmanship there (Varro in Pliny *Nauralis Historia* 35.157; Livy 156.1), and a number of inscriptions of a private nature were written in Etruscan. A turning point in Latium would occur when the Etruscan army, headed by

Arruns, son of Porsenna, was defeated in Aricia in 504 B.C.

Other Etruscan settlements on the Italian peninsula are on record, although they were neither as massive nor as lasting. One example is Fermo, where researchers have discovered two necropoleis from the Iron Age that were similar to their contem-

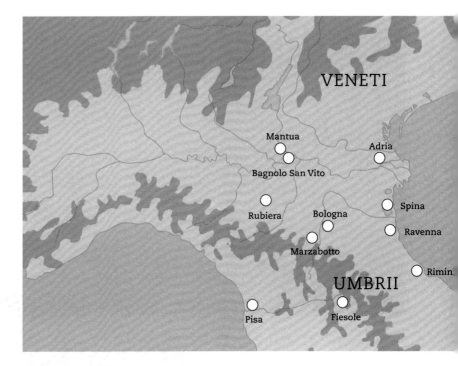

Etruria in the Po Valley, including the main Etruscan cities

poraries in Etruria, or in Busca (Cuneo), Verucchio (Rimini), or Ravenna, where we find Etruscan inscriptions. In these cases the Etruscan presence is securely attested during this period.

Even outside of Italy, the presence of Etruscans was not altogether rare, as we know from certain incidental facts. Some

The countryside around Volterra (Pisa), where hills alternate with valleys and plains

evidence

of these Etruscans were merchants, as the abovementioned inscription from Pech Maho would lead one to believe; we have similar evidence from Aleria on Corsica. In other cases it seems there were consistent groups who moved for political reasons, as the written strips from the Zagreb mummy from Egypt or the border *cippi* from Oued-Miliane in Tunisia lead one to conclude (see p. 101).

The Landscape

Etruria is mostly made up of hills separated by valleys and plains. The few mountains in the region, such as Amiata, Cetona, and Falterona, are situated exclusively in northern Etruria and seldom reach heights above a thousand meters (3,300 ft.). The plains are not very extensive and tend to appear along the coastline, mostly as alluvial deposits at river mouths. Depending on the altitude,

Albegna, the Ombrone, the Bruna, the Cornia, the Cecina, and the Secchio. The history of Etruscan river cities was intimately tied to their watercourses. Their corresponding valleys contained important roads from earliest antiquity. There are numerous lakes, as well, some of them quite large (Bracciano, Bolsena, and Trasimeno). Those in southern Etruria are almost exclusively of volcanic origin (Bracciano, Mantignano, Monterosi, Vico, and Bolsena). Those along the Tyrrhenian coast are ancient inlets or lagoons that have since been closed to the sea. Some lake basins, if they were not replenished by tributaries or underground springs, became swamps over the course of the centuries, and eventually dried up. This was the case with Prile Lake, between Roselle and Vetulonia, which became the plain of Grosseto.

Therapeutic springs in Etruria were renowned and numerous (Vitruvius *De architectura* 2.6.4; Symmachus *Epistulae* 7.39): Aquae Nepesinae (Nepi) was reputed to cure ailments of the stomach and urinary tract, while Aquae Careretanae (Cerveteri) and Aquae Tauri (near Civitavecchia) were both quite hot and thought to cure bone diseases. Others are known only by name, although their locations can sometimes be deduced: Aquae Apollinares (Vicarello on Lake Bracciano), Passerianae (south of Lake Bolsena), Vetuloniae, Populoniae, and Volaterranae. It is often forgotten that a fragmentary bronze statue of huge dimensions from the fifth century B.C. was found at the famed springs of Chianciano Terme, Acquasanta. It was probably an ex-voto to a god of health, and we may therefore infer that this spring was used in antiquity as it is today.

these plains were either forested or cultivated, the latter chiefly for wheat, wine grapes, and olives. The coastline is interrupted by three headlands—Argentario, Punta Ala, and Piombino—that form natural ports. Many rivers cut through the region. In addition to the Tiber, the Arno, and their tributaries, others that disgorge into the Tyrrhenian Sea are: the Mignone, the Marta, the Arrone, the Fiora, the

Etrurian bedrock varies considerably. Tufaceous rock (nenfro) dominates southern Etruria; in northern Etruria, it is mostly sandstone and limestone. Nenfro, being quite soft once it has been extracted from the quarry, can be worked evenly, while the other stone is quite hard and can only be roughly cut. For this reason burial chambers in the tombs of southern Etruria were carved into the rock, while those in northern Etruria were built with huge slabs or large unshaped stones.

Natural Resources

The ancient sources join in celebrating the fertility of the land and the agricultural production of Etruria. A revealing statement by Diodorus Siculus (5.40.3) expressly describes the land there as producing fruit of every kind and in great quantity. Etruria also sup-plied Rome with grain during times of famine (see p. 61). In 308 B.C., the consul P. Decius Tarquinia forced Tarquinia to pay war reparations by providing the Roman army with grain (Livy 9.41.5). In 205 B.C., Caere, Volterra, Arezzo, Perugia, Chiusi, and Roselle contributed grain to P. Cornelius Scipio's expedition as he prepared to face Hannibal in Africa (Livy 28.45.15–18). Agricultural goods were one means by which Etruria entered into international trade. Sources often mention the excellent returns that Etruria gained from its vineyards and the fame of Etruscan wine, which was exported to various regions in central and northern Europe beginning at the end of the seventh century (see pp. 51, 87ff., 113ff.). In the early years of the fourth century, wagons loaded with wine, oil, and dried fruit departed for Gaul from Chiusi, a city whose economy was primarily agricultural (see p. 64). The frequency with which the cultivation of fields is represented in Etruscan art, throughout the entire arc of its development, is also significant. Among the scenes that adorn the frame of a wheeled bronze incense-burner from Bisenzio, dating to the final decades of the eighth century— scenes mostly pertaining to the occupations of the upper classes (the hunt, warriors fighting, a group of nobles)—is a depiction of plowing. A beautiful bronze sculptural group of a ploughman from Arezzo, dating to the end of the fifth or the beginning of the fourth centuries, almost certainly was created for a votive deposit. We find many agricultural tools, such as plows, scythes, or hoes, together with weapons in a votive deposit in Talamone (Grosseto), dating between the second and first centuries. It is sometimes forgotten that Romulus, when he founded Rome, marked off the area of

the future city with a furrow made by a plow, following a suggestion from Etruscan experts who had been gathered for the occasion (Plutarch *Romulus* 11.1).

Scenes that refer to breeding various animals, especially the strong and steadfast ox (Columella *De re rustica* 6.1.2), have been a part of the Etruscan figurative tradition since its very beginnings. A ram's head was a frequent motif for decorating the handles of impasto bowls during the Villanovan period. Armed dancers, a hunter, and a figure with an ox, all rendered in full relief, adorn the top of a lid of a biconic bronze vase from the final decades of the eighth century in Bisenzio. Sculpted groups of horses at the trough or a lord breaking two horses, the so-called *despotes hippon,* were reproduced on the rims of a number of impasto cups from the second half of the eighth century in the Faliscan *agger.* A herdsman watching over a herd of boars occupies an entire frieze that is incised upon a gilt-silver "bucket" from Chiusi

lization, cattle-breeding was both widespread and socially highly esteemed.

The forests of antiquity must have occupied far more terrain than they do today. The ancient writers often mentioned them: for example, the forests of Capena (Virgil *Aeneid* 7.697), the wooded mountains of Volsinii (Juvenal 3.191), and the thick forests of Gravisca (Rutilius Namatianus *De reditu* 1.281–84). These stands of timber were of vital importance. They provided habitat for game: Boar, elk, rabbit, and deer hunting were frequent subjects in Etruscan art, from the most ancient to the most recent examples. These various representations primarily signify the strength (or power) of the object's recipient, but the goods obtained from hunting—meat, hides, bones, or animal fat—may have had significant commercial value as well.

The most valued forest product was undoubtedly wood, which was used for building houses and boats, for carpentry work, and as fuel for blast furnaces, kilns, and so forth. The high value placed on wood, which is explicitly recorded in the ancient sources (Strabo 5.2.5), derives from the fact that, in the dry Mediterranean environment, forests with tall trees were rare.

Salt was another of Etruria's great resources. It was either mined, as in Volterra, or extracted from seawater in evaporation ponds that were set up along the Tyrrhenian coast. Between Ostia and Pisa the location name *Saline* is often found, a name testifying to an activity that has extremely ancient roots in the area. Indeed, wars between Rome and Veii that date back to the time of Romulus (Livy 1.14–15; Dionysios of Halikarnassos 1.55; Plutarch *Romulus* 25) were fought over the

dating to the middle of the seventh century. These subjects are reprised on other prestigious goods and feature animals that were either used for fieldwork or raised for wool or meat. The works probably allude to the occupations of their purchasers; indeed, from the earliest centuries of Etruscan civi-

possession of saltworks, which were quite productive near the mouth of the Tiber.

Fishing, on rivers, lakes, and the sea, must also have augmented the region's economy. Once again the figurative evidence shows images of fish or fishing from the eighth century B.C., and these images might allude to the owner's prowess in this activity and/or to fish as a source of his affluence. Literary evidence, admittedly from a much later period, records a bounty of fish in the Tiber, particularly pike (Varro in Macrobius *Saturnalia* 3.16.12–13; Horace *Satirae* 2.2.31–33); the abundance of fish in Etruria's lakes (Strabo 5.2.9); repopulating these waters with saltwater fish (Columella *De re rustica* 8.16.2); the use of the headlands of Piombino and Argentario as sighting posts to spot passing schools of tuna (Strabo 5.2.6–8); the demanding capture of a monstrous fish, an *aulopias,* from the waters of the Tuscan Archipelago (Aelianus *De natura animalium* 13.17); and the supply of Rome's market with fish from Pyrgi (Athenaeus *Deipnosoph* 5.224c).

The most consistent profits, however, came from mines, especially metalliferous ones that supplied iron, copper, tin, silver, lead, and zinc: expensive items all (Pliny *Naturalis Historia* 33.1). Writers from the late Republican and Imperial periods often referred to the mines of Populonia (Strabo 5.2.6) and the Isle of Elba (Diodorus Siculus 5.13.1–2; Virgil *Aeneid* 10.173–74; Strabo 5.2.6; Silius Italicus 8.615–16; Pliny *Naturalis Historia* 3.81, 34.142; Pseudo-Aristotle *De Mirabilibus auscultationibus* 93; Servius Auctus *Ad Aeneidum* 10.174; Rutilius Namatianus *De reditu* 351ff.). The picture, however, was much broader than the ancient writers suggest and included the Apuan Alps, the Cecina Valley in

Volterrano, the Colline Metallifere (south of Volterra), a spur on the island of Elba, the Rognosi Mountains in Aretino, the massive Amiata, and Tolfa Mountains. The emphatic reports of mines on the island of Elba by the writers cited may result from the fact that they lived during a period when a powerful Roman decree had prohibited mining activity in the territory of the Italian peninsula but perhaps not on the

On the following pages, the rear wall in the second chamber of the Tomb of Hunting and Fishing, from the final decades of the sixth century B.C. Tarquinia, Monterozzi necropolis. The pediment is painted with a scene of a symposium and a nuclear family. On the wall below is a depiction of fishing and bird-hunting with a sling.

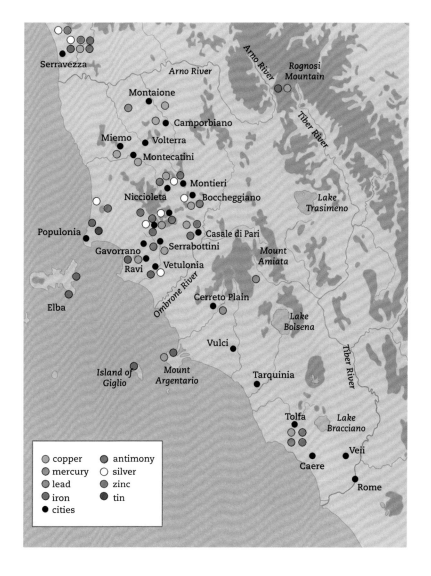

islands (Pliny *Naturalis Historia* 3.138, 32.78). One of the most striking things in reviewing the entire archaeological record of Etruria back to the most ancient times is the enormous quantity of metal utensils, mostly iron or bronze. However, this vast production tells us little about where the raw materials came from. The unnamed author of *De Mirabilibus auscultationibus*, sometimes called Pseudo-Aristotle, in stating that everything in Etruria was made of bronze, suggests the general impression that the ancients had of Etruria in this regard. The high market value of these minerals and metals were very helpful in paying for the refined products of artisans of the Near East and Greece. Etruscan metal ingots were part of the cargo on a ship that sank near the island of Giglio toward the end of the seventh or the beginning of the sixth centuries.

The abundance of primary resources in the region was the driving force behind the intense trade activity of the Etruscans, both on land and on the sea. The various cities were connected by routes that primarily followed the river valleys; in some stretches, at least in southern Etruria, these routes were even tunneled through rock. On the Tyrrhenian coast, the inlets or estuaries of the rivers became ports, and these saw both commercial traffic and collateral activities such as religious observances.

The vigorous economy, which we have only briefly outlined here, was sufficient to stimulate the birth and development of a great civilization.

A Historical and Cultural Profile

Origins The people whose civilization developed in the territory of Etruria can only be defined as Etruscan from the start

of the seventh century B.C., when the first inscriptions in Etruscan were written. The alphabet used for these was Euboean in origin and was in all probability transmitted through Pithecusae and Cumae, two Euboean settlements in southern Italy. This transmission was the end result of commercial and cultural exchanges that began during the third quarter of the eighth century, bringing in wine, clay jars for storing wine, and expert potters. The written documents that have survived from the first half of the seventh century number around ten; they were inscribed on luxury goods such as painted pottery, fine bucchero, ivory, and precious metals. The inscriptions denote an audience with elevated social status, although their linguistic and graphic tradition certainly reflects the region's general situation.

Cultural evidence from the seventh century B.C.—from tombs to houses, settlement structures to manufactured goods, and monumental works to the decorative repertory, all of which will be discussed in more detail later—differs significantly from

Ivory plaque inscribed with the most ancient Etrurian alphabet known, from about the middle of the seventh century B.C., from the Circle of the Ivories in Marsiliana d'Albegna (Grosseto). The tablet was found together with other ivory writing instruments: two scrapers and two styli. Grosseto, Museo Archeologico e d'Arte della Maremma

On the facing page, a *tagliata* (cut), a narrow road dug between high rock walls, in the Sovana necropolis (Grosseto)

On the facing page, impasto
hut urn, ninth or eighth
century B.C., from Vetulonia
(Grosseto). The urn reproduces a dwelling from the
Villanovan era. Florence,
Museo Archeologico

that of the eighth or ninth centuries.
Nevertheless, we can point to certain similar expressions that persist from the first
period to the second. For example, there is
a type of trench tomb and a circular tomb
made of stone slabs driven into the earth,
with various depositions (seen, for example,
at Vetulonia), both of which came into use
during the first half of the eighth century
and continued to spread through the century that followed. We also see certain linear developments, so to speak, such as
fibulae shaped like inflated arches, leeches,
or boats, which began in the eighth century
and continued during the seventh. It is also
highly significant that, at a number of
places, necropoleis from the seventh century continue to function at the same sites,
with about as many deposits, as in the
eighth and ninth centuries. Although we
know far less about the cities of the living
than about those of the dead, we may infer
that the people who lived in the adjacent
areas and buried their dead in the necropoleis were a steady population from the
ninth through the seventh centuries. Even
without written proof, therefore, one can
speak of "Etruscans" in the ninth and
eighth centuries.

The culture in Etruria and Etruscanized
areas during those early centuries is commonly called "Iron Age" or "Villanovan."
The latter term derives from a place,
Villanova (near Bologna), where the first
necropolis from this period was discovered
in 1856. Little is known of its inhabitants
due to the perishable nature of their construction materials. Nevertheless, based on
the few surviving remains and on indirect
testimony (small models of houses), we can
establish a few points with certainty.
Settlements were made up of villages of a

few hundred or, more rarely, a few thousand inhabitants. The villages were often
situated near one another, not more than
two kilometers (1.25 miles) apart, and faced
a common center. A typical dwelling was a
hut built with branches that were supported by poles and covered with clay. The
hut was roofed with straw that was bound
to a framework of poles, which projected
out over the walls. Its plan was either circular, semicircular, or, more infrequently,
rectangular. The interior, whose surface
area ranged between thirty and eighty
square meters (320–860 sq. ft.), was generally a single room that was sometimes
divided in two. A hearth would have occupied its center, and the residents would
have arranged a modest collection of
furniture—beds, a table, and a cupboard—
along the walls. Dishes were made of
impasto and possibly wood; the most valuable were bronze.

The world of the dead yields more
information. The necropoleis outside the
inhabited areas were made up of pit tombs
of between 80 and 150 centimeters (2.5–5
ft.) in depth, which were used for cremated
remains. Beginning in the eighth century
B.C., we start to see trench tombs used for
burials. For cremation rites, the ashes of
the deceased were placed in handmade
impasto urns of biconic or spherical shape,
normally between thirty and forty centimeters (12–16 in.) in height. The single handle
of this vessel was usually positioned hori-
zontally, which made it impractical for
everyday use. It was decorated with stamps,
incisions from a multi-pointed instrument,
or applied metal laminae. Ornamentation
was generally restricted to the upper part of
the vessel's neck and the widest part of its
belly and was composed of Geometric

motifs: points, lines, angles, triangles, quadrilaterals, swastikas, meanders, circles, semicircles, and so on. Only rarely were there narrative scenes, such as the two seated figures, one in front of the other, that were incised on the handle of certain ash urns, perhaps intended as a farewell from the deceased's closest relatives; or the two embracing figures seen on the lid of an ash urn from Chiusi, which had a similar meaning. Few objects were found among the grave goods, but these are often sufficient to suggest the gender or social status

ous items of tableware. The decorations on these works were either incised or embossed and were quite refined. They featured animal or human figures or occasionally a narrative scene, most commonly a boar or deer hunt that celebrated the owner's skill at the chase. Besides these representations, which were at first quite realistic, others indicated an openness to the figurative tradition of other cultures. For example, the motif of the "solar boat" (two opposing protomes of stylized birds that were joined by a straight or semicircular

of the deceased, as when a razor or a weapon identifies a male, or a spindle or bracelet a female.

Fine bronzework began to appear in the second half of the ninth century B.C. and included razors, helmets, swords, shields, knives, horse bits, belts, fibulae, and vari-

line) is linked to the "urnfield culture" of the Carpathian-Danube environment. Other bronze works refer to models from the same region, such as conical or crested helmets or antenna swords; the make is definitely Etruscan, but the types of objects betray central-European origins. Today it is widely held that bronze workers came to Etruria from central Europe, attracted by the abundance of raw materials, bringing a number of successful innovations to the art. Thus we can affirm that central-European groups were ensconced in the Etruscan territories during the ninth and eighth centuries.

There seems to have been an eastern Aegean component within the Etruscan culture from the eighth century as well. A mirror uncovered in a pit tomb of Tarquinia and dated to the first half of the ninth century B.C. is considered to be Aegean-Cypriot in origin and may point to a marriage between a Tarquinian and someone from the eastern Mediterranean. However, a marriage in the ninth century between populations that were so far apart geographically almost certainly signifies another kind of relationship, especially a commercial one, between two groups with mutual interests. Indeed, as we will see, imports of Near Eastern manufactured goods were on the increase over the course of the eighth century.

Sardinia was another important player. A group of three bronzes from Sardinia uncovered in a pit tomb in Vulci—a figure of a chief, a stool, and a basket, all miniatures—are thought to be wedding goods. However, the recovery in Vetulonia and its surrounding territory of more than forty small impasto pitchers with elongated and off-centered necks, a style typical of Sardinian culture since the Iron Age, can better be explained if we posit a consistent population of Sardinians at Vetulonia continuing to use the vases of their homeland at their new location. Pitchers of this same type have also been found in small numbers in other Etruscan cities, such as Caere,

Tarquinia, Vulci, Bisenzio, Chiusi, Populonia, and Volterra.

These are just a few examples, but they elucidate the situation in Etruria during the ninth century B.C. The region was open to input from many different cultures and races, which in turn adapted to local people

Impasto pitcher with an elongated, off-center neck, beginning of the eighth century B.C., from Vetulonia (Grosseto). This vase was either made in Sardinia or created locally after a Sardinian model. Florence, Museo Archeologico

Small bronze portraying a chief, end of the ninth century B.C., from a tomb from the Cavalupo necropolis in Vulci (Viterbo). The bronze was found among grave goods together with two Sardinian bronzes, and a miniature stool and basket. Rome, Museo di Villa Giulia

and practices. The arrival of these foreign elements must have been neither massive nor sudden. On the contrary, it was a steady influx of small groups spread out over time, as we may deduce from the fact that none of these linguistically diverse groups imposed their language in Etruria. Instead, they adapted to the local language. The end result of this process was the formation of the Etruscan people.

The local component, however, cannot in and of itself explain the birth of this people. There are relationships between the oldest Villanovan expressions and those of the late Bronze Age in Etruria. For example, the ash urns are consistently biconic, although their shapes are stockier than those of the late Bronze Age. However, evidence from this era is not continuous with the early Iron Age before it, particularly from the topographic and demographic points of view.

The rise of Etruria in the ninth century B.C. coincided with the discovery and development of agricultural and mineral resources, which help explain the region's demographic increase (including the influx of foreigners) and cultural ascension. One natural resource often aided in the exploitation of another: the discovery of iron in the ninth century, for instance, led to the manufacture of agricultural tools, especially the plow, which in turn allowed people to till the land and grow more food.

If we examine the problem of the origins of Etruscan civilization in the light of direct sources, we end up at odds with the ancient writers. They insisted that the Etruscan people existed before the first histories, but they debated whether the Etruscans immigrated to the Italian peninsula or were native to the region.

Hellanicus (in Dionysios of Halikarnassos 1.28.4) defined the Etruscans as Pelasgians, that is, of northern Greek descent. Herodotus (1.94) recapitulated the story that they were originally Lydians who migrated from that country in the wake of the Trojan War. Anticleides (in Strabo 5.2.4) considered that the Etruscans were Pelasgians who first immigrated to the islands of Lemnos and Imbros in the Aegean and then joined with the Lydians on their voyage to Italy. Dionysios of Halikarnassos opposed these theories (1.29–30), claiming that the Etruscans had no cultural affinity with those peoples. Thus, he said, those who think them an indigenous people are in the right. Until the middle of the twentieth century, scholars viewed this problem along the lines that the ancient writers had laid out, accepting their statements as a point of departure and using the direct sources to support either one theory or another. They even added a third theory, according to which the Etruscans arrived in Italy from central Europe. This theory presumed that the Raeti, a people native to the Danube Basin, were in fact Etruscans, an idea that several writers had explored (Livy 5.33.11; Pliny *Naturalis Historia* 3.133; Pompeius Trogus in Justinus *Epitome* 20.5.10; Stephanus Byzantius, s.v. "Rhoithoi").

Each of these theories has valid points that keep us from eliminating them entirely from the discussion. Stating the problem along the parameters of ethnicity instead of provenance, as the most recent generation of scholars has done, is a way of appreciating all three theories, or rather, their respective contributions to the debate. Nevertheless, the ancient sources beg further explanation.

Below, painted cup that was made in Euboea in the Geometric style and uncovered in Veii, second half of the eighth century B.C. Rome, Museo di Villa Giulia

On the facing page, lebes on a conical bronze stand of Syrian make, second quarter of the seventh century B.C., from the Barberini Tomb in Praeneste (Rome). Rome, Museo di Villa Giulia

Provenance from the Aegean basin, from northern Greece or Lydia, in the period immediately following the Trojan War places the Etruscan story within the picture of the *Nostoi,* that is, the heroes who fought at Troy and later migrated toward the western basin of the Mediterranean (Aeneas, Antenor, Odysseus, Diomedes, and others). Dionysios of Halikarnassos, who sought to prove that the Romans were of Greek origin, campaigned hard for the idea that the Etruscans were an indigenous people. The Etruscans, he asserted, were not like any other people in language and culture, and could not have originated from the Aegean world as the Romans had done. Provenance

from central Europe cannot be based on defining the Raeti as Etruscan, inasmuch as this draws from an expansion movement by the Etruscans from the south toward the north that occurred during the sixth century B.C.

In the eighth century B.C., the phase following the Villanovan era, we can pick up

signs of a noticeable change in Etruscan lifestyle. The grave goods contained more objects, and of higher quality, compared to those of the ninth century; bronzework became more common; amber and gold, imported from abroad, began to be used in certain ornamentation; the tombs were grouped to signify society's organization into *gentes* (family groups); and local works began to show exotic influences. This change involved a particular sector of the population, an emerging class dedicated to exploiting resources on a large scale. The small number of known narrative scenes in figurative works—of hunting, warrior dancing, duels, and family groups—allude to the growing status of this class. Commercial relations with highly cultured foreigners were starting to influence the locals.

Foreign goods become widespread in this period. A bronze cup decorated with animal friezes (Vetulonia) and a clay pitcher with a narrow neck (Tarquinia) came from Phoenicia. A bronze *lebes* whose handles were decorated with a lotus flower (Vulci) came from Cyprus. From Egypt came the area's first scarabs and tiny idols in faience, found at Veii. These same types of objects were uncovered in other parts of Italy (Sybaris and Pithecusae); their importers were most likely Phoenician sailors who may also have transported Sardinian works such as conical buttons, daggers, and swords to various locations on the Tyrrhenian coast.

The most consistent imports came from the Euboean world, either Aegean or colonial, and they reached coastal cities (Tarquinia and Vulci) as well as inland ones (Veii, the Faliscan *agger,* and the Rome of the Latini). Among these were cups and Geometric kraters that were used to serve wine. Provided that their context is known, these can usually be linked to other locally produced impasto vases that were made for the symposium, a ceremony in which participants drank wine. All of this leads one to conclude that wine was also imported into Etruria from Euboea (in perishable wine-skins) and the practice of the symposium, which was widespread and appreciated among the aristocracy, came along with it. The Euboeans themselves must have been the transporters: They traded the same products along the southern Tyrrhenian coast, where they had also established emporia and colonies (Pithecusae and Cumae). They may even have brought the practice of winegrowing itself to Etruria, importing skilled Euboean vinedressers. The Etruscans, for their part, contributed to this trade metals and salt from cities in the lower Tiber valley.

Meanwhile vases for wine were starting to emerge from workshops in southern Etrurian cities. Kraters, *olpai*, *hydriae*, pitchers, and stands were all decorated with motifs derived from the Euboean repertory. These products are attributed to masters who arrived from the Euboean world and started to work for the rich local clientele. Master potters created vases using a fast wheel, introducing this technical innovation into Etruria. Of particular significance is the fact that pottery production, requiring specific skills, was removed from the home environment and placed in the hands of specialized artisans.

No less significant was the progress made in bronzeworking, due in part to masters who had arrived from the Carpathian-Danube region. Products such as helmets, shields, and horse bits were eventually exported to various regions of continental

Europe and to the greater Greek sanctuaries such as Olympia, Delphi, Dhodhóni, and Samos (see pp. 83ff.).

Ancient sources date the first armed conflicts between Rome and Veii over the control of saltworks at the mouth of the Tiber to the final decades of the eighth century B.C. (Livy 1.14–15; Dionysios of Halikarnassos 2.55; Plutarch *Romulus* 25). Current opinion, however, is that tradition had projected into the faraway past events that were in fact much more recent. It is difficult to believe that there could have been wars between cities that did not yet exist as urban entities, although there may indeed have been clashes (and possibly armed engagements) between clans or families who managed productive and commercial activities in their respective cities.

The Orientalizing Period The long-range trading circuit in which Etruria had significant interests during the late Villanovan period, and its resulting cultural and social transformations, visibly broadened between the end of the eighth and the seventh centuries B.C. Numerous exotic objects, originating in the Near East, Greece, central Europe, and Sardinia, appear among grave goods, evidently bought by wealthy private customers. The most valuable items came from the Near East, from trade involving the Aegean basin and the western Mediterranean, giving the name "Orientalizing" to art of the seventh century that originated in those regions. By the ninth century, the Phoenicians had sailed for the mineral district of Tartessus on the southern Iberian Peninsula and had established colonies on the coast of western Sicily, North Africa, southern Sardinia, and on the Iberian Peninsula itself. Phoenician sailors were also responsible for transporting luxury goods from various Near Eastern cities to Etruria. A few examples will suffice: from Egypt, a faience vase bearing a cartouche with the name of the pharaoh Bocchoris (from the second to last decade of the eighth century), with tiny faience idols that were part of a collection; from Assyria, a bronze *situla* with a lion's head; Phoenician gilt-silver cups decorated with incised and embossed figurative friezes; from Syria, huge bronze *lebetes* decorated with animal protomes, as well as embossed bronze double-walled bowls and ivory jewel-boxes decorated with reliefs; finally, from Cyprus, silver pear-shaped pitchers and bronze candelabras. Pottery continued to reach Etruria from Greece, no longer from Euboea, but from eastern Greece and Corinth: wine vessels (*kotylai, skyphoi*, and jugs) and ointment jars (*aryballoi* and pyxides).

Amber, which was widely used in ornamental objects such as necklaces and pendants, originated in the Baltic area. Bronze *situlae* with characteristic decorations incised along the border, and the cross-shaped fasteners of furniture handles that were found in a number of circular tombs in Vetulonia, are works from the Carpathian-Danube region and the Hallstatt culture. The original models of large *situlae* with fixed vertical handles, of the so-called Kurd type, also came from this region.

Works from Sardinia from the Orientalizing period have also been unearthed in Etruria. For example, the bronze boats from Vetulonia's Tomb of the Leader, the *Tomba della Navicella* (Tomb of the Little Ship), and the *Tomba delle Tre Navicelle* (Tomb of the Three Little Ships) are of Sardinian origin. Some have asserted that these specimens must have arrived

back in the ninth and eighth centuries B.C.: A number of bronzes from Sardinia were uncovered among Etruscan grave goods of that age (see p. 37). These are just a few examples to give a flavor of the provenance and type of the Orientalizing goods. Such objects tended to be linked either to the symposium ceremony or to the care and adornment of the body, two clear modes of aristocratic display.

Master artisans from these far-flung areas began to emigrate to Etruria and work for the local clientele. For example, a number of ivory works were found in an Etruscan

context from the seventh century B.C., some of which had been imported from the Near East and others made locally. The ivory itself was obviously imported from the Near East; in all probability masters came with it (along with their tools) and began to work with a material that had been previously unknown in Etruria. Among the grave goods of Tomb 928 in Pontecagnano and the Tomb of the Leader

At left, Protocorinthian pyxis with Geometric decorations, first half of the seventh century B.C., from the Tumulus of the Cylindrical Pyxides in Populonia (Livorno). Florence, Museo Archeologico. At right, a Protocorinthian *kotyle* with Geometric decorations, first half of the seventh century, from the right chamber of Tomb 2 in the Tomb of the Ship in Caere (Rome). Rome, Museo di Villa Giulia

On the facing page, a faience vase with hieroglyphic inscriptions that include the name of the pharaoh Bocchoris, end of the eighth century B.C., from the Tomb of Bocchoris in Tarquinia (Viterbo). The vase was made in Egypt and was probably brought to the area by Phoenician traders. Tarquinia, Museo Archeologico

in Vetulonia were, respectively, a silver *kotyle* and another of gilt-silver, both of which are quite similar to Phoenician precious-metal cups in their materials, their make, the technique of their incised decoration, the types of animal and vegetal motifs that make up their decorative friezes, and their use of hieroglyphics for decorative purposes. The similarities are such that in all probability the master moved to Etruria from the very Phoenician city where these types of cups had originated. We have also both direct and indirect evidence of Greek masters who were active in Etruria, some of whom we know by name. The potter and ceramic decorator Aristonothos worked in Caere during the second quarter of the seventh century and placed his signature upon a krater. Eucheir, Eugrammos, and Diopos

were Corinthian artists who, according to Pliny the Elder (*Naturalis Historia* 35.152), came to Etruria just before the year 650 B.C. following the rich merchant Demaratos; there they introduced sculptural techniques for terra-cotta. We may also theorize that masters arrived from the area of the Hallstatt culture. A group of bronze *lebetes*, found in a number of locations in Italy and even at Olympia, can be attributed to a workshop in Vetulonia thanks to their particular ornamentation and animal protomes. One of these examples has ornamentation incised beneath its rim that reveals the involvement of a bronzeworker from the Hallstatt region.

These foreign masters helped to open the Etruscan world to their lands of origin. Local painted vases, in bucchero or

On the facing page, amber necklace (reassembled), beginning of the seventh century B.C., from the Circle of the Jewelry in Vetulonia (Grosseto). Florence, Museo Archeologico

Below, a krater signed by the potter and ceramic decorator Aristonothos, portraying the blinding of Polyphemus, first half of the seventh century B.C., from Caere (Rome). The master was a Greek who worked in Etruria for the local clientele. Rome, Musei Capitolini

impasto, began to mimic the shapes of
models that originated in the Near East or
Greece, partly because they were destined
for the same buyers. The decorative repertory consisted of freehand drawings: motifs
of plants and animals—real or imaginary—
and human figures busy in narrative or
mythological scenes. These decorations
were usually charged with symbolic meaning. Take, for instance, the "lord of the animals" motif—a man taming a pair of
lions—that recurred in a variety of costly

works (gold work, ivory, tomb paintings).
We may deduce that such items alluded to
their owners' power.

Examining certain works can help to
illuminate the activities of masters who
were working in Etruria and who made
noteworthy contributions to Etruscan art.
The gilt-silver *kotyle* from the Tomb of the
Leader in Vetulonia, mentioned above, has
a shape that was originally Protocorinthian
or Corinthian and ornamentation that
recalls the repertory of Phoenician cups.
An oval *aryballos* in bucchero of unknown

provenance, preserved in Berlin, also has a
Protocorinthian or Corinthian shape and a
frieze with horses and riders derived from
Phoenician cups. A gilt-silver "bucket"
from Chiusi also has frieze figures that
stylistically recall Phoenician cups,
although some of the warriors wear
Corinthian helmets. The mixing of such
different traditions within the same work
is possible only in an environment such as
Etruria, where these two traditions commingled. It was a significant trend within
Etruscan art.

With the first half of the seventh century B.C., certain painters emerged in the field of ceramic decoration who reproduced friezes of animals and narratives scenes that evoked Cycladic pottery (the Cranes Painter and the Heptachord Painter). Many objects for personal adornment, such as fibulae, pins, bracelets, earrings, and so on, were made from gold sheets (the raw material was imported) and decorated with motifs from the Orientalizing repertory. These were executed with the refined techniques of embossing, filigree, granulation, and fine gold dust (*pulviscolo*), techniques that may have been introduced into Etruria by goldsmiths from the Aegean or the Near East. In bronzeworking, the technique of embossing animal and vegetal motifs on sheet metal became widespread; so too did bronze casting, which was used to render tall, narrow figurines for votive offerings. A variety of works in metal were exported (see pp. 84ff., 112ff.).

The Etruscan residence in this period was transformed from a hut into a house of masonry, elongated and organized into

The Tomb of the Chariots, first half of the seventh century B.C., at the San Cerbone necropolis in Populonia (Livorno)

Stone head and bust from
a statue of a woman in
mourning, second half of
the seventh century B.C.,
from the tumulus tomb
of Pietrera in Vetulonia
(Grosseto). Florence, Museo
Archeologico

different spaces. It had stone foundations, walls of lattice or unfired bricks, and a tile roof. Based on what we find in tombs, furniture included beds, tables, thrones, and footrests. Weapons hung on the walls. The tomb, an expression of aristocratic power, interred the qualified members of *gens* either inside a circular structure ringed by upright stones, or in a chamber built or cut into rock. Outside, the tomb resembled a monumental mound of earth.

In tombs from this period we also find evidence that writing was beginning to take hold, with the first brief inscriptions marking the ownership of valuable goods. The first examples of monumental stone or terra-cotta statues, linked to domestic cults, appear housed inside the tombs: for example, those from the Tomb of the Statues in Ceri, the Tomb of the Five Chairs in Caere, the Pietrera Tomb in Vetulonia, and the necropolis of Casalmarittimo. The great tradition of tomb painting also began in the Orientalizing period: the *Tomba delle Anatrelle* (Tomb of the Little Ducks) in Veii, the Tomb of the Painted Animals, and the Tomb of the Painted Lions in Caere.

This archaeological record leads us to deduce the rise of an upper class that grew rich on the abundant natural resources of the region, participated in a wide trade circuit, and invested its profits in luxurious and costly goods. This class was obviously only a part of the population of Etruria, but the Orientalizing impetus was largely their prerogative. This movement showed different features in different cities. The coastal settlements with greater access to foreign influences and trade, and those with healthy economic prospects, had direct and continual contact with more sophisticated cultures, from which they adopted ideas

and models. They often transmitted these acquisitions to the lesser or inland cities, with the result that the latter were often late in taking up the prototypes, or diluted them with local elements.

During the second half of the seventh century imports from the Near East, central Europe, and Sardinia decreased while those from Greece increased. The years around 630 B.C. marked the arrival of two ceramic painters to Vulci: the Swallow Painter, from eastern Greece, and the Bearded Sphinx Painter, from Corinth, who worked for a number of years both in keeping with their respective training and also integrating each other's experience. The Bearded Sphinx Painter founded a school; he instigated the Etruscan-Corinthian tradition, which lasted for almost a century. Other ceramic works of the time worth mentioning are polychrome vases from Caere and Veii, which featured incised and painted ornamentation on a dark-gray monochrome background, and other works in bucchero with incised decorations from a number of southern Etruscan cities, whose repertory consisted of animal friezes and a few narrative scenes.

During the seventh century, a kind of middle class emerged, consisting of specialized artisans (goldsmiths, bronzeworkers, potters, dyers, and builders), farmers, and small-time merchants, who were no longer completely dependent on the magnates of industry and trade. In the course of a few decades, they acquired considerable autonomy. Wealth was no longer concentrated in the hands of a few rich people, but was more evenly distributed and, as a result, we see a decrease in extravagant gestures. The new middle class, corresponding to the Greeks' *demos*, adopted certain aristocratic customs, beginning with the nobility's

organization and writing. Its members entered decisively into public, political, and social life. In residential areas, we see a new emphasis on public works: roads that followed a regular layout, designated neighborhoods for artisans' workshops, squares for secular assemblies, temples for religious gatherings, paved public spaces, sewers, enclosure walls, port structures, necropoleis, and so on. These urban achievements were a reflection of a new urban ideology. Thus the city was born, and it asserted itself as a political entity. Like the Greek *poleis*, the history of Etruria is that of individual cities. Consequently, we can accept or at least justify the tradition that wars were fought by lone Etruscan cities during this period. For example, in 606 B.C., Chiusi, Arezzo, Volterra, Roselle, and Vetulonia joined forces with the Latini against the Roman

king, L. Tarquinus Priscus (Dionysios of Halikarnassos 3.51.4).

The Archaic Period Between the end of the seventh and the beginning of the sixth centuries B.C., the Phoenicians were definitively edged out of their role as the Etruscans' chief trading partners. This redounded to the benefit of the Corinthians and eastern Greeks, who continued to export from their native countries goods such as wine and ointments in their characteristic containers. Kraters, amphorae, pitchers, *kotylai, aryballoi,* and *alabastra* were brought from Corinth, while Rhodian bronze pitchers, cups, and horse bits came from eastern Greece. These vessels and their decorative repertory were widely copied in local ceramic production in Etruria, including painted pottery, bucchero, and red impasto.

The effects of these two schools—the Corinthian and the eastern Greek—can be easily seen in the great stone sculptures from the first half of the sixth century B.C. Statues such as *The Centaur* and the so-called *Isis of Vulci* combine characteristics of the Daedalic tradition—cubic, flat heads; large foreheads with bangs cut straight across; and pronounced chins and cheekbones—with the eastern Greek tradition. In *The Centaur*, the latter tradition shows in the plump flesh that hid the bone structure; in the *Isis*, the clothes give a unified structure to the piece. This combination of styles continued in the sculptural production of other cities, such as Ischia di Castro or Chiusi, which was clearly influenced by that of Vulci.

The Phokaians of Ionia, who according to Herodotus (1.163.1) discovered the western Mediterranean basin, held a privileged position among the eastern Greeks. Their first great accomplishment was to found Massalia (Marseilles) around 600 B.C., at the terminus of a great trade route that followed the valley of the Rhone and its tributaries and connected the Mediterranean to central Europe. It is no accident that the Rhodians were already frequenting the area in the last decades of the seventh century (Pseudo-Scymnus 204ff.), and the Etruscans as well (amphorae for shipping and bucchero vases for wine). Massalia consolidated its position and installed various lesser colonies along the coast, from Ampurias (Empória) in Catalonia to Nice (Nikaia) along the Côte d'Azur, and finally to Aleria (Alalía) on Corsica.

Together with Corinthian and eastern Greek pottery, Attic and Laconian ceramics also began to reach Etruria. The latter would increasingly conquer Etruscan markets to the detriment of other types of works, causing inevitable competition. The Attic exports were impressive for both their quantity and quality. Masterpieces such as the François Krater were found in Etruscan tombs, as were, from the second half of the sixth century, vases painted by Exekias, the Amasis Painter, or by pioneers of the new red-figure technique. Goods from the farms and mines of Etruria were valued as profitable compensation for such articles.

Cities assumed an increasingly important role in political administration and urban planning. Meanwhile, the figurative tradition has preserved the memory of struggles between these cities. A fresco from the François Tomb in Vulci, dating from immediately after the middle of the fourth century B.C., represents two heroes in combat.

A large bowl by the Swallow Painter, from the final decades of the seventh century B.C., from Vulci (Viterbo). Rome, Museo di Villa Giulia

The loser in the conflict is identified by an inscription with his personal and family name as well as an adjective identifying his city. The winner's inscription bears only his personal and family name, from which we conclude that he was Vulcian. The names of a number of figures in the frieze, such as Caelius and Aulus Vibenna, Mastarna (Servius Tullius), and Cn. Tarquinius Romanus, recall historical episodes from the middle decades of the sixth century. If the chronological references are similar for all of the groups, we may deduce that they allude to wars that the Vulci fought (and won) with other cities who fell during the sixth century: a sort of town epic.

The coastal metropoleis—Caere, Tarquinia, and Vulci—supported their sea trade with port structures and related infrastructure. Great trading sanctuaries were erected at Pyrgi (Caere) and Gravisca (Tarquinia), frequented by both Etruscans and foreigners such as Greeks and Carthaginians, who enjoyed considerable freedom in this free-trade zone, so to speak. The inscribed gold tablets of Pyrgi, written in Etruscan and Phoenician-Punic, contain the text of a dedication (it is not clear of what) to the goddess Uni-Astarte that was made jointly by both Etruscans and Carthaginians. Vases from the sanctuary of Gravisca contain dedicatory inscriptions in both Greek and Etruscan to various deities (Hera, Aphrodite-Turan, and Apollo). Ships transporting the works of Etruscan industries to the western basin of the Mediterranean, especially wine and ointment (see pp. 87ff.), departed from these ports, or at least stopped over there. Since sanctuaries in general and coastal ones in particular were major hubs of trade, they were also places where ethni-cally diverse groups met, where their respective cultural experiences were exchanged. In such places, the process of acculturation was more immediate, direct, and intense.

The interests of three economic powers became concentrated in the basin of the Tyrrhenian Sea: the Etruscans; the Phokaians; and the Carthaginians, who in some ways continued the tradition of their Phoenician ancestors. A clash was inevitable, and, naturally, two of these powers allied themselves against the third. Matters came to a head when a new contingent of Phokaians reached Aleria (Corsica) from their motherland after the Persian occupa-tion of Asia Minor (546 B.C.) and began to plunder the entire region. The Etruscans and Carthaginians joined forces against them. They clashed on the Sardinian Sea, and the Phokaian fleet was destroyed, forc-ing them to desert Corsica and settle in the lower Tyrrhenian Sea at Velia. Thereafter each of the three powers controlled separate sectors of the Tyrrhenian Sea: the Phokaians the upper and lower Tyrrhenian, the Carthaginians Sardinia, and the Etruscans the middle Tyrrhenian and Corsica (Herodotus 1.165–67). The Caeretans, who played a primary role in the conflict, imme-diately sent a delegation to Delphi to ask the oracle how they could protect themselves from a plague that had broken out among the Phokaian prisoners and was spreading throughout the local population (Herodotus 1.167.1–2). (Caere had always had a privi-leged rapport with Delphi, to the point of having a *thesaurus*—a treasury building—in the sanctuary there.)

The battle on the Sardinian Sea was only an isolated episode and did not substan-tially damage trade relations between the

The François Krater, second quarter of the sixth century B.C., from Chiusi (Siena). Florence, Museo Archeologico. The vase, which is signed by its maker (Ergotimos) and its painter (Kleitias), is one of the masterpieces of Attic black-figure pottery.

Etruscan coastal cities and the Phokaians. Artisans continued to reach Etruscan cities on the Tyrrhenian coast from various cities of Asia Minor, once again as a result of the Persian occupation there. They produced works of good quality, such as Caeretan *hydriae* and bell-shaped *dinoi* at Caere, Pontic vases at Vulci, and late-Archaic tomb paintings at Tarquinia. The Etruscan commercial movement directed toward the Gulf of Lion, on the other hand, experienced a decline in favor of Massalia, especially in the wine trade; the Massaliot amphorae are seen gradually replacing Etruscan works. At the same time, Etruscan wine exports found their way into continental Europe through the Po Plain and the Alpine valleys. This traffic intensified during the fifth century, when Celtic princes began to receive gifts of wine; wine vases of Etruscan origins have been found in their tombs and residences, including *lebetes, stamnoi,* and pitchers with elongated necks (see pp. 122ff.).

The most ancient known Etrurian temples date back to the sixth century B.C. In addition to the *oikos* variety temples (on a quadrangular plan), we find the first buildings with a tripartite plan—Vitruvius called them Tuscan (*De architectura* 4.7)—on the hill of Piazza d'Armi in Veii dating to the start of the sixth century. They were built on a podium with a front colonnade and a rear section with three *cellae,* or just one *cella* and two wings. They represent the monumentalization of an architectural form that was known previously from the chamber tombs of southern Etruria, especially in Caere and in residences from the sixth century. Some of these temples are quite renowned, such as the sanctuary of Portonaccio in Veii, Temple A in Pyrgi, or the Temple of Jupiter on the Capitoline Hill in Rome. Significant sculptural works are preserved in these temples, such as the terra-cotta statue of Jupiter in the central *cella* of the temple of the same name in Rome, which was made by the sculptor Vulca from Veii (Pliny *Naturalis Historia* 35.157), or the terra-cotta statues from the end of the sixth century that decorated the top of the temple at Portonaccio, which illustrated legends of Apollo such as the struggle with Herakles for the Ceryneian Hind and the slaying of Python.

Tomb painting saw an extraordinary efflorescence in Tarquinia beginning in the years around 540 B.C., after other somewhat tenuous attempts during the first half of that century. It is one of the most striking displays of Etruscan art and one of the few happy cases in which ancient paintings have been preserved. The subjects here are from mythology (Achilles and Troilus in the Tomb of the Bulls) or are related to funerary rites: the laying out of the deceased, athletic competitions, dances, hunts, and symposia—all opportunities for the work's sponsor to portray himself in an exalted or even heroic light.

The prevailing style at the end of the second half of the sixth century originated in eastern Greece. The figures were created with fluid outlines and surfaces that were toned down. The figures' limbs tended toward heaviness, with receding profiles, rounded skulls, large foreheads, almond-shaped eyes, and gently smiling mouths. During the final decades of that century, the Greek goods exported to Etruria were mostly Attic (vases and fabric), and the transporters were Attic or Aegean. At this point the Attic influence on local art gained the upper hand. The iconographic patterns and stylistic characters became those of

The back wall of the Tomb of the Augurs, from the final decades of the sixth century B.C. The two mourning male figures stand on either side of the fictitious door, which may represent the tomb's door or a portal to the afterlife, from the Monterozzi necropolis in Tarquinia (Viterbo)

Attic pottery: the structural features of the body, conceived in a more organic way, began to intrude on eastern Greek style. The profile straightened, and the mouth lost its smile.

The so-called lesser arts are no less interesting than the masterpieces. There are black-figured vases, works in bucchero decorated with reliefs, bronzes either made of hammered sheets or cast (utensils and figurines), and goldwork. Many objects, although not of the highest quality, aimed at a display of luxury by members of the middle class: items for symposia, toiletries, or personal jewelry. Even products made of costly materials, such as gold, formed part of this class of goods. We no longer see the large fibulae, bracelets, or breastplates of the seventh century but mostly lighter articles like earrings and rings that, while revealing the artisans' technical skill and interest in figurative designs, were less pretentious.

In the sixth century B.C. the Etruscans expanded into the Po Plain and toward Campania (see pp. 22ff.). While their presence in Bologna dates back to the ninth century, when the Villanovan period began, it was between the sixth and the beginning of the fifth centuries that the great cities of Adria, Spina, Marzabotto, and Mantua were founded. Bologna itself was refounded during the second half of the sixth century with the addition of a new urbanized city structure that tradition attributed to heroes from Perugia (Silius Italicus *Punica* 8.599–600; Servius Auctus *Ad Aeneidum* 10.198). The success of the port cities of Adria and Spina was linked to the trade in grain from the Po Plain and the distribution of Greek vases to the inland regions of Emilia and the Po Valley. In Campania the situation was no different. Other than the

Gold earrings, second half of the sixth century B.C., provenance unknown. Florence, Museo Archeologico

On the facing page, the left wall of the Tomb of the Leopards with musicians, dancers, and servants, first half of the fifth century B.C. Monterozzi necropolis in Tarquinia (Viterbo)

Villanovan cities of Pontecagnano and Capua, where archaeological evidence dates from the Villanovan period through the second half of the fifth century, the other coastal and inland cities had their Etruscan period during the sixth and fifth centuries (see pp. 22ff.).

Two momentous changes occurred at the end of the sixth century B.C., changes that were destined to have serious consequences for Etruscan history in the centuries to follow. Etruscan expansion experienced its first severe blow when the last Etruscan kings of Rome—L. Tarquinius Superbus and L. Porsenna, according to the sources—lost power and were expelled from the city. The Etruscan army, commanded by the same Porsenna and his son Arruns, was later wiped out by Ariccia in 504 B.C. Secondly, the smaller inland cities that depended on the coastal metropoleis were gradually abandoned as urban migration picked up speed.

The Classical Period After the battle on the Sardinian Sea, the strength of the Etruscans on the sea began to decline. The coastal cities attempted to extend their control to the lower Tyrrhenian (expansion toward the

Ligurian Sea was barred by the presence of Massalia and its colonies). In the early years of the fifth century B.C. they directed their attention toward the Lipari Islands, which could have become a base for further protection. This action ultimately failed, however. Over the course of the conflict both the Etruscans and the Liparians scored victories: Each side offered votive gifts at the sanctuary of Delphi on the occasions of their respective triumphs. In the end, though, the Liparians would not be conquered. Meanwhile Anaxilas, the tyrant of Rhegion (modern Reggio di Calabria), fortified the Point of Scilla with a rampart and equipped a naval base to defend the strait from the Etruscans (Strabo 6.1.5). During those same years the Etruscans attempted to occupy the "Felici Islands" (possibly the Canaries), beyond the Pillars of Hercules in the Atlantic, but they were thwarted by the Carthaginians.

Meanwhile a new naval power arose in the Mediterranean basin: Syracuse. Its first battle, which ended in victory, was fought against the Carthaginians at Himera in 480 B.C., the same year the Athenians defeated the Persians at Salamis. Control of the Mediterranean basin was divided between two powers: the eastern part was in the hands of the Athenians, the western in those of the Syracusans. In 474 B.C. the latter came to the aid of Cumae in a naval battle there against the Etruscans, which ended with the destruction of the Etruscan fleet. On this occasion the tyrant of Syracuse, Hieron, offered a number of helmets that had been taken from his Etruscan enemy to Zeus at Olympia. The next year a defensive wall was erected on the island of Pithecusae in order to counter any further Etruscan attacks.

These episodes marked the beginning of a crisis among the Etruscan cities along the Tyrrhenian coast, a crisis worsened by the Syracusans' victorious expedition against Etruria's mineral district on the island of Elba in 453 B.C. and the founding of a Syracusan port on the eastern coast of Corsica. The ports of the southern Etrurian metropoleis, which had benefited enormously from commercial activity, were closed off to Greek trade, and thus Syracuse struck indirectly at the economy of its rival, Athens. Etruscan inland cities remained beyond the reach of these events and they were busy on other fronts: Between 483 and 474 B.C., Veii repeatedly clashed with Rome, which was famously defended by the *gens* Fabia (Livy 2.42.9–2.54.1).

The port of Populonia, on the other hand, which primarily distributed minerals and metals, received a boost, perhaps due to the support of the Syracusans themselves. Indeed, Populonia experienced a period of greatness between the middle of the fifth and the third centuries B.C. It was the only Etruscan location where Greek vases by talented masters (the Meidias Painter, the Codrus Painter, the group of the Marlay Painter, and the Meleager Painter) continued to arrive, albeit in small numbers. The metallurgy industry, which had already been active since the sixth century, began to operate on a grand scale. Dozens of acres of land around Baratti, Populonia's port, were covered with slag heaps, burying tombs from the previous centuries. The slag was left over from the smelting of ferrous minerals from the island of Elba, as described by Varro (in Servius Auctus *Ad Aeneidum* 10.174). The metalworking industry also began to develop a high profile, chiefly producing iron,

Silver coin with the Gorgoneion (obverse), fourth century B.C., from Populonia (Livorno). Florence, Museo Archeologico

bronze, and lead utensils. Coins issued there are among the oldest from Etruria: gold coins with a lion's head, silver with the head of Medusa, and bronze with the heads of various deities.

Another port that took advantage of the blockade of the southern Etruscan ports was Spina in the upper Adriatic. It was the grain port for the Po Plain, and some have said it was the clearinghouse for Etrurian minerals and metals during the fifth century B.C. Here, too, masterpieces of Greek pottery from the fifth and fourth centuries arrived, destined for local customers as well as those in inland cities on the Po Plain and in Emilia (Marzabotto, Bologna, and Mantua). A number of Attic vases uncovered in Etrurian inland cities may have been routed there via Spina. The city's relations with the Greek world were excellent: A number of sources even call it a Greek city (Pseudo-Scylax 17; Strabo 5.1.7), and it had a treasury at Delphi.

The consequences of the crisis in the coastal cities, however, were grave, as we can tell from the artistic production of the time. For example, the painters decorating the tombs of Tarquinia were no longer influenced by Greek models—particularly painted vases. They kept reworking Archaic iconography and stylistic elements, which became rather sloppy. The outlines of figures, which had been thin and elegant in Archaic execution, now became broad and barely effective aesthetically. This fact is noteworthy because Greek art in this period, thanks to a number of outstanding masters—Myron, Polyclitus, Phidias, and Alcamenes in sculpture, and Micon, Polygnotus, Parrhasius, and Zeuxis in painting—used devices such as foreshortening, perspective, "bold" outlines,

chiaroscuro, and tonal values in color to give figures three-dimensionality. In coastal Etruria, however, artisans focused on bronze utensils that did not rise beyond the level of craft. Nevertheless, some of these products found an export market: Vulcian long-beaked pitchers appear in continental Europe (see pp. 122ff.) and the mirrors, censers, and candelabras are mentioned in literary tradition (Pherecrates in Athenaeus *Deipnosoph* 15.700c).

The inland cities located along the valley of the Tiber and its tributaries—Veii, Falerii, Volsinii (Orvieto), Chiusi, and Arezzo—were primarily agricultural economies and they benefited from the crisis of the coastal cities. On a number of occasions during the fifth century B.C., these cities supplied Rome with wheat in times of need. These cities also had well-proportioned sculptures in stone, terra-cotta, and bronze in their tombs and sanctuaries, works that echoed the achievements of Classical Greek art. It is worth mentioning a few of these. At the temple buildings of Belvedere or Via San Leonardo in Orvieto, fragments of terra-cotta statues reflect the achievements of Greek sculpture

The back wall of the Tomb of the Leopards featuring a symposium scene, first half of the fifth century B.C., from the Monterozzi necropolis in Tarquinia (Viterbo)

during the third quarter of the fifth century: the hair and beards punctuated by comma-like locks, the protruding eyebrow arches, and the robust anatomy. The *Mars* from Todi, a bronze statue of a warrior that unites the deliberation of Polyclitus with the majesty of Phidias, has been attributed to a workshop in Volsinii.

Etruscan continued to ply the seas during the fifth and fourth centuries B.C., although some sources described their activities as piracy. Despite their weakness, the coastal cities hastened to make up for their loss to Syracuse at the earliest opportunity. During the Peloponnesian War, when the Athenians laid siege to Sicilian cities between 415 and 413 B.C., several Etruscan cities banded together to support the besiegers. Their contribution to the effort—a mere three

ships—shared the disastrous fate of the Athenian fleet. The Syracusans, encouraged by their success, pursued policies against both the Etruscans and the Greeks and took control of the seas. Around 390 B.C. they removed colonies from crucial points along the Adriatic Sea, such as Ancona, Adria, and Issa; in 384 B.C., on the pretext of clearing Etruscan pirates from the sea (in reality they were collecting funds for war against the Carthaginians), they raided the sanctuary at Pyrgi in the Tyrrhenian and carried away considerable riches (Diodorus Siculus 15.14.3–4; Pseudo-Aristotle *Oeconomica* 1349b; Aelianus *Varia Historia* 1.20; Polyaenus *Strategemata* 5.2.21). Between 383 and 373 B.C. they settled in the acropolis of Croton on the Ionian Sea.

The trade in Greek pottery was dramatically affected over the course of the fifth century B.C. by Etruria's new strategic situation. Vases produced in Attic workshops could no longer gain access to international markets through Etruscan ports, which were essentially reduced to Populonia on the Tyrrhenian Sea and Spina on the Adriatic. A number of potters and ceramic decorators emigrated during the second half of the fifth century toward southern Italy, Sicily, and the Pontus Euxinus regions. In the early decades of the fourth century, they also reached Etruscan areas at Falerii, where there were several active workshops. Other affiliates would eventually detach from these workshops and establish themselves in other Etruscan cities (Vulci, Tarquinia, Caere, Orvieto, Chiusi, and Volterra).

Two major events marked the history of ancient Italy between the end of the fifth and the first centuries B.C.: the descent of the Gauls into the Italian peninsula and the Romanization of Italy.

Chalice-shaped, red-figured krater with scenes of the Sack of Troy (the slaying of Neoptolemus and Priam, and Menelaus recovering Helen), by the Nazzano painter, from about the middle of the fourth century B.C., from Falerii Veteres (Viterbo). Rome, Museo di Villa Giulia

According to tradition, the Gauls were encouraged to migrate into Italy by an Etruscan from Chiusi named Arruns, who enticed them with offers of wine, oil, and dried fruit (Livy 5.33.1–6; Dionysios of Halikarnassos 13.10; Plutarch *Camillus* 15.3–4). This version of events would explain why the Gauls stopped at Chiusi: Perhaps they expected the local inhabitants to give them land to cultivate before they continued on to sack Rome (390 B.C.). The Gauls remained in Italy from then on, and they wove relationships that alternated between friendship and enmity with a variety of Italic peoples, including the Etruscans. Their actions were often tied to Syracuse's expansionism: the founding of the Syracusan colony of Adria in the early years of the fourth century, for instance, may have been part of a (hypothetical) Gallic-Syracusan plan against the Etruscans. The Syracusan assault on the sanctuary of Pyrgi in 384 B.C. took place three years after a clash between Gauls and Caeretans, and it is possible that the Syracusans may have taken advantage of the Caeretans by attacking the sanctuary of their port. Battles between Gauls and Romans ensued, with Etruscan participation, and some had significant consequences. The battle of Sentinum in 295 B.C. marked the defeat of the populations of central Italy—the Senones, Umbri, Samnites, and Etruscans—and Roman power asserted itself over the entire region. That power would be consolidated in 283 B.C. when the Romans defeated the Etruscans and the Boii at Lake Vadimo (near Ameria).

The Roman occupation of Veii in 396 B.C., after a decade-long siege, was the first step in the Romanization of Etruria, a process that would take three centuries to complete. The war for Veii ended with the fall and destruction of that city; its lands were annexed into Roman territory in Rome's first expansion beyond the Tiber. In the two years that followed, another two Etrurian cities were conquered: Capena in 395 B.C. and Falerii in 394 B.C. These were the only cities to have fought alongside Veii, since they were the closest and the most endangered by Roman aggression.

The Etruscans attempted to control the lower valley of the Tiber by removing two colonies that were under Latin law: Sutri in 383 B.C. and Nepi in 373 B.C. Both were absorbed into the territory of Tarquinia, which during the first half of the fourth century engaged in various skirmishes with Rome. The conclusive conflict between Tarquinia and Rome occurred between 358 and 351 B.C., ending in a forty-year truce that was renewed in 308 B.C. The other great metropolis of southern Etruria, Caere, never directly took the initiative to go to war with Rome, and indeed always sought a neighborly relationship. It was rewarded with *civitas sine suffragio*, that is, its people became Roman citizens lacking only the right to vote. By the middle of the fourth century, all of southern Etruria was definitively under the control of Romans who turned their attentions to the Latini, the Samnites, and the Gauls.

Etruscan cities along the Tyrrhenian coast felt the effects of this new situation. The aristocracy, probably extracting profit from the land, began to reassert itself. Inland regions once again saw their populations rise as agriculture was reintroduced, including areas characterized by the so-called rock necropoleis (Blera, Norchia, Castel d'Asso, Grotta Porcina, San Giuliano, San Giovenale, and Tuscania). A number of the tombs at city necropoleis

belonged to the new wealthy class; they are typically large, featuring rich decorations of paintings and sculpture with characteristic subjects (banquets, weapons and domestic furnishings, and mythological series). Examples include the Tomb of the Reliefs in Caere; the Tomb of the Underworld, the Tomb of the Shields, the Tomb of the Giglioli, and the *Tomba della Mercareccia* in Tarquinia; and the François Tomb in Vulci. Included in this class are a number of sarcophagi of Parian marble, uncovered in various tombs at Tarquinia, which were often painted with tempera. This social renewal may have had external support from the Roman Senate, which had a close and willing partner in the Etruscan aristocracy.

The Hellenistic Period Between the end of the fourth century and the third quarter of the third century B.C., sources record a series of clashes between the Romans and Etruscans from the cities of central Etruria. These battles usually ended in Roman victory. In 310 B.C., as previously noted, an Etruscan army was defeated near Lake Vadimo; in 302 B.C. the Roman army intervened in Arezzo when it was shaken by a slave uprising and restored the aristocrats to power; in 294 B.C., after a variety of skirmishes, Volsinii, Perugia, and Arezzo signed a truce with Rome; in 293 B.C. the consul Lucius Postumius Megellus definitively took Roselle; in 280 B.C. the consul Tiberius Coruncanius celebrated a triumph over the Vulcians and Volsinians; in 264 B.C. Volsinii (Orvieto) was occupied and destroyed by the consul M. Fulvius Flaccus, and its surviving populace was displaced; Falerii suffered the same fate in 241 B.C., with its inhabitants relocated to the plain at Falerii Novi.

By this point, central Etruria had lost its autonomy. The region was kept under control by a policy of repopulating the countryside with farms and small rustic settlements that were loyal to Rome and by founding colonies that were true breeding grounds for Roman spirit: Cosa in 273 B.C., Castrum Novum in 264 B.C., Alsio in 247 B.C., Fregene in 245 B.C., Pyrgi in 191 B.C., Gravisca in 181 B.C., Lucca in 180 B.C., Luni in 177 B.C., and Heba-Magliano between 167 and 157 B.C. Roman citizens arrived to take possession, bringing with them masters who were subsequently employed in building and decorating public works. The consular roads of Aurelia, Clodia, Cassia, Flaminia, and Amerina, many of them retracing old Etruscan routes, acted as pathways for Roman influence and were used for the rapid transfer of troops.

By the second half of the third century B.C., the Etruscan cities were no longer actively resisting Rome. People of the lower classes, who were often unemployed, emigrated to the capital and found work there by enrolling in the Roman professional army; those of the upper classes, such as the Caecina family of Volterra, also emigrated there to move into politics. It is no accident that two great battles fought by the Romans against their enemies during the last quarter of the third century took place in Etruscan territory, and with the Etruscans' consent. One was against the Gauls at Talamone in 225 B.C., the other against Hannibal's Carthaginians near Lake Trasimeno in 217 B.C. Moreover, when P. Cornelius Scipio was equipping his expedition to face Hannibal in Africa in 205 B.C., many Etruscan cities contributed goods from their respective economies. Caere provided wheat and provisions; Populonia iron;

Tombs of the rock necropoleis of Norchia (Viterbo), fourth or third century B.C.

The Tomb of the Reliefs, second half of the fourth century B.C., from the Banditaccia necropolis in Caere (Rome). Furnishings from an aristocratic house are reproduced in stucco upon the walls and pilasters.

Tarquinia wheat and sailcloth; Volterra wheat and lumber; Arezzo wheat and a large quantity of iron tools and weapons; and Perugia, Chiusi, and Roselle offered wheat and fir timbers for shipbuilding (Livy 48.45.14–18). The Etruscans and other Italic peoples now sought integration into Roman society: Cumae petitioned Rome in 180 B.C. for the privilege of using the Latin language for their public acts and auctions (Livy 40.42.13).

Despite the broad assertion of Roman power, Etruscan art continued along traditional lines. Incised mirrors continued to be produced. Their decoration, however, was cursory, obsessively repeating patterns and iconography such as the Dioscuri, the Lasa (female demons), or an erotic version of the Judgment of Paris. Bronze figures of offering bearers or divinities, primarily found in votive deposits, echo Greek art of the fourth century B.C. They feature embellished faces that are slightly tilted, with thin, elongated necks and bodies that are disproportionately long from the waist down. Among these, a group made with anti-Classical tastes—flat and extremely elongated bodies—stands out. These figures originated in various locations in central Italy. Some are from Volterra, including the masterpiece of the series, the so-called *Ombra della Sera* preserved at the Museo Guarnacci at Volterra.

Coins from the third century B.C. are exclusively bronze and were mostly issued by cities with mining economies. Looking beyond their artistic merit, they give some indications of rituals and local situations. For example, there is one from Volterra with the head of a two-faced deity on its front, and another from Populonia with a hammer and pincers on its reverse.

For the most part, pottery was intended for symposia. Other than those imitating red-figured works, the vases were black-painted or silver-plated. What ornamentation they had was composed of striations, tiny stamps (normally palmettes), or friezes with reliefs. This trend persisted between the fourth and first centuries B.C., when Arretine pottery began to be made.

Painting, especially in Tarquinia, includes a number of famous examples, such as in the Tomb of the Typhon, the *Tomba del Convegno*, and the Tomb of the Cardinal. Their common subject was funerary, often peopled with demonic figures.

The works that best represent Etruscan art of the Hellenistic period are the burial sarcophagi of southern Etruria and the small cinerary urns of northern Etruria. They were made of local materials and therefore varied from site to site. The sarcophagi were concentrated in Tarquinia and Tuscania; very few came from other cities. Those in stone were made of nenfro, the volcanic tufa that is so common in southern Etruria. The deceased was shown lying upon the lid in a supine position (fourth century B.C.), obliquely (third century B.C.), or partly upright (the end of the third and second centuries B.C.). The latter mimics the position of participants at a symposium, and indeed the deceased is shown holding a bowl for wine. The casket, which was decorated with reliefs, presented subjects from the netherworld (demons, monsters, and the journey to the afterlife) or from myths that were often reinterpreted from a funerary angle. Terra-cotta sarcophagi were a specialty of Tuscania.

The practice of cremation gave rise to a somewhat different tradition. Small ash urns were mainly produced in Volterra, Chiusi,

and Perugia. The deceased on the lid was either partly reclining (first half of the third century B.C.), mostly upright with a naked torso (second century), or wearing a tunic (end of the second and first centuries). The deceased was generally posed as a symposium participant, holding a drinking vessel if male and a mirror or fan if female. In Volterra, the urns were made of tufa or alabaster. Urn decorations in tufa showed the journey to the Underworld, while those

Clay urn showing a hero using a plow as a weapon, second century B.C., from Chiusi (Siena). Florence, Museo Archeologico

in alabaster, which could be carved in full relief, primarily featured subjects from Greek mythology, into which Etruscan demons were often inserted. In Chiusi carvers used alabaster to create decorations in high relief with figures that remain attached to the background, or travertine to illustrate Greek myths. During the second century many urns were fashioned in terracotta with stamped decorations, such as one

On the facing page, a pilaster with a painting of Typhon standing as a telamon at the tomb of the same name, from about the middle of the second century B.C. Monterozzi necropolis in Tarquinia (Viterbo)

showing the fratricidal duel of Eteocles and Polyneices, a hero who fights with a plow. In Perugia, urn production began toward the end of the third century, generally using travertine. The shape of the urn tended to be cubic rather than parallelepiped, and its lid was shaped like a roof with a pediment at the rear. It was decorated in partial relief, and the subjects depicted were either mythological or funerary.

The popularity of Greek myths, especially episodes from the Trojan and Theban cycles, has its counterpart in Latin tragedy from the Archaic period, when these Etruscan urns were being produced. Representations on a number of urns from the Volterran series preserve elements reminiscent of theatrical tradition, such as landscape backgrounds, the placement of scenes between columns or statues, and artificial backdrops propped up by supports as if for a stage. (The name of one Etruscan tragedian, Volnius, has passed down to us [Varro *De lingus Latina* 5.40.5].)

The style that prevailed in urn depictions may have originated on parchment: bowed, expressive heads; projections and indentations in body structure; fluttering drapery; and baroque accents. We see the same tendencies in architectural terra-cottas during the second century B.C., such as those from Catona (Arezzo). Moreover, there is abundant evidence of a Classical style with Attic origins, such as organically structured and slender bodies, which had reached Etruria indirectly through Rome.

These sarcophagi and urns raise the question of portraiture: To what extent were these representations individualized? Representing the deceased on a lid would seem to personalize the funerary monument, but in fact the statue's features were generic and did not represent individual faces or bodies. Evidently the carver's workshops were supplied with an assortment of urn lids bearing images that a master could retouch as the occasion demanded, adding features such as baldness, wrinkles, or dimples. True portraits did exist, such as statues in homage of high-profile citizens. One of these is the *Orator* from Pila (Perugia) that dates to the second century B.C. Based on the inscription on the toga's hem, the statue appears to have belonged to the Etruscan world even at this late date, although its costume, shoes, and realistic expression were already tilting toward the Roman.

The epilogue to this process of Romanization was the Social War (90–88 B.C.), which ended with the Romans granting the right of Roman citizenship to the Italic peoples (*lex Julia* and *lex Calpurnia*). This event marked the end of the various political and cultural entities that had characterized the history of ancient Italy over the course of the last millennium B.C. From that moment on, the inhabitants of Etruria had the same rights as Roman citizens, and Latin became the official language in Etruria. Etruscan history merged with Roman history.

Later History

According the sources (Censorinus *De die natali* 17.5.6), the Etruscan world is supposed to have spanned ten centuries. However, these "centuries" did not always last exactly a hundred years. The last two Etruscan "centuries" were said to have begun after the Social War. The penultimate one began in 88 B.C., with a violent trumpet blast that frightened the entire population, namely the Civil War (Plutarch *Sulla* 7.3). The final period (which was quite brief) began in 44 B.C., heralded by the appearance of a comet.

During that momentous first century B.C., we find a number of sepulchral epitaphs that are bilingual, written in both Etruscan and Latin. The texts are almost always limited to the name of the deceased.

On the facing page, the *Orator*, bronze statue of the second century B.C., from Pila (Perugia). Florence, Museo Archeologico

Terra-cotta head of a young man wearing a Phrygian cap, first half of the second century B.C., from Catona (Arezzo). Florence, Museo Archeologico

One from Pesaro, from the second half of the first century B.C., refers to a certain L. Cafatius, who was a haruspex and interpreter of lightning (in Latin *haruspex fulguriator*, in Etruscan *netśvis trutnvt frontac*). The deceased's line of work was naturally conservative and highly prestigious in the Etruscan world, and the addition of the Etruscan text is in line with his position.

References by the ancient writers to Etruscan haruspices, who were still active during the late Republican and Imperial periods and even during the High Middle Ages, were both explicit and frequent (Cicero *De divinatione* 1.2.3; 1.41.92; *De legibus* 2.9; 2.21; Tacitus *Annales* 11.15.1; Ammianus Marcellinus 23.5.8; Zosimus 5.41.1; Procopius *De bello Gothico* 8.21.16). The science they safeguarded (the *disciplina etrusca*) was recorded in books that were regularly consulted on important occasions.

These small signs are enough to confirm that firmly rooted Etruscan traditions persisted in the new age. These traditions were not (and could not be) suddenly erased through some legislative act. Furthermore, alongside the remaining forms that continued without interruption, a movement to revive Etruscan culture emerged during the first century B.C. Latin translations were made of books that set down the rules of the *disciplina etrusca*, and specialized works on the Etruscans were written. Both types of literature, unfortunately, have been lost (see p. 16). But people started to collect Etruscan bronzes (Horace *Epistulae* 2.2.180–83), and Virgil gave the Etruscans a determining role in the birth of Rome in his *Aeneid*, a work written for Emperor Augustus. Livy, among others, insisted that the contributions of Etruscan culture to Rome's origins be recognized in official

The bronze statue of the *Chimaira*, end of the fifth century B.C., from a votive deposit at Porta San Lorentino in Arezzo. The wounds visible on the monster's body suggest that the *Chimaira* must have been part of a sculptural group that included its slayer, Bellerophon, riding on Pegasos. Florence, Museo Archeologico

historiography, and institutions such as the council of the Etruscan peoples and the order of seventy haruspices were resurrected. Etruscan cities celebrated the notable figures of the past with honorific statues and eulogistic inscriptions, as with the Spurinna family in Tarquinia during the Julio-Claudian era. The columns of the ground-level portico of the Colosseum even continued the Tuscan order of architecture. The list could go on much longer.

Interest in the Etruscans did not abate during the Middle Ages, when Etruscan urns were used to contain the relics of saints. For example, in 1140 the remains of Saint Clement were deposited in an urn that is today preserved at the Museo Guarnacci in Volterra. It was with Humanism and the Renaissance, however, amid the fervor of rediscovering the ancient world, that a genuine mythology began to surround the Etruscans in Tuscany and Lazio. They became a model for civil and moral reform programs in cities such as Florence and Viterbo, which both sought antecedents for their contemporary achievements in their Etruscan past.

At first the Etruscans were merely figures from the literary and historiographic tradition. But toward the middle of the sixteenth century evidence from their buried monuments began to gain appreciation. Cosimo I de' Medici acquired for his collection a number of great bronze statues that had been dug up in Etruria, such as the *Minerva,* the *Chimaira* of Arezzo, and the *Orator* of Pila. In their dominating cultural role, the Etruscans were seen as the Medicis' predecessors. It should be remembered that Cosimo I, when he finally managed to

become the Grand Duke of Tuscany in 1569, took the official title of *Magnux Dux Etruriae,* making sly reference to a region that was much larger than Tuscany and hinting at his expansionist agenda. The distinction between Tuscany and Etruria was fudged once again when the son of his second successor, Ferdinando I, charged Leonida Pindemonte of Verona in 1596 with creating the first geographic map of Tuscany. The work was entitled *Geografia della toscana e breve compendio delle sue historie* (The Geography of Tuscany and a Brief Outline of Its History), although the cartographic reproduction and the treatment of the subject regarded Etruria in its entirety.

Antiquarians in the eighteenth century (F. Buonarroti, A. F. Gori, S. Maffei, G. B. Passeri, and M. Guarnacci) followed the same lines. They devoted themselves to every aspect of Etruscan culture—language, inscriptions, religion, art, and so on—and utilized monumental and figurative sources as well as literary ones. They formulated exalted judgments about the Etruscans that bore no relationship at all to history.

Their work was poorly received and derided as "Etruschery" (*etruscheria*) instead of Etruscology. Such misplaced enthusiasm undermined research on the Etruscans for a long time. This impediment was finally overcome by serious scholars working in the first decades of the nineteenth century— L. Lanzi and G. Micali in Italy and K. O. Müller in Germany—who undertook the scientific study of Etruscan history. They helped formulate directions for research that, in combination with more recent developments, persist to the present day.

On the facing page, bronze pitcher with a biconic body and a human-shaped handle, end of the fourth century B.C., from the Tomb of the Gold in the Peschiera necropolis in Todi (Perugia). Rome, Museo di Villa Giulia

The Etruscans in the Mediterranean

| GIOVANNANGELO CAMPOREALE

[handwritten annotations:] meaning p96. pirates try to steal the wine trade by estab. naval supremacy.

[handwritten:] named after → Etruscans

An Etruscan *hydria* showing Etruscan pirates being transformed into dolphinmen after abducting Dionysos, from the end of the sixth to the beginning of the fourth century B.C., provenance unknown. Toledo, Museum of Art

The Etruscans had many ties to the sea, including trade, piracy, fishing, naval engagements, and port structures and infrastructure. It is no accident that the Tyrrhenian Sea takes its name from this ethnic group (the Greeks, as we will remember, called them the Tyrrhenoí) and that the Adriatic took its name from Adria, an Etruscan colony (Livy 5.33.7–8). The Etruscans' first expeditions on the Tyrrhenian, or more generally the Mediterranean—those that we have been able to reconstruct or know from ancient sources—date back to the origins of their civilization. However, we must scrutinize the evidence of these expeditions carefully, judging each case on its own merits, and making sure that alternative theories and caveats also get an airing.

A number of manufactured goods from the late Bronze Age, items that were made in Sardinia or Cyprus and brought to the Italian peninsula via Sardinia, should be set aside from this discussion; we have only fragments of these objects, uncovered in deposits at Piediluco in Contigliano and San Francesco in Bologna. Etruscan works in Sardinia dating back to the ninth century B.C.—for example, a double-edged razor from a shipwreck in Nurra and a crescent-shaped razor from Laerru or Cuglieri—are more solidly attested, as

On the previous page, the headland of Monte Conero in the mid-Adriatic; its inlets provided landings for Greek merchant ships that transported goods for trade.

are Sardinian works in Etruria. The latter include miniature figurines of a chieftain, a stool, and a basket from a tomb in the Cavalupo necropolis in Vulci; a bronze dagger from a trench tomb in the Poggio alle Birbe necropolis in Vetulonia; and the earliest impasto pitchers with elongated and off-centered necks from the Villanovan tombs of Vetulonia. The flow continued during the eighth century, with Etruscan bronze fibulae of various kinds in Sardinia, and Sardinian conical buttons and impasto pitchers in Etruria. However, the question remains open as to whether this traffic was due to Etruscan traders who reached Sardinia or to Phoenician sailors who voyaged across the entire western basin of the Mediterranean during the ninth century, setting up colonies and emporia at many coastal locations in northern Africa, Spain, Sardinia, and Sicily.

Ephorus (in Strabo 6.2.2) asserts that the Greeks delayed their colonization of eastern Sicily for fear of being raided by Etruscan pirates. Keeping in mind that the oldest Greek settlements on the coast of the Italian peninsula and islands date to the first half of the eighth century B.C. (the emporium at Ischia around 775 B.C.; the colony of Cumae around 750 B.C.), and that those on the eastern coast of Sicily date to the second half of the same century (Syracuse in 734 B.C.; Megara Hyblaea in 728 B.C.), Ephorus's statements must have referred to the middle decades of the eighth century or before. One plausible theory, often proposed, is that the historian was projecting a contemporary situation into the remote past, since Etruscan piracy must have been common during his own time (the fourth century B.C.).

The Etruscans' vital relationship with the sea during the early years of their history manifests itself in many different ways. Impasto vases in the shapes of small boats, dating to the ninth century B.C., were among a number of Villanovan grave goods from cities on the Tyrrhenian coast (Caere and Tarquinia). Boats frequently appear on the oldest painted Etruscan vases, datable to between the last decades of the eighth and the first decades of the seventh centuries. A sea battle between two ships—possibly commemorating a conflict in which the vase's Etruscan owner was involved—is painted on a krater from the years around 660 B.C. It was found in Caere and signed by Aristonothos, a master of Greek origins who probably worked in Etruria. A ship is painted in a tomb, also in Caere, from around the middle of the seventh century and may allude to the deceased's profession. Thus we can infer that the Etruscans, at least those in coastal cities, must already have had an interest in the sea in the ninth to seventh centuries. Whether their activities constituted trade or piracy is of less concern, especially since the two were not easy to distinguish in those early centuries. According to certain ancient writers (Thucydides 1.5.1; Pompeius Trogus in Justinus *Epitome* 43.3.5), piracy at that time was more a source of glory than of shame.

Greeks from the island of Euboea had been trading since the first half of the eighth century B.C. with cities on the central and southern coast of the Tyrrhenian. These important exchanges led to the founding of colonies and emporia in the lower Tyrrhenian Sea (Ischia and Cumae), although not yet in the middle Tyrrhenian. Similarly, the Phoenicians, whose products

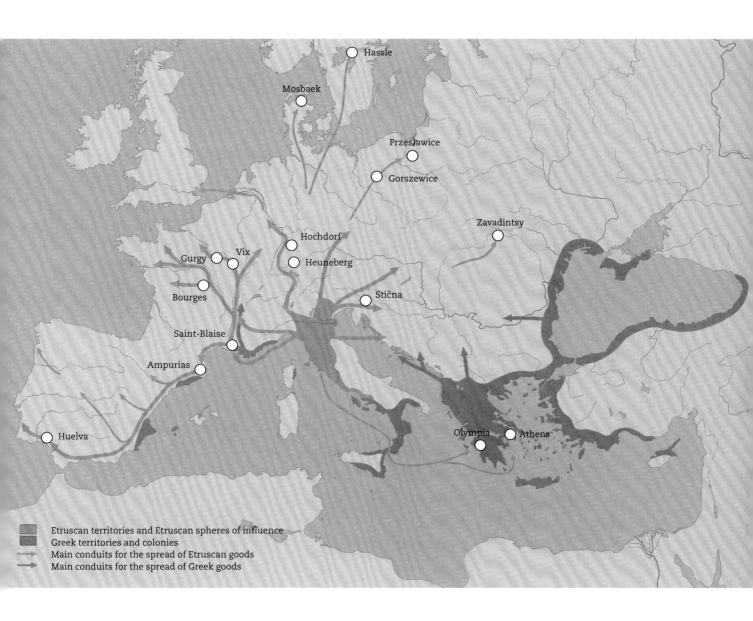

Map of Europe indicating the directions that Etruscan and Greek products took

can be found in tombs in Etruscan cities along the Tyrrhenian coast (Tarquinia, Vulci, and Vetulonia) beginning with the middle decades of the eighth century, had not yet established settlements there. Evidently the Etruscans defended their coasts from foreign interference that might have compromised their maritime ventures.

Although Etruscan expeditions to various Mediterranean regions, beginning with the Tyrrhenian islands (see later chapters on Corsica, Sardinia, and Sicily), were mostly commercial, they inevitably had cultural implications. To reconstruct the picture accurately, data from historiographic and literary traditions and from archaeological research must be sifted

Map legend:
- Etruscan territories and Etruscan spheres of influence
- Greek territories and colonies
- Main conduits for the spread of Etruscan goods
- Main conduits for the spread of Greek goods

Map labels: Hassle, Mosbaek, Przesławice, Gorszewice, Zavadintsy, Hochdorf, Gurgy, Vix, Heuneberg, Bourges, Stična, Saint-Blaise, Ampurias, Huelva, Olympia, Athens

Krater signed by the potter and ceramic decorator Aristonothos depicting a naval battle, first half of the seventh century B.C., from Caere (Rome). The battle probably alludes to a conflict between the vase's owner and a competing merchant's ship. Rome, Musei Capitolini

thoroughly for validity and legitimacy. The archaeological finds are generally works of artistic craftsmanship, usually of sufficient quality to be sold on foreign markets. These works were sometimes shipped by themselves, as rarities or curiosities. But more often they traveled together with goods that ended up being consumed or transformed, and which are thus difficult to quantify. The merchants who shipped these goods—foodstuffs, wood, minerals, or metals, which Etruria had in abundance—may or may not have been Etruscans. In either case, the acculturation process in the region where the manufactured goods were shipped was likely more intense if Etruscans were there, especially if they were there for significant stretches of time. Two fragmentary crested bronze helmets, uncovered in sanctuaries at Olympia and Delphi, constitute the earliest evidence we have of the Etruscan thrust into the Mediterranean basin. These resemble others uncovered in Villanovan tombs from the end of the ninth or the first half of the eighth century B.C. Goods were flowing in both directions by this time, since an Aegean or Cypriot mirror (which may have been restored in ancient times) was found in a trench tomb in Tarquinia from the middle of the ninth century, and we know of other similar examples in Sicily (Pantalica) and in Sardinia (Santadi). The clearest examples of Greek exports to Etruria date to the third quarter of the eighth century: Euboean cups that were probably brought by merchants who frequented the lower Tyrrhenian, founding emporia and colonies (see pp. 8off.). The Euboean colonies in the lower Tyrrhenian may have been the middlemen in the distribution of these cups throughout Etruria, since Etruscan goods from that time have been found in Ischia (impasto amphorae with spiral decorations) and in Cumae (sheet-bronze shields). (It seems prudent to leave out of consideration an Etruscan bronze belt, today in the Bibliothèque Nationale in Paris, which was acquired in Euboea but may have been unearthed elsewhere.) The final decades of the eighth and the first decades of the seventh centuries saw a steady influx of Etruscan bronze weapons into a number of Greek sanctuaries: two shield fragments in Dodona; a shield fragment and an antenna sword in Samos; and shields and spear points (eighteen fragments) in Olympia. These finds are obviously votive offerings, although we cannot ascertain whose they

were or who brought them to Greece. We can extract a few clues from the nature of the finds themselves, however. Since they are weapons, they may have been spoils of war. But in fact the shields in question are made of such thin sheets of bronze that they would have crumpled beneath the blows of an attacking weapon, even if they had been reinforced with leather. (In any case, we have found no traces of leather.) In addition, the shields were furnished with a carrying handle, which means that they could be grasped but not worn. In short, these armaments—more impressive for their rich ornamentation

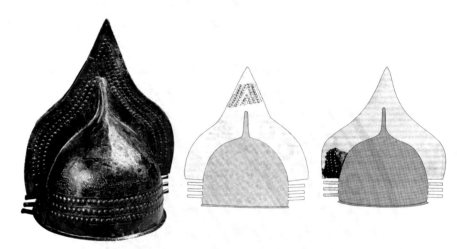

of concentric bands than for their efficacy as military implements—were much more likely used as parade weapons. We can make similar deductions regarding the spear points, which were quite long (one of them would have measured over a meter long if its tip were intact) and thus ill suited for use in battle.

Weapons such as these, and others mentioned below, were uncovered among

Crested bronze helmet, second half of the eighth century B.C., from the Tomb of the Warrior in Volterra (Pisa). The drawings highlight two fragments of crests from similar Etruscan helmets that were discovered in Greek sanctuaries at Olympia and Delphi. Volterra, Museo Guarnacci

At left, Attic black-figured amphora of the so-called Nikosthenic type, second half of the sixth century B.C., from Caere (Rome). Similar amphorae were produced in the Athenian workshop of the potter Nikosthenes after Etruscan models. Rome, Museo di Villa Giulia

At left, Attic black-figured amphora of the so-called Nikosthenic type, second half of the sixth century B.C., from Caere (Rome). Similar amphorae were produced in the Athenian workshop of the potter Nikosthenes after Etruscan models. Rome, Museo di Villa Giulia

At right, Euboean transport amphora from the first half of the seventh century B.C., from the Tomb of the Hut in Caere (Rome). Amphorae such as these were used to transport oil and wine. Rome, Museo di Villa Giulia

Villanovan grave goods. They indicate the elevated social status that the deceased enjoyed in life, and conceivably they had the same ideological value when they were offered as ex-votos at a sanctuary. Similarly, a variety of bronze fibulae attributable to Etruscan workshops have been

found in these same sanctuaries. These were coeval with the weapons, objects of personal adornment that were used with garments or, more generally, fine textiles. The latter, being of animal or vegetal fibers, have long since turned to dust. But we know from many literary references that textiles were often presented as offerings to gods. To take just one example, Homer (*Iliad* 6.90–93; 6.293–95) writes that Hecuba offered the most beautiful peplos she possessed to Athena. In other words, these weapons and articles of clothing may well have been valued equally as offerings.

The substantial number of shields found at Olympia and other sanctuaries, and their chronological distribution ranging between the last decades of the eighth century B.C. (examples with Geometric motifs) and the early decades of the seventh (with Orientalizing motifs), tells us that they arrived in Greece and were designated as offerings at a fairly steady pace. The same can be said of the fibulae. We can imagine that these items served as some sort of compensation, albeit partial, for merchants who brought wine vases from Greece (Euboea and Corinth) and probably wine as well (see pp. 40ff.). But this is merely a theory. What is certain is that the donors, regardless of their nationality, brought these objects to Greece as offerings, and in significant quantities. It is worth affirming that Etruscan manufactured exports are in fact representative of the national culture. They were made of bronze, a material that was widely used in Etruscan works from the ninth century B.C. on; as we have noted, its constituent materials—copper and tin—were mined close by. As the ancient writers affirmed (Pseudo-Aristotle *De Mirabilibus auscultationibus* 93), bronze was used for every sort of utensil in Etruria.

The helmets and shields, we know, were made in southern Etruria, and perhaps more precisely in Tarquinia. The cities of southern Etruria, or rather the magnates of these cities, were actively exporting the commercial valuable resources of the territory (salt from saltworks at the mouth of

Clay ash urn with a modeled representation of a banquet on its lid, from about the middle of the seventh century B.C., from Montescudaio (Pisa). This is the oldest example of a banquet scene of the Etruscan figurative tradition in which the guest is seated at table rather than lying on a bed as in scenes from previous centuries. Florence, Museo Archeologico

the Tiber, minerals and metals from the mountains of Tolfa). By the eighth century B.C., they had already penetrated a broad market and were trading directly with Greek merchants.

During the first half of the seventh century B.C., Etruscan handmade bronzes continued to be deposited in the great sanctuaries of Greece, although their origin and nature changed. A horse bit and two *lebetes* from Vetulonia, with handles decorated with lotus flowers and lion cubs, were discovered in Olympia; a similar *lebes* (with only its handle preserved, at the National Museum of Athens) was found in a sanctuary in Attica or Greece; and the end of a (*situla?*) handle and a crown of blooming lotus flowers on a pyxis lid, also made in Vetulonia, were discovered in the Heraion of Samos. These offerings were primarily part of services for symposia and, as such, they were valuable goods that interested the upper class. In most cases the objects were made in Vetulonia.

We should also mention, at least in passing, the fragmentary bronze basins with beaded rims, more than ten in number, that were uncovered during excavations in the sanctuaries of Olympia and Isthmia. These should be considered western imports, even if they cannot clearly be ascribed to either Etruscan cities, southern Italy, or Sicily.

Other handmade bronzes from the Vetulonia workshops, also linked to the symposium, were exported to a variety of locations outside Etruria, such as Italy and northern and central Europe (see pp. 112ff.). We have, for instance, the tripods with legs shaped into eyelets from Bologna, Este, and Novo Mesto (Slovenia);

a pyxis and a fluted bowl from the pit tomb of Tumulus I in Appenwihr (Alsace); and the fluted bowls of Hallstatt, Lyon, or Frankfurt am Main.

Context is very important where these objects are concerned. When found in tombs (as was the case with the tripods from Bologna, Este, and Novo Mesto), they could suggest that the ceremony for which they were designed—the symposium—along with its aristocratic ideological implications, had been introduced among the local elites. When found in a (Greek) sanctuary, their presence simply indicates that the owner, almost certainly someone of the upper class, wanted to offer a valuable object. The cultural implications of the offering differs, depending on whether the offering bearer was an Etruscan who had purposely come to the sanctuary, a Greek, or an Etruscan residing in Greece. In either of the last two cases, it can be theorized that the objects, before being dedicated to a deity, had been kept for a time in private homes and used in ceremonies similar to those practiced where the object itself had been made. Common opinion holds that the custom of the symposium was introduced into Etruria from Greece; the use of such objects in everyday practice may thus be attributed to Etruscans who had reached Greece by the seventh century B.C., importing this Eastern custom when they returned home. The intense commercial relations between the two countries, each of which depended on the other's raw materials and finished products (see pp. 26ff.), would facilitate this exchange. In addition, we have historiographic, epigraphic, and cultural evidence of Greek individuals who integrated into Etruscan society during the seventh century. Demaratos, for example, a rich trader from Corinth, was exiled from his homeland; he settled in Tarquinia and married a local noblewoman (Cornelius Nepos in Pliny *Naturalis Historia* 35.16; 35.152; Dionysios of Halikarnassos 3.46.3–5; Strabo 5.2, 2; 8.6.20). *Rutile Hipukrate*, a name found in an Etruscan inscription from Tarquinia (TLE 155) and derived from a Greek personal name (Hippokrátes), reveals the Greek origins of some of the nobility. Finally, Greek potters, ceramic decorators—the above-mentioned Aristonothos and various Euboeans—or artists in the company of Demaratos were active in various cities of southern Etruria. The question of who transported what materials where is destined to remain open for the time being. Sources state that the merchant Demaratos regularly traveled between Greece and Etruria with loaded ships (Dionysios of Halikarnassos 3.46.3). It is highly likely that Etruscan traders did the same.

Beginning with the final decades of the seventh and for much of the sixth centuries B.C., Etruscan trade in the Mediterranean basin burgeoned, chiefly in wine. The trading network extended across a vast geographic area, from the Pillars of Hercules (the Strait of Gibraltar) to the coast of Syria and the Black Sea. Evidence of commercialized products comes, albeit indirectly, from impasto amphorae used for transport and bucchero vases, or pottery painted in the Etruscan-Corinthian style that were used to draw, pour, and drink wine and were sold as wine services. Wine vases were among the earliest Greek imports to Etruria, at first from Euboea (eighth

century) and then from Corinth and Ionia (between the end of the eighth and the seventh centuries). In all probability, wine was also brought to Etruria from Greece along with these wine services, certainly in transport amphorae and perhaps also in wineskins, which, alas, have not survived. The symposium ceremony, in which participants drank wine, and the social implications connected with it, had by now become established in Etruria. Already toward the end of the eighth century, wine vases that imitated Greek models began to be produced in the workshops of Etruria. It is most likely that the first masters to work in these shops were Greek immigrants; they would have had local apprentices who eventually continued production on their own. In the meantime the cultivation of wine-producing grapes was also introduced in Etruria, perhaps by Greek vinedressers attracted there by the brisk trade in wine. Notably, one of the first narrative scenes of Etruscan art, dating from the middle decades of the seventh century, is a banquet modeled on the lid of a clay ash urn from Montescudaio in the *agger* of Volterra. A rich lord, aided by an attendant (or is it a flute player?), sits pompously before a table laid with various victuals and a large container of wine. In the span of a few decades, the wine produced in Etruria must have reached high levels of quality and quantity; at that point, it became a widely traded commodity.

The first exports were to Corsica, Sardinia, Sicily (see related chapters below), and Carthage. The oldest Etruscan goods that have been discovered in these places are bucchero vases used for wine: amphorae with spiral decorations,

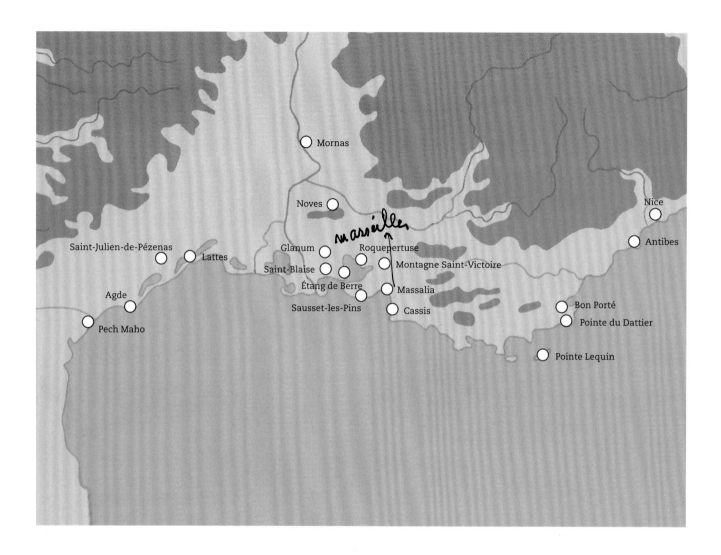

Mornas

Noves

marseilles

Nice

Saint-Julien-de-Pézenas

Glanum
Roquepertuse
Antibes

Lattes
Saint-Blaise
Montagne Saint-Victoire

Étang de Berre
Massalia

Agde
Sausset-les-Pins
Bon Porté

Cassis
Pointe du Dattier

Pech Maho
Pointe Lequin

The Ligurian Sea and the Gulf of Lion, indicating the areas involved in trade with Etruria during the Archaic period

Phoenician or Protocorinthian pitchers, *kotylai* that date to immediately after the seventh century B.C., and *kantharoi* and other vases for drawing wine dating between the end of the seventh and the early decades of the sixth centuries. In Carthage these items are found in both tombs and residences, although in the latter the vessels are in fragments. We conclude, therefore, that the vases were used in the ceremonies of everyday life. In shape they resemble other examples from southern Etruria, especially Caere, which may have been the departure point for this traffic.

Beginning with the end of the seventh century B.C., the greater part of Etruscan wine exports were directed toward the coastal region of southern Gaul (Provence and Languedoc). Archaeological finds there—transport amphorae, bucchero and Etruscan-Corinthian vases—are quite numerous and once again were uncovered at both residences and necropoleis. In certain locations, such as Saint-Blaise, they number in the thousands. At the same time, other bronze wine vases reached Etruria: Rhodian-type pitchers and basins with beaded rims. In all probability, as we have said, the symposium and its related ideology arrived along with these vases of wine. In early times, given the scant number and value of the imported bronze vases, these shipments may have consisted of exchanges between chieftains. But from the first half of the sixth century on, they had become a genuine trade.

To complicate the picture, Greek pottery—Corinthian, Ionian, and Attic—was uncovered in the region that dated between the end of the seventh and the sixth centuries B.C. According to the sources (Pseudo-Scymnus 204ff.), at the end of the seventh century the area was frequented by Rhodians and then by Phokaians, who founded the colony of Massalia (Marseilles) around 600 B.C. Moreover scholars have inferred that Massalia had a number of subcolonies, located along trade routes and dating to the first decades of the sixth century: Ampurias (Empórion), Agde (Agáthe), Antibes (Antípolis), and Nice (Nikaia).

If historiographic and cultural evidence from the coast of southern Gaul points to permanent and organized Greek nuclei, it becomes difficult to disassociate the striking evidence of Etruscan material from a fixed outpost of Etruscans there, at least as agents of trade though perhaps not rising to the level of colonists. Etruscan graffiti on a number of vases from the second half of the sixth century B.C. from Lattes in Languedoc spell out a local woman's name that has been Etruscanized (*vcial*); per-

The recto and verso sides of a lead sheet inscribed with commercial texts in Greek and Etruscan, respectively, from the middle decades of the fifth century B.C., from Pech Maho (Aude). Sigean, Musée des Corbières

haps she was a native who had married an Etruscan merchant. We also have the inscription from Pech Maho on lead sheet from the first half of the fifth century, which was part of a commercial text in Etruscan on one side and in Greek on the other. Although it dates to a period more recent than the time in question, it offers further proof that Etruscans were integrated to some degree with the people of the region.

Shipwrecks and their cargo have been recovered from the shallows off Provence, a short distance from the coast, from the first half of the sixth century B.C. These shed some light on maritime traffic there. A wreck discovered off Cap d'Antibes yielded about 180 huge amphorae for wine that have been attributed to workshops in southern Etruria (Caere and Vulci), dozens of bucchero vases and Etruscan-Corinthian pottery that constituted wine services and were also made in southern Etruria

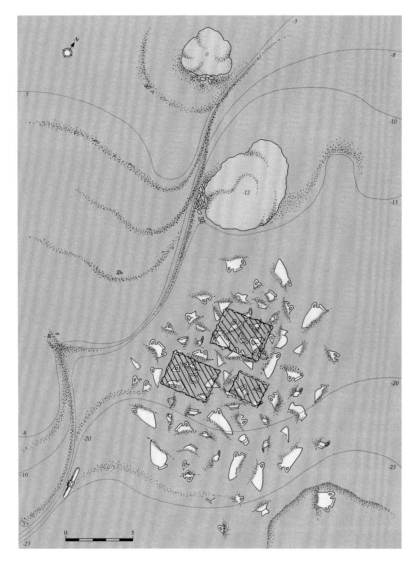

(*kantharoi*, cups, and pitchers), an Ionic cup, and a Punic oil lamp. The ship had surely set out from an Etruscan port. The Ionic cup could be part of Etruscan material of the time, since similar specimens have been found in great numbers in Etruria. The Punic lamp may provide a clue as to the nationality of the ship's owner or crew. Other wrecks, for example those of Bon-Porté and Pointe-du-Dattier, had

cargoes with wine amphorae of Etruscan, Massaliot, Ionian, and Corinthian make. The varied provenance of the cargo leaves us guessing as to the nationality of those who managed this maritime traffic, although it does indicate that ships journeyed short distances at a time, loading and unloading a variety of goods at the ports where they docked. It is important to remember that the ships, in departing

Lyre-shaped handle of a bronze funnel-shaped strainer (*infundibulum*) with a ram's head, first half of the sixth century B.C., from Cancho-Roano (Estremadura). Badajoz, Museo Arqueológico Provincial

from or docking in Etruscan ports, could at any point have also taken on Greek goods, which must have been quite common at Etruscan ports. Obviously, Greek goods may also have shipped directly from Greece to cities of southern Gaul, given the numerous Greek colonies in the area. What is certain is that the process of Greek acculturation in the region, which began immediately with the arrival of Greek

The Cévennes range and the Black Mountain (Montagne Noir), which are in the surrounding areas of Languedoc, are mineral districts that have been exploited since ancient times and were important sources of copper. Minerals or unrefined copper, which always had considerable market value, could readily have reached ports on the Gulf of Lion from inland areas. Workers in the mining and metal-

On the facing page, above, plan of the underwater excavation of a shipwreck from the first half of the sixth century B.C., Cap d'Antibes (Provence). The ship transported impasto amphorae, bucchero and Etruscan-Corinthian painted vases. At right, two impasto amphorae from the wreck at Cap d'Antibes

products, was at least partly mediated through the Etruscans. Greek and Etruscan goods were valued and destined for natives who had the desire and financial resources to buy them.

The problem then becomes one of determining the motivation behind such a large Etruscan (and Greek) expansion into southern Gaul. The answer, obviously, is the region's natural resources.

lurgical fields—skilled or unskilled— could have accompanied these products from the mines (Caesar *Bellum Gallicum* 3.21). Moreover, the Rhone River fed into the Gulf of Lion and in turn connected it to other river valleys (the Saône, the Loire, the Seine, and the Garonne) that reached the tin-mining areas of the Loire and even, through the channel at Manche, Cornwall. While it is true that Etruria

Bronze Etruscan mirror decorated with the incised Judgment of Paris, from about the end of the fourth century B.C., from Ampurias (Catalonia). Barcelona, Museu Arqueológico de Barcelona

was already rich in metals, the high degree of development that the metal industry achieved during the seventh and sixth centuries B.C. leads one to suppose that there was a continuous demand for raw materials. It may have been more economically advantageous to import them rather than continuously exploiting local mines. (Situations of this kind are common in the modern world.) The Etruscan ships had to return home with some sort of cargo, and given the coastal navigation that was common at that time, these foreign metals may also have been unloaded at other Mediterranean ports. Following this same reasoning, the ships that reached the Gulf of Lion may have taken on loads of wood or salt—commodities that Etruria already had in abundance— in order to transport them to other regions.

The Etruscans exported wine vases for transport or table to the Iberian coast as well, though in smaller quantities. The markets ranged from Catalonia to Cadiz and Huelva along the Atlantic coast, beyond the Pillars of Hercules, to ports in the mineral district of Tartessus, which Greeks and Phoenicians had frequented since the early centuries of the first millennium B.C. A number of finds deserve mention: an Etruscan wine service comprising an impasto amphora, a bucchero *kantharos*, and an Etrusco-Corinthian dipping vessel was uncovered in a residential building in Ullastret (northeast Catalonia); a bronze funnel-shaped strainer (*infundibulum*) with a handle shaped like a lyre and terminating in a ram's head—an Etruscan handmade article from the first half of the sixth century that was used for pouring and filtering wine—was discovered at a lordly palace in Cancho-Roano (Estremadura), again in the mineral district of Tartessus. And it is often forgotten that a bronze offering bearer, today in Leiden and belonging to a series commonly seen in Arezzo and Volterra, may have come from the area around Barcelona. Could it have been a gift from Etruscan merchants to their Iberian partners?

Etrusco-Corinthian ointment jars, mostly *aryballoi*, have been found in some cities along the Iberian coast, for example in Ampurias, and also in Carthage. This fact extends the range of Etruscan commerce beyond what we previously supposed. Today various work-

shops for these ointment jars have been identified in Vulci, Tarquinia, Caere, and perhaps even Vetulonia. Any discussion of these containers must also take into account their contents: perfumes and ointments. Toward the end of the seventh century B.C., it seems that Etruria not only produced and exported these articles, but must also have cultivated the plants that are their primary materials: at a minimum, grapevines for vinegar and olive trees for oil.

Carthage also yielded an ivory plaque in the shape of a boar. It is a *tessera hospitalis*, a sort of chit acknowledging mutual hospitality. It bears an Etruscan inscription (TLE² 724) that refers to a Carthaginian

(*Puine Karthazie*), who may have been in Etruria for commercial reasons.

We now know, on the basis of Etruscan grave goods from the second half of the seventh and sixth centuries B.C., that transport amphorae, vases for wine, and ointment jars continued to reach Etruria from various regions of Greece (Corinth, Ionia, Laconia, and Attica), despite the fact that Etruria was now exporting these items. Undoubtedly it was a matter of quality and price. Etruria imported high-quality products from Greece that were destined for a discerning upper class. It also exported similar goods of inferior quality to areas of the western Mediterranean basin. The latter were

perhaps destined for a poorer and less exacting clientele.

Etruscan manufactured goods also reached the eastern Mediterranean basin between the end of the seventh and the first half of the sixth century B.C. These, however, were far fewer than imports of Greek goods that were reaching Etruria, or Etruscan goods that were sold in the western basin. The eastern finds were always linked to the consumption of wine and generally came from sanctuary areas: bucchero *kantharoi* from Ithaca, Amicle, Corinth, Perachora, the Athenian Agora, Chios, and Samos; bronze funnel-shaped strainers from Olympia, the Acropolis at Lindus, the Temple of Apollo Erethimios

road between Corinth and the port of Lechaeum, excavations turned up vases from Corinth, Chios, and Rhodes, Ionic oil lamps, and more than thirty bucchero *kantharoi*. In its variety, this collection was not much different than cargoes in shipwrecks, which indicates that Etruscan materials were circulating in foreign trade and that, once they arrived at their new location, they were bought by local people for use either in domestic contexts (houses or tombs) or public ones (sanctuaries). Proof of this comes from epigraphs written on a number of pieces. A bucchero *kantharos* from the sanctuary of Perachora, for example, bears a dedicatory inscription in Greek by a Greek (*Near[chos an]etheke*:

A drawing of the armlet of an Etruscan shield, second half of the sixth century B.C., from Olympia. Olympia, Archaeological Museum

on Rhodes, and the Temple of Artemis Ephesia at Panticapaeum (on the Crimean peninsula). Bucchero *kantharoi* have also been found in tombs (Corfu, Delos, Rhodes, and Kition) and in residences (Corinth, Smyrna, and Ras-el-Bassit). An Etruscan-Corinthian cup from the group of Poggio Buco in Amathus (Cyprus) can also be added to the list. In every case, the examples amount to only a few units in each location.

In the so-called "merchant complex," a storehouse that was located on the

Nearchus offers me). The funnel-shaped strainer from Panticapaeum also has a dedication to Artemis Ephesia in Greek (*Son [anetheken] Artemi Efes[ei]*: Son offers me to Artemis Ephesia).

Certain finds dating to the sixth century B.C. clarify aspects of the Etruscan expansion into the eastern Mediterranean basin in general and the Greek world in particular.

An enormous quantity of Greek vases painted in red- and black-figure techniques have been uncovered in Etruria, some of which are either authentic signed masterpieces or can be attributed to illustrious masters. They were destined for displays of luxury, such as symposia, or for a woman's personal toilet. Some of these, black-figured works from Attic workshops of the second half of the sixth century B.C., are deemed to be model shapes that had been used in Etruscan bucchero production. For example, amphorae by the Athenian potter Nikosthenes featured rings on their bellies; certain drawing vessels had a conical body with ribbon handles above them; and semicylindrical supports had flared feet. The choice of vase shapes reflected market study: The Athenian workshops produced vases that responded to the specific needs and tastes of their Etruscan clientele. Etruscan tastes undeniably affected Greek production, but obviously other factors impinged on the highly sophisticated Greek ceramic industry.

Potters from Etruria may also have traveled to Athens and worked in local workshops. An Etruscan inscription on a fragment of a Laconian black-painted cup dates to the third quarter of the sixth century and originated at the sanctuary of Athena Aphaia in Aegina; the fact that the text was written on a Greek-made vase hints that the dedicator may have been an Etruscan living in Greece. In a similar conundrum, we find an inscription in Doric dialect, *Tyrsanos* (i.e., Etruscan), written on the base of an Attic *lekythos* from the early fifth century from the Athenian Agora. A theory that this refers to a hellenized Etruscan has been discounted.

Among the evidence of Etruscans in the eastern Mediterranean, we may include a Homeric hymn to Dionysos (probably dating to the end of the sixth or beginning of the fifth centuries), which describes how Etruscan pirates abducted that god. According to this legend, the pirates abducted a handsome young man from the seashore without realizing his divine nature. They carried him aboard ship and threatened to bring him to Egypt and Cyprus unless he or his relatives paid a ransom. The god then assumed the form of a lion and attacked the sailors, who dove into the water to save themselves. There they were transformed into dolphins. Myths, as is well known, are "poetic" elaborations on the episodes of everyday life. Here, the story of the Dionysos' abduction alludes to circumstances that must have prevailed in the Mediterranean world during the sixth century. Etruscan piracy and the Etruscan ships had swept through the western and eastern Mediterranean basins in competition with Greek and Punic ones. Seafaring was linked to the wine trade (Dionysos is the god of wine), and the Etruscans attempted (but failed) to remove the Greek monopoly on this product. The myth confirms the Etruscan expansion toward the eastern Mediterranean, and its attempt to establish naval supremacy.

The earliest evidence in the ancient sources of Etruscans frequenting Greek sanctuaries dates to the sixth and fifth centuries B.C. After the battle on the Sardinian Sea (about 540 B.C.), the Caeretans sent a delegation to Delphi to ask the Pythia how to mitigate a plague that had broken out in the city. The plague arose from the unburied bodies of Greek prisoners, who had been put to death by stoning (Herodotus 1.167.1–2).

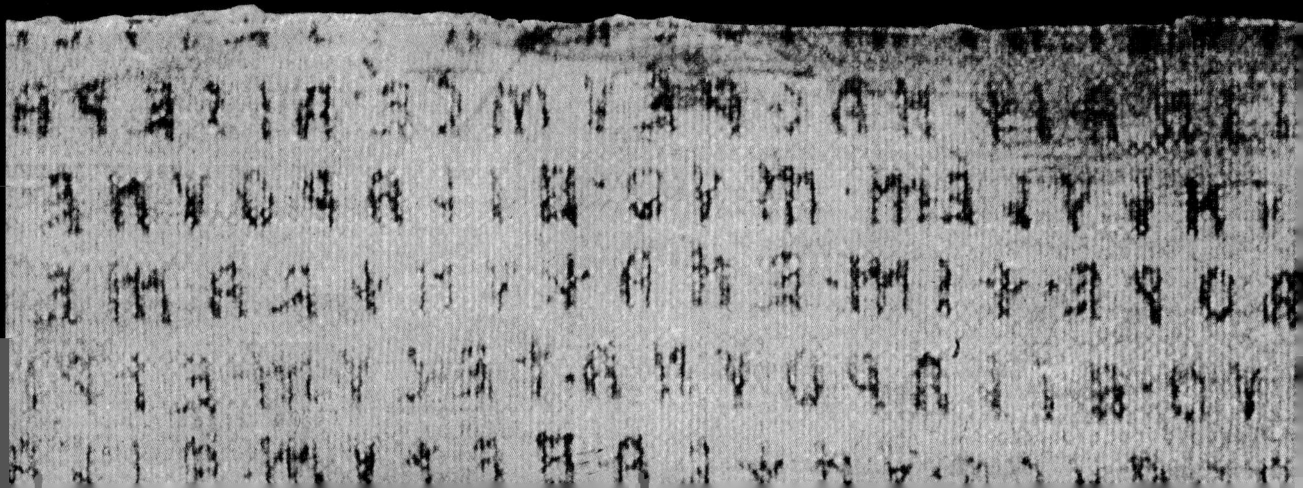

Some have linked this event with the installment of the Caeretan treasury building in the sanctuary at Delphi (Strabo 5.2.3). The Etruscans from Spina had a treasury building in the same sanctuary that probably dated to the first half of the fifth century (Strabo 5.1.7; 9.3.8; Pliny *Naturalis Historia* 3.120). At this time Spina, the port for grain grown on the Po Plain, had close ties with the Greek world. Romans also frequented the sanctuary of Delphi in the second half of the sixth century, during the reign of Tarquinius Superbus, who, of course, was a king of Etruscan origin. He sent gifts to the sanctuary after taking Sessa Pomezia (Cicero *De republica* 2.24.44); he also sent his sons, Titus and Arruns, and his nephew Brutus to interrogate the oracle about certain miraculous and extraordinary events, such as a serpent emerging from a wooden column (Livy 1.56.4–7), and a plague that raged through the city (Dionysios of Halikarnassos 4.69.2). Perhaps this initiative can be considered the Roman equivalent of the actions by the Caeretans described above. Between the end of the fifth and the early years of the fourth century, in the time of Marcus Furius Camillus, the Romans continued to have contact with the sanctuary of Delphi, and they dedicated a great golden vase there (Diodorus Siculus 14.93.3–4; Livy 5.15–28; Plutarch *Camillus* 3–8; Appian *Italica* 8).

A number of inscriptions in an Etruscoid language (not Etruscan!), dating to the Archaic period and discovered on the island of Lemnos, have been evaluated in a number of ways. Some have thought them to be a highly convincing indication that Etruscan groups had arrived on the island; others have held that they reflect an ancient linguistic stage in the Mediterranean, from which Etruscan and Lemnian developed. In addition, one tradition (Strabo 5.2.4) maintains that a group of Pelasgians from Lemnos joined the Lydians and, led by Tyrrhenus, colonized Etruria. For the moment the question must remain open.

During the second half of the sixth and fifth centuries B.C., Etruscan trade toward southern Gaul was in decline (the Etruscan amphorae for wine were gradually supplanted by Massaliot wares), although not in the rest of the Mediterranean. More than ten fragments of bronze pitchers with elongated spouts from this time, part of wine services, were found in Carthage. There was also a fragment of a tripod leg of a Vulcian metal ingot, also linked to symposia. But the most widespread Etruscan object during this period was a wooden casket revetted with plaques of ivory or bone and decorated with animal or mythological figures, primarily from Vulci. These objects have been found at Tharros and Nora (Sardinia), Ibiza (Balearic Islands), Malta, the Athens Acropolis, Delos, Rhodes, and Cyprus, as well as in Etruria and the Italian peninsula. In addition, the sanctuary at Olympia has Etruscan bronzes that date between the final decades of the sixth and the beginning of the fifth centuries: a decorated shield with armlet; the boss of a shield with a mask of Achelous; and an embossed sheet with a scene from the legend of Herakles. Pausanias (5.12.5) informs us that the Etruscan Arimnestos, whom he called a king, frequented the sanctuary and offered a throne to Zeus. He also specifies that the monument was situated in the temple pronaos. Recently scholars have tended to think that this was a work in wood and ivory rather than bronze, similar to other Etruscan works from the seventh century; it would have dated to the early fifth century, just before the great temple was built. Information about a Greek named Telemachus from Thessaly that was found in an epigraph also dates from this period. He participated in the games at Delphi, defeated "the strongest of the Etruscans" in a fight and killed him. It follows that the Etruscans not only frequented the sanctuary but were also admitted to contests there.

After the battle on the Sardinian Sea, Etruscan naval power was well established. Foreign merchants and goods flocked to their ports. In the port sanctuary of Pyrgi, for example, Etruscans and Carthaginians made a joint offering to the goddess Uni-Astarte, as inscriptions incised on gold tablets in their respective languages demonstrate. In the port sanctuary of Gravisca, Etruscans and Greeks made dedications to Aphrodite, also in their own languages. Tradition hints at commercial treaties, such as those between the Etruscans and the Carthaginians, for instance (Aristotle *Politica* 3.5.10–11). However, beginning with the early fifth century, records speak of Etruscan actions against Carthage and Greece interests in the lower Tyrrhenian and even beyond the Pillars of Hercules. These did not reap positive results. Their first goal—to conquer the Lipari Islands—precipitated a number of clashes, of which the Etruscans won some and lost others. On the occasion of their respective victories, both the Etruscans and Liparians offered gifts at

the sanctuary in Delphi. Coinciding with these events, the tyrant Anaxilas of Rhegion fortified his city with ramparts and prepared a naval base in order to defend the Strait of Messina from the Etruscans (Strabo 5.1.5). The Etruscans also apparently attempted to occupy the Felici (Canary?) Islands, but the Carthaginians thwarted them (Diodorus Siculus 5.20.4). In 480 B.C. they suffered a serious defeat in Himera at the hands of the Syracusans, who became the dominant force in the western Mediterranean basin. In fact, just a few years later, in 474 B.C., Syracuse, in league with the Cumaeans, defeated the Etruscans in the waters off Cumae (Pindar *Pythian* 1.71–75; Diodorus Siculus 11.51). The tyrant Hieron of Syracuse offered a part of the spoils to Zeus at Olympia, including a number of helmets with dedicatory inscriptions. Another blow to Etruscan naval power was inflicted in 453 B.C., again by the Syracusans, when they raided the mineral regions of northern Etruria (including Elba) and practically blocked the great ports of the coastal metropoleis, except that of Populonia, from importing Attic goods.

At this point, the Etruscans were no longer a major sea power. Their involvement during the Peloponnesian War— three ships flanking the Athenians at the siege of Syracuse (415–413 B.C.)—ended in failure, as did the Athenian expedition as a whole (Thucydides 6.88.6; 6.108.2). Some have suggested that their involvement in this debacle was linked to events described in a eulogistic epigraph from the Julio-Claudian period, according to which the Tarquinian Velthur Spurinna was the first Etruscan to lead an army into Sicily. This hypothesis is difficult to accept, both because the Etruscans had previously intervened in Sicily and the Lipari Islands, and because it would make little sense to eulogize a person's role in leading a failed expedition.

Thereafter, the Etruscans continued storming through the Mediterranean, but only as pirates. Ancient writers make numerous and explicit references to this practice. Indeed, when the Syracusans assaulted the sanctuary at Pyrgi in 384 B.C., seizing many valuables in order to underwrite a war with the Carthaginians, they undertook this operation on the pretext of freeing the seas of Etruscan pirates.

Despite an increasing state of crisis, Etruscan goods continued to reach Greek sanctuaries in the fifth and early fourth centuries B.C. For example, bronze candelabras or censers (only their feet have been recovered) were dedicated at Olympia and Lindus. Other examples were uncovered in Cyprus and Tell Sukas (Syria). It becomes difficult to say who transported these products because the southern Etruscan ports were blocked from trading with Greece. Greek writers of the fifth century relate bits of information about the exportation and diffusion of Etruscan works in Greece. Critias (in Athenaeus *Deipnosoph* 1.28b) cites golden cups and bronze objects that decorated houses. Pherecrates (in Athenaeus *Deipnosoph* 15.700c) praises the Etruscans' skill in bronzeworking, especially in making candelabras. Aeschylus (*Eumenides* 567–68) and Sophocles (*Ajax* 16–17) mention an Etruscan horn. Pollux (*Onomasticon* 7.28.86, 92), referring to the age of Pericles, asserts that Etruscan footwear was renowned in Athens.

The Etruscans must also have been known in Greece for their religious practices, because in the fourth century B.C., Plato urged people not to alter ceremonies and rites, no matter what their origin: local, Cypriot, or Etruscan (*Leges* 5.9.738).

Only scant records survive of an Etruscan presence in the Mediterranean from the fourth century on. From the western basin, two silver coins from Populonia are on record; these were uncovered in a lagoon in Berre, near Marseilles. There is also a mirror from Ampurias depicting the Judgment of Paris from the end of the fourth century. From the eastern basin, a pot-bellied bronze pitcher from a residential context in Al Mina on the Syrian coast, some scarabs from the fourth and third centuries from Panticapaeum (the Crimea), and a mirror with a portrait of a Lasa (female spirit) from the end of the fourth century from Olbia on the Black Sea, stand out.

The Etruscans may simply have lost interest in the Mediterranean, with the obvious exception of their piracy. They were quite busy inland: fighting the Romans, who were beginning to penetrate into Etruria (the fall of Veii dates to 396 B.C.), and fighting the Gauls, who since the early fourth century had been in central Italy, first battling against the Etruscans and then joining forces with them against the Romans.

We find traces of the Etruscan civilization during its final phase in two North African countries, Egypt and Tunisia: written texts that are of primary importance for understanding the language, religion, and history of the Etruscans. The longest Etruscan inscription known comes from Egypt (about 1,130 words survive,

corresponding to about half of the original text), written on a sheet (*liber linteus*) that had been cut into strips and used to wrap the mummy of a young woman. The text, which dates to the second and first centuries B.C., is a religious calendar with a series of ritualistic precepts, and therefore intended for community use. This "book" may have been brought to Egypt already written, and was only used for the mummy when it had outlived its religious usefulness. Today it is preserved at the National Museum of Zagreb. In Oued-Miliane, in the Tunisian inland region, three *cippi* with Etruscan inscriptions were discovered. They establish the borders of a private property and place it under the

protection of a supreme divinity (Tinia, the equivalent of the Greeks' Zeus). They indicate the presence of an Etruscan community there, not just because there were three of these *cippi* but also because they were written in a language that had to be intelligible to the neighbors.

The presence of Etruscan groups in certain African regions has been linked to the wars between Marius and Sulla, when the cities of northern Etruria sided with Marius and were punished by the victor, Sulla, in various ways, particularly through the imposition of a military colony. In those circumstances, many Etruscans could have taken the path of exile and reached Egypt and Tunisia.

View of the Gulf of Baratti (Livorno), where the port of Populonia was located. Necropoleis from the Archaic period and an industrial quarter are located close to the coast.

The Etruscans in Europe

| GIOVANNANGELO CAMPOREALE

The interior of an Etruscan red-figured cup with a depiction of satyrs, provenance unknown, fifth century B.C. The Etruscan inscription *Avlesvpinas* is written on the cup and refers to a member of the Vibenna family. Paris, Musée Rodin

On the facing page, wheeled bronze incense-burner used for rituals, from Strettweg (Upper Styria), seventh century B.C. Graz, Steiermärchisches Landesmuseum Joanneum

Relations between Etruria and "barbarian" northern and central Europe have, even in recent times, been the subject of considerable debate in publications, conventions, and exhibitions. According to current understanding, the picture of Etruscan expansion into the central European regions—which naturally will continue to evolve as new discoveries come to light— is already quite developed, complex, and rich with cultural implications. Our reconstruction is based primarily on data from archaeological surveys—if we include epigraphic evidence in this cate- gory. Historiographic and literary traditions are also important, especially for the second half of the millennium B.C., that is, the period when the Gauls descended into the territory of the Italian peninsula. It is important to emphasize that objects often arrived in a new area in company with their relative uses and underlying ideologies. In other words, the objects themselves were vehicles in a process of acculturation, which was amplified and fortified if people moved with them. An Etruscan object, if found in a tomb, had almost certainly been used in everyday life before becoming part of someone's grave goods, as we know from their traces of wear and tear or ancient repairs. And even though an object might be found in a votive deposit—riverbeds were used for this purpose in much of continental Europe—it may have had a previous domestic, or at least private, use. See, for instance, the bronze crested helmet taken from the bed of the Tanaro River near Asti (p. 147).

reindeer & antlers man →

Etruscan goods can be found in many museums of northern and central Europe, especially in the museums of small cities that normally preserve local finds. Unfortunately, these often remain unpublished or are published in catalogues of local distribution. The praiseworthy initiative of the French magazine *Caesarodunum* in creating a census of Etruscan and Italic works uncovered in the area of ancient Gaul has proven that these items are far more numerous than we might have expected: They are no less interesting from a historical and cultural point of view for being relatively inconspicuous. Such is the case with Etruscan fibulae from the eighth and seventh centuries B.C., which were quite widespread in central Europe and were probably as broadly distributed as Etruscan fabrics. These fibulae also suggest that some people in the area of the finds were dressing differently than most of their peers (see pp. 80; 84–85). These are the types of objects that tell us the most about the Etruscan presence in continental Europe. At the same time, we must make certain qualifications. The Etruscan (or Italic) finds in small central European museums often come with no information as to their provenance. While it is usually assumed that they were found in the immediate area, sometimes they are relics of old collections, which may have been formed in any number of ways. When the provenance is uncertain, or when an object's origins—Etruscan, Greek, Magna-Graecian, or even central European—are open to debate, it is unwise to make deductions of a general nature. This was the case, for instance, with an iron tripod and a bronze *lebes* decorated with griffon

protomes, dating to the Archaic period and found in a tumulus tomb of St. Colombe (Côte d'Or), and also with the renowned bronze krater of Vix (Côte d'Or). Works from Greece or Magna-Graecia may sometimes have reached continental Europe through Etruria, or have been brought north together with Etruscan products; this can only be ascertained by the context of the find. The situation is quite different when we find local copies of Etruscan goods in cities of northern and central Europe. Sometimes even their models are known in the same location, such as the bronze pitchers with elongated spouts from the end of the sixth and fifth centuries B.C., which were imitated in central European works in clay and bronze. At other times there is only a copy from a local workshop, as with a number of razors or horse bits from the eighth century, which can be explained by positing the arrival of models or bronzeworkers from Etruria. In such cases, obviously, the central Europeans' acculturation toward Etruscan civilization was more advanced.

The picture that follows, given its inherent uncertainties, cannot be exhaustive, but it is indicative of the principal trends regarding the exportation of products or the emigration of groups of people from Etruria toward central and northern Europe.

The first Etruscan exports to move into Europe date back to the Villanovan period and are analogous to those that were then being sent to the great Greek sanctuaries (see pp. 83ff.).

Crested helmets were often used in the ninth and eighth centuries B.C. in Etruria as covers for biconic ash urns. They were

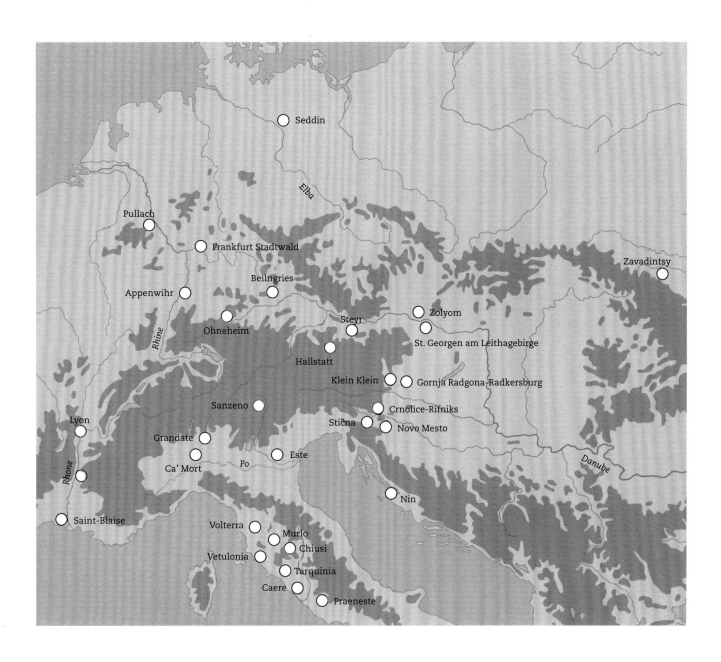

- Seddin
- Pullach
- Frankfurt Stadtwald
- Beilngries
- Appenwihr
- Ohneheim
- Steyr
- Zolyom
- St. Georgen am Leithagebirge
- Hallstatt
- Klein Klein
- Gornja Radgona-Radkersburg
- Sanzeno
- Crnolice-Rifniks
- Lyon
- Stična
- Novo Mesto
- Grandate
- Ca' Mort
- Este
- Zavadintsy
- Saint-Blaise
- Nin
- Volterra
- Murlo
- Chiusi
- Vetulonia
- Tarquinia
- Caere
- Praeneste

Rhine
Elba
Rhone
Po
Danube

Above, map showing the distribution of Etruscan and Greek products in the central European region

At left, bronze antenna sword from the ninth or eighth century B.C., from Steyr (Austria). Vienna, Naturhistorisches Museum

clearly signs that the deceased had elevated status in society. This type of artifact had actually originated in central Europe, although it was widely produced in Etruria in both terra-cotta and bronze, especially in southern Etruria. The Etruscan examples, chiefly the bronzes, are characterized by a wavy or arched-shaped crest and two horizontal bands of studs arrayed along the helmet's base. It is probable that this new helmet design from Etruria was introduced and further developed by northern masters who emigrated to Etruria. This type of work was then exported to various parts of ancient Italy (Sala Consilina, Fermo, and Asti) and Europe, where it was found at Zavadintsy in the Ukraine and in Hallstatt in Austria. Similarly, antenna swords, which also had originated in central Europe, were largely copied in Etruria with some added distinctive traits, such as antennae with only one curve. Swords of this kind were uncovered at Steyr (Upper Austria) and at Seddin (Brandenburg), as well as in Este, Italy. In both cases, the first products exported from Etruria were high-quality bronzes linked to the ideology of the warrior, which, as is well known, had aristocratic connotations.

Another Villanovan bronze article that was widespread in central Europe was the razor. The earliest examples are crescent-shaped with an interrupted curve, datable to the end of the ninth and the first half of the eighth centuries B.C. They were uncovered at St. Georg am Leithagebirge (Austria), Pralognan (Savoy), and Bourges (central France). Local copies of this item were also made: An example from Nin (Dalmatia) featured a handle that was small and flat rather than rod-shaped.

Finds in bronze, iron, and impasto from tombs dating to the Villanovan period, ninth and eighth centuries B.C., from Tarquinia (Viterbo). Florence, Museo Archeologico

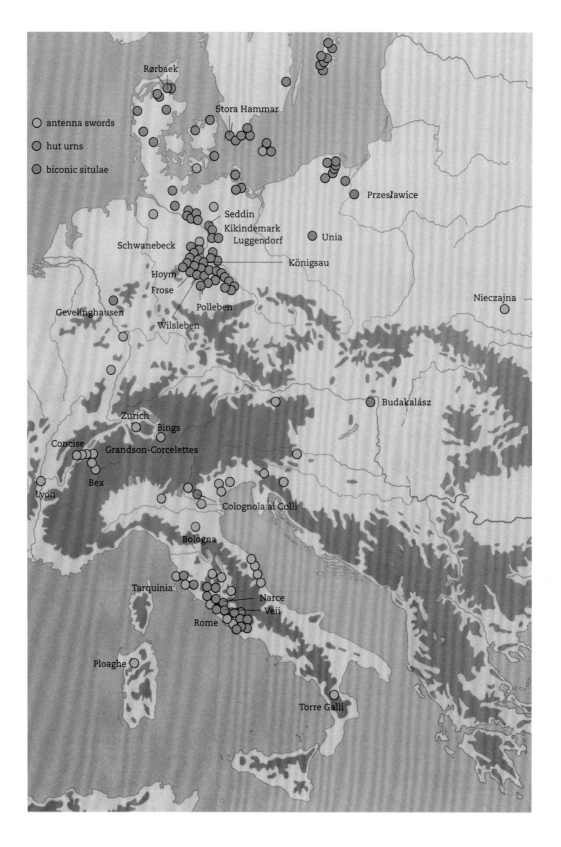

Map showing the spread of hut urns, biconic *situlae*, and antenna swords in central Europe.

antenna swords

hut urns

biconic situlae

Rørbaek

Stora Hammar

Przesławice

Seddin
Kikindemark
Luggendorf

Schwanebeck

Unia

Königsau

Hoym
Frose

Gevelinghausen

Polleben

Wilsleben

Nieczajna

Budakalász

Zurich

Bings

Concise

Grandson-Corcelettes

Bex

Lyon

Colognola ai Colli

Bologna

Tarquinia

Narce
Veii

Rome

Ploaghe

Torre Galli

It pays to recall that Etruscan razors were also discovered at Este on a road that runs toward Dalmatia. This object continued to be exported during the second half of the eighth century, and crescent-shaped examples with continuous curves were discovered at Brison St. Innocent (Savoy), Mörigen (Switzerland), the Harth forest in Mulhouse (Alsace), and Clayeures (Lorraine).

One product found in Villanovan contexts from later periods in southern Etruria is a bronze biconic vase with a mostly stocky body. It was decorated with studs of various sizes, distributed in concentric bands that are joined by the motif of the "solar boat." Two similar

Wörgl near Kufstein (Austria). This object, which was used for personal adornment, was often found in Villanovan female burials from the late Villanovan period. This was another item that was exported to other locations on the Italian peninsula, such as Este and Cologna Veneta in Veneto.

Regarding objects for personal adornment, Etruscan and Italic fibulae from the eighth and seventh centuries B.C. deserve special mention. Fibulae of a variety of designs—some with enlarged arches, others shaped like leeches, boats, or dragons—have been found at scattered locations in northern and central Europe. They were quite numerous, spread

Gold fibula with decorations and inscriptions that were made through the granulation technique, dating to the middle decades of the seventh century B.C., from Castelluccio La Foce in the surrounding area of Chiusi (Siena). The inscription records the piece's owner and donor. Paris, Musée du Louvre

examples were found at Gevelinghausen (Westphalia) and at Przesčawice (northern Poland). The vase was also exported to the Po Plain, where it was found at Cologna Veneta (Verona) and in the Carrettino Tomb at Ca' Morta (Como) among grave goods from the early seventh century B.C. The latter provides indirect evidence of the trajectory taken by Etruscan works toward the regions of northern Europe.

There are reports that a rhombus-shaped bronze belt from the seventh century B.C. was found in a tomb in

throughout a vast area from Austria to Germany, Poland, and France. They indicate that fabric and wool from Etruria, destined to be made into clothing fastened with these fibulae, were also distributed throughout northern and central Europe.

Let us consider the works reviewed up to this point. For the most part they are made of bronze, a noble material, and they are of high quality, requiring specialized professional competence for their manufacture. They are either weapons or objects for personal adornment, that is, precious goods that reveal the elevated social status of those responsible for the exchange. Some of them emulate models from central and northern Europe in their shape (crested helmets, antenna swords) or their decoration (the "solar boat" motif on biconic vases). As has already been suggested, northern models probably reached Etruria, yet interestingly, examples of Etruscan works were exported to the northern and central European environ-

Relatively few objects were exported, though these select items were distributed over a vast territory that ranges from the Ukraine to central France. The explanation usually given is that these were gifts exchanged between leading figures in their respective regions. Yet it is unlikely that these exchanges would have been limited to this short list of precious objects; quite likely there were other goods involved that were perishable, subject to change, or otherwise impossible to trace. Payment

ment. This was a sort of return trip, a clear indication that the northern world appreciated Etruscan metalworking in the ninth and eighth centuries B.C. These Etruscan goods were also discovered in various Mediterranean sites (crested helmets at Olympia, antenna swords on Samos). They were almost certainly products of workshops in southern Etruria, especially Veii and Tarquinia, which during the period in question were the cities most active in bronzeworking and trade.

for these commodities, which would have made up the bulk of the trade goods, may have taken the form of Baltic amber, which had already reached Etruria (and Italy in general) in the eighth century B.C. But one such product on its own cannot have made up the only compensation used in these exchanges, since Etruscan goods reached east and west far beyond the presumed "amber path." In addition, amber had already reached Italy in the late Bronze Age, before the emergence of

the Etruscans, as attested by finds at Frattesina in Fratta Polesine and the surrounding area (Romagna). The presence of bronze biconic urns at Como and Cologna Veneta, the crested helmet at Asti, and the crescent-shaped razors and belts at Este—all halfway between their point of manufacture and the places where they have been found in northern and central Europe—raise the question of trade brokerage. Handing their goods over to an intermediary would, among other things, have allowed the Etruscans to avoid the arduous crossing of the Alps, a route that even in the time of Julius Caesar (*Bellum Gallicum* 3.1) still involved serious risks and onerous tolls for traveling merchants.

A similar consideration applies to objects that reached Etruria from the Transalpine area. Take, for example, a bronze cart that was discovered in Tarquinia, whose bird-shaped body sprouts two quadruped heads. Comparable works can be found among examples from Sokolac (Bosnia) or Orastie (Transylvania). However, a terra-cotta copy found in a tomb from the eighth century B.C. in Este suggests that a bronze model had reached that area, which lay on the route between the Balkans and Etruria.

Between the end of the eighth century B.C. and the years around the middle of the seventh, Etruscan handmade goods continued to radiate into continental Europe, although most of these items were not produced in southern Etrurian cities.

Two horse bits from Zolyom (Romania) and Alpenquai (Zurich), with modeled uprights in the shape of foals, are thought to imitate an original made in Vetulonia, as do a series of bronze discs with interior openwork from a tumulus tomb in Stična (Slovenia), which must have been used for a harness. The latter match others uncovered in the Circle of the Trident in Vetulonia. A number of bowls decorated with flattened grooves can probably also be ascribed to the Vetulonian environment; these were recovered from tumulus tombs in Poiseul-la-Ville (Côte d'Or), Frankfurt am Main, Appenwihr (Alsace), and around Lyon that were quite rich in bronzes. The example from Frankfurt is linked to a bronze *situla* whose base is attached to the body with anchor plates that are quite similar to those found on the base of a *situla* of the so-called Kurd type (to be discussed below) from the Tomb of the Leader in Vetulonia. Whether Vetulonian or central European, the one from Appenwihr stands apart from the others for having a bell-shaped handle that is in turn inserted inside two rings.

A bronze pyxis was part of the grave goods in a tomb in Appenwihr and was similar to the so-called Vetulonian censers. Scholars agree that the work derives from Vetulonia, but they differ on which workshop made them. Some hold that it was imported from Etruria, while others think that it was a local copy of an Etruscan model. In truth, some characteristics of the pyxis, such as the absence of a chain to attach the handle to the lid and the presence of an embossed frieze of cats, cannot be found among works from Vetulonian workshops. This could credit the theory that it was locally produced after a foreign model. Nevertheless, two bronze Vetulonian-type objects were also found in the tomb in Appenwihr, with particular characteristics that distinguish them from other comparable Etruscan works. One can then imagine that a bronzeworker who trained in Vetulonia and relocated to central Europe might be responsible for other bowls from the same region. (Two bowls of the same type were found in the Carrettino Tomb at Ca' Morta, already mentioned, and they too are connected to other bronze dishes found en route from Etruria to the Rhine valley.)

An andiron and twelve skewers—an iron service for roasting meat—were found in a rich "chariot" tomb (*a carro*) in Beilngries (Germany). It is one of the oldest services known in the central European region and it resembles others recovered from Etruscan tombs of the Orientalizing period.

Etruscan expansion was also directed toward Eastern Europe. A bronze tripod with legs twisted into eyelets was found in a tomb in Novo Mesto (Slovenia); it belonged to a group that is generally agreed to be Vetulonian. In addition to other cities in Etruria itself (Chiusi, perhaps Vulci), similar examples were exported to Oria (Brindisi), Bologna (the *Tomba dell'Arsenale*), and Este (Tomb Pelà 49). The latter is located on the road between Vetulonia and Novo Mesto.

Etruscan exports to continental Europe during the seventh century B.C., like those of the preceding century, were generally bronzes of good quality, mostly from Vetulonia. As with the Mediterranean trade, exports from the ninth and eighth centuries can be ascribed to cities in southern Etruria.

Etruscan exported goods were linked to horsemanship and the banquet-symposium. The transmission of these objects was a clear indication that their corresponding activities and aristocratic ideologies had arrived from Etruria. Horse trappings, of course, allude to the ownership of horses, which in a military engagement or parade undoubtedly conferred distinction and social elevation on the owner. Banquet or symposium services indicate the adoption of a rarified custom, a form of high-level socializing, that reached Etruria from the Near East and Greece and which passed from there to the Transalpine region as an Etruscan— or Etruscanized—custom. Those interested in trade were members of the upper class, people who used luxury goods to establish and strengthen relations and friendships that frequently had a commercial aspect.

The arrival of Etruscan wine-service vases most likely implied the arrival of Etrurian wine as well. Historiographic sources provide explicit evidence of this commerce for the fourth century B.C. (see pp. 126ff.), though in all likelihood it goes back at least to the seventh century. In that period the princes of northern and central Europe began to enjoy Etruscan wine in preference to local beverages such as beer or mead. The Nordic peoples as a whole increasingly favored it: Diodorus Siculus (5.26.3) relates that the Gauls exchanged a slave for an amphora of wine. From this we can imagine a line of trade: wine on one side, slaves on the other. Granted, we have not found transport containers for Etruscan wine in northern and central Europe. But the containers that survive, clay amphorae, began to be produced in Etruria only at the end of the seventh or the beginning of the sixth

Bronze tripod with legs decorated with eyelets, seventh century B.C., from Novo Mesto (Slovenia). This piece is Vetulonian in type and probably arrived from that city. Ljubljana, Narodni Muzej

Pitcher with painted decorations (since disappeared), end of the seventh century B.C., from the Tomb of the Situla in Stična. Ljubljana, Narodni Musej

Bronze pitcher with an elongated spout, second half of the fifth century B.C., from the Bourges area (central France). The piece belongs to a class of Etrurian goods that were primarily exported to and imitated in central Europe. Bourges, Musée de la Ville

Bronze *situla* with embossed decorations, dating from the sixth century B.C. but discovered in a tomb with materials from the early fifth century. The *situla* was used as an ash urn. Tomb 68 in the Certosa necropolis at Bologna. Bologna, Museo Civico Archeologico

chalices were pre A.D.

centuries; before that, wine was transported in wineskins, which have not survived. In the seventh century, wine was definitively a carrier of Etruscan culture into the northern and central European regions.

Etruscan manufactured goods from the seventh century B.C. discovered in the Transalpine region come from tombs, while those found in Greek areas are from sanctuaries. This fact had consequences for the process of acculturation, which was more intense in the North. There, the objects were not kept merely for a certain period of use but were also deposited as grave goods in the owner's tomb, signifying a strong attachment to them and their associations.

Certain products that reached continental Europe, for example fluted bowls (Como) or tripods with eyelet legs (Este), have also been found in tombs in southern Italy. These once again raise the question of mediated and indirect contacts. But regardless of how these products arrived at their destinations, their influence on the Transalpine population, or more precisely on the lifestyles of the higher social classes, is beyond dispute. Nordic copies and certainly the likely presence of Etruscan masters in northern regions are convincing indications of this influence.

Commercial and cultural activity between Etruria and the Transalpine area ran both ways in the seventh century B.C. We have previously mentioned the possible trade in slaves and in raw materials, and we know that amber had already reached Etruria by the second half of the eighth century, probably from the Balkan regions. Imports of this resin peaked dur-

ing the seventh century, especially into cities such as Vetulonia or those of the *agger* of Falerii and Capena, where local artisanship was quite advanced. In the early times, master cutters almost certainly came to Etruria with their specialized tools, adapting to the local cultural climate and the needs of their Etruscan clients.

Hallstatt-culture *situlae* from the Carpathian and Danube regions also reached Etruria (Vetulonia and Bologna). They can be distinguished from local works by the characteristic decorations incised along their rims and their cross-shaped fasteners. *Situlae* of the so-called Kurd type (huge containers with conical bodies and eyelet sheet handles nailed to the lip and back) can probably be attributed to bronzeworkers from the same area. These were found in a number of Etruscan and Italic cities (Vetulonia, Populonia, Chiusi, Veii, Fabriano, Praeneste, and Pontecagnano). A group of *lebetes* with handles decorated with tiny cats or animal protomes, which came from a workshop in Vetulonia and spread to various cities (Populonia, Fabbrecce-Città del Castello, Praeneste, and Olympia), can also be attributed to the same bronzeworkers. One of these shows decorations on the rim that were typical of the repertory of the Hallstatt culture. A *lebes* from Este in Veneto that was almost certainly produced locally shows an identical decoration with a grazing stag above it. In this case, too, one could imagine a master from the Hallstatt culture who came to Etruria from the Transalpine area. These examples provide evidence of intermediate stops on the route between the Transalpine area and Etruria.

A reconstructed tumulus
tomb from the first half
of the sixth century B.C.,
Hochdorf (Baden-
Württemberg)

Between the end of the seventh and
the first three-quarters of the sixth centuries B.C., trade between the Etruscan
and the Transalpine worlds continued
along the lines of previous centuries. Two
Etruscan-Corinthian terra-cotta pitchers
that were produced in southern Etruria,
perhaps in Vulci, were found in the Tomb
of the Situla in Stična and at Haguenau
in Alsace (the date of this last provenance
is not completely certain). A bucchero
kantharos with flared feet that was found
in the area around Kósiezlec (central
Poland) belongs to this same cultural
horizon. It was discovered during the
nineteenth century under unclear circumstances; it is certainly a southern Etruscan

type, many examples of which were
exported to multiple sites in the Mediterranean basin (see pp. 88ff.). Other
fragments of bucchero vases belonging to
wine services, though these were few and
isolated and discovered under unknown
circumstances, have been reported here
and there in Europe: Freiburg, Saxon-
Sion, Hallstatt, Enns, and Alte Gleisberg.
However, given that we lack precise
knowledge as to the circumstances of
their discovery, we must exercise caution
in using them to reconstruct a general
historical picture. A bronze funnel-
shaped strainer has been associated with
the grave goods of Tomb 7 in the Archaic
necropolis of Trebeniste. It belongs to

Etruscan production from the first half of the sixth century, and examples of its type were exported to various sites in the Mediterranean (see pp. 89ff.). Bronze pitchers of the "plumpe Kanne" variety were recovered from a number of "chariot" tombs in ancient Gaul and fall within Vulcian production from the first half of the sixth century. A bronze pitcher of the same kind is reported to have been in Tomb 3145 in Santa Lucia di Tolmino (Slovenia). In Tomb 2850 and Tomb 1008 at the same Slovenian location were two Ionic cups—Type A2 according to a Vallet-Villard classification—which may have come from Etruria. Rhodian-type pitchers, commonly considered of Etruscan make, have been found in tumulus tombs in Inzigkofen and Kappel in Baden-Württemberg and in Hatten in the lower Rhine.

Large *lebetes* from Hassle (southern Sweden), St. Colombe (Côte d'Or), and Hochdorf (Baden-Württemberg) have been judged to be Greek works, though they could have been distributed through Etruria. A huge bronze krater from a rich tumulus tomb in Vix, part of the goods belonging to a female buried on a cart, and other related materials (two Attic cups from the final decades of the sixth century B.C. and *lebetes* that may have been Etruscan from the same period) could have also arrived via Etruria.

Bronze statuettes of haruspices from the Hellenistic period characterized by pointed head-coverings and cloaks that are fastened with buckles, from the area around Siena. Göttingen, Archäologisches Institut der Universität

Each of these vases is linked to the ceremony of the symposium and the consumption of wine, continuing a cultural tradition among the princes of Central Europe that had taken root during the previous century through Etruscan influence. These goods were produced in southern Etruria, probably Vulci. Although these items are quite refined, they are few in number, almost insignificant compared to the thousands of bucchero vases of Etruscan-Corinthian pottery. These transport amphorae were found in Provence, Languedoc, or Catalonia and carried Etruria's wine exports to the northern coasts of the western Mediterranean basin. Ointment jars (*aryballoi* and *alabastra*) with their aromatic contents also reached these areas from Etruria.

Etruscan exports to the northern coasts of the Mediterranean, then, were part of a vigorous, steady trade. By contrast, two Etruscan-Corinthian pitchers from Stična and Haguenau and the bucchero *kantharos* from Kósiezlec mentioned above, similar to Etruscan vases from the Gulf of Lion region, were alone in their respective findspots. This suggests that the Etruscans had largely failed in their attempts to penetrate the markets of continental Europe with their less precious trade goods.

The spread of Etruscan luxury goods into the European, Transalpine, and Mediterranean regions may be related to the various sociopolitical structures that were forming in those regions. The Transalpine area was ruled by various princes, each controlling his own territory, whose relations with the Etruscans ran much as they had in the seventh century B.C., that is, as exchanges between leaders. The area that faces the western Mediterranean basin, which was in contact with Greek colonies of the same area, experienced an early urbanization and the rise of a middle class. The latter consumed most of the wine and vases sent up from the South.

Beginning in the final decades of the seventh century B.C., another class of Etruscan bronzes—human and animal statuettes made by casting—reached central and northern Europe. A group of five small bronzes—two oxen, two female figures, and a warrior—were found in a deposit at Thorignéen-Charnie (Maine, France). The closest comparable works are statuettes from the end of the seventh century, of which a small number have been found in the area around Arezzo and Volterra and which have been attributed to workshops from those cities. Similar statuettes of a more recent date (from the end of the sixth and fifth centuries)— either kouros, kore, or Diskobolos types—come from various locations in Upper Savoy, Franche-Comté, Burgundy, and Nivernais. The geographic distribution of these bronzes indicates that a trade route ran as far as the mineral district of Loire, which supplied tin to the demanding Etruscan bronze industry. Etruscan merchants may have given these statuettes in payment for tolls. In any event, they ended up as ex-votos, as did similar ones in Etruria. They have now been found even farther afield: bronzes of this type were found in England at Blandford and Uffingham, cities near the tin district of Cornwall, and in Ireland at Sligo. According to the National Museum of Dublin, this last piece may have arrived from France or Germany during the second or first centuries B.C.

Etruscan black-figured amphora with a representation of Herakles pursuing the Minotaur, of unknown provenance, from the beginning of the fifth century B.C. The substitution of Herakles for Theseus, the Athenian hero who, according to myth, killed the Minotaur, is probably due to a personal choice on the part of the Etruscan master. Paris, Musée du Louvre

We may recall that two lion's-head shield bosses were discovered toward the end of the nineteenth century, perhaps around Vienne (near Lyons). These bronze items were made in Tarquinia between the end of the sixth and the beginning of the fifth centuries B.C. The finds, made under unknown circumstances, are the only examples of their kind to be recovered in continental Europe and came from tomb contexts.

One extremely important record is an inscription on a fragmentary impasto vase from Montmorot, at the foot of the French side of the Jura Mountains. It was locally made and found in a context that dates to the second half of the sixth century B.C., though the writing and the object itself may be much older (late seventh to first half of the sixth centuries). The text is written in an alphabet that may have originated in northern Etruria and contains an abbreviated personal name of Gallic origin: *pris.* Among all the known inscriptions of Gallic origin, which are admittedly few, the Montmorot piece is the most ancient. Its early date implies that the alphabet arrived in that area at the end of the seventh century: a fact of enormous cultural significance, showing the multifaceted penetration of Etruscan culture into the Transalpine region. The text names a person, probably the vase's owner, and thus recalls the oldest Etruscan epigraphic records (seventh and sixth centuries), which often bear the inscribed name of the object's owner in their formulae of ownership or giving. These objects were usually of good quality with a high sales value. Inscriptions during this period in Etruria were used to emphasize one's personal prestige; the

same is true of the vase from Montmorot. Montmorot dominated the plain of Bresse, an area of great economic interest because of its saltworks and its key location at the crossroads between the Rhone valley and the valleys of the Ill and Rhine rivers, which were vital trade routes in antiquity.

After the battle on the Sardinian Sea (about 540 B.C.), exports of wine and ointment, which previously left Etruria by sea toward the Gulf of Lion, showed a considerable decline. The Etruscans held on to and consolidated control in the middle Tyrrhenian Sea, while the Massaliots kept the Ligurian Sea and the Gulf of Lion. In various inland regions of Provence and Languedoc, large amphorae of Massaliot wine began to appear and gradually supplanted the Etruscan variety. They are often associated with Ionic cups of the B2 type (according to the Vallet-Villard classification) in gray Massaliot ware and Attic black-figure pottery, which were always for wine. Apparently vineyards planted on the French coast of the Mediterranean had reached maturity, allowing the region to export its surplus wine to central Europe. However, this did not entirely extinguish the trade in Etruscan wine to the north and east; they continued to utilize the Alpine passes and river-valley routes that run northward in a variety of directions (the Rhone, Saône, Doubs, Loire, Rhine, Inn, Isar, and Danube). There are indications that they used bronze wine-service vases rather than amphorae for transport.

The most common of these vases was a pitcher with an elongated spout, which is usually called by its German name, "Schnabelkanne." Its production has been

Handle from a pitcher in the shape of a lion seizing the head of a young man in its teeth, from a princely tomb in Castel San Mariano (Perugia), from around the middle of the sixth century B.C. Munich, Antikensammlungen

attributed to Vulci and dated between the final decades of the sixth century and the entire fifth century B.C. Today there are hundreds of known examples, more than half of which come from the Transalpine region. Their area of diffusion ranges from the Po Plain to Switzerland, western France, Germany, Poland, and the Balkan Peninsula. The exported examples include a large number with decorative additions. We see the usual palmette, figurine, or sileni heads that were modeled and attached to the base of the handle, and tiny pearls or eggs on the rim, but also incised friezes of either leaves, braids, spirals, or palmettes and lotus flowers were added to the neck and body near the base. This fact can easily be explained from a commercial standpoint, since products destined for exportation were normally more elaborate and valuable than the run of the mill. Sometimes the ornamental friezes were tacked on by central European masters, who sought to raise the resale value of the vase after it had reached its destination.

Central European imitations of this pitcher are significant. Terra-cotta examples that slavishly reproduce the bronze models of the Etruscans have been found in a number of tombs that date to the final phase of the Hallstatt culture or the beginning of the La Tène culture (fifth century B.C.). Bronze copies were found in certain royal tombs or residences from the same period. These may be distinguished from Etruscan models by their smaller, slimmer bodies and by their excessive indulgence in decorative elements, such as elongated lips, embossed floral motifs, and bands of braids or checkerboard patterns made by overlays

of coral and red enamel. On the handles we find full reliefs of animals, some of which are shown biting human heads. At the lower end of the handle, a silenos head is embellished with stylized vegetal elements, volutes, or S-shaped motifs that are often assembled in a bizarre composition.

Another pitcher with a biconic body that was quite widespread in Etruria during the fifth and fourth centuries B.C.—bronze and terra-cotta examples emanating from workshops in Vulci, Falerii, Populonia, and Volsinii—was exported to the Transalpine region. Known examples of this kind amount to only a few units and, unfortunately, we know nothing of the circumstances surrounding their discovery. One is from the area of Cujk (the Meuse region in the Netherlands), another from Fécamp (upper Normandy), and from Port-Clouet (Lorraine). All three belong to a Vulcian series and date to the fifth century.

A bronze rod tripod from a rich tumulus tomb in Bad Dürkheim is also of Vulcian make and dates to the first half of the fifth century B.C. This handmade work belongs to a class of objects that were destined for local and foreign markets; we have examples from Spina and the Athenian Acropolis (see p. 98).

The repertory of fifth-century Etruscan bronze vases that were found in central Europe also includes large wide-mouthed containers: *stamnoi* and *cistae a cordoni* with ropelike ornamentation. These are comparable to others from the Po Plain, especially Felsina (Bologna) and Spina, where some *cistae* of central-European make have been recovered. These vases were often found together among grave goods, sometimes in combination with Attic red-figured or black-painted cups, for the most part in monumental tumulus tombs where the deceased was interred on a carriage. Among the Greek vases, St. Valentin-type cups were among the most popular, with their highest concentration in the Po region: Dozens of examples, once again associated with wine services for symposia among the privileged classes—have been found in the necropoleis of Spina and Felsina. Resin deposits were found inside some of the *stamnoi*, proving conclusively that they were used to contain wine.

As we have seen, between the end of the sixth and fifth centuries B.C. trade and Etruscan culture radiated toward continental Europe from at least two centers: Vulci and the Po Plain. It may be that the new prominence of the Po Plain resulted from its role as intermediary in distributing Vulcian products to the northern regions, which it had been pursuing since the end of the seventh century. This same period saw the founding, refounding, and renewal of Po cities, from Marzabotto to Felsina (Bologna), probably as a result of this expanding commercial activity.

One anecdote, handed down by various historiographic sources (Livy 5.33.1–6; Dionysios of Halikarnassos 13.10; Plutarch *Camillus* 15.3–4) and dating back to the years between the end of the fifth and the early fourth centuries B.C., concerns the reasons for the Gauls' descent into the Italian peninsula. It also touches on the subject at hand. Arruns, a well-to-do resident of Chiusi, had taken into his home a young man named Lucumo who had been entrusted to him by a dying friend. The

Fragment from a stone sculptural group with a lion and a severed human head, second century B.C. (?), from Osuna, Spain. Madrid, Museo Arqueológico Nacional

Stele with a fifth-century
A.D. runic inscription, from
Matebo (Sweden). Visby,
Gotland Museum

young man behaved properly at first, but then had an affair with Arruns's wife. In order to flee the mockery of his fellow citizens, Arruns deserted his native city and set out toward Gaul with wagons laden with wine, oil, and dried fruit. He offered these first fruits of the season to the Gauls, and when they asked him where they had come from, he told them they derived from Etruria, adding that the region would be easy to conquer since it was ruled by women. Pliny the Elder (*Naturalis Historia* 12.5) linked the story of Arruns to another one, which concerned a Helvetian (thus a Gaul) named Helicon: After working as a blacksmith in Rome for a time, he returned to his native land, bringing dried fruit, grapes, oil, and wine with him.

Both stories give precise indications of the nature and consistency of Etruscan trade toward Gaul (think of Arruns's wagons), which was based on agricultural products and especially on wine. It seems obvious that the two traditions describe a broader phenomenon rather than a single moment in time just prior to the Gauls' descent onto the Italian peninsula. In other words, they describe trends that had been in play for some time. It follows that the figures of Arruns and Helicon express a general situation rather than the acts of a few isolated individuals.

The ancients also repeated a tradition that the ancient Raeti, who lived in the valleys of Trentino-Alto Adige and Grigioni, were an Etruscan people (Livy 5.33.11; Pliny *Naturalis Historia* 3.133; Justinus 20.5.10; Stephanus Byzantius, s.v. "Rhoithoi"). The Etruscans were thought to have arrived from central Europe, specifically the Danube region, and the

Raeti were thought to be the surviving members of a group that had started moving in a north–south direction and who had stopped along the way. Without entering into the merits of this question (see p. 113), it is worth noting that epigraphic evidence of the Raeti is written in an alphabet of Etruscan origin. It may be that as the Etruscans moved south, the Raeti moved north. The alphabet is the most obvious proof of this inverse movement. The middle of the fifth century B.C. saw the beginnings of Celtic art. Its figurative repertory consisted primarily of monsters with bodies of serpents or lions (sphinxes and griffins), palmettes, and lotus flowers. These were all Orientalizing motifs, almost certainly transmitted from the southern Mediterranean, which found favor in Gaul more than two centuries after they had flourished in places such as Greece, Italy, or Iberia. The references between Celtic and Etruscan works are undeniable, even if we cannot assert any direct dependence. For example, the Celtic modeled lion from the second half of the fifth century, represented in the act of seizing a human head between its teeth, appears on the handle of a pitcher with an elongated spout from Dürrnberg (Salzburg). It is similar to another pitcher handle from Castel San Mariano in Munich that is older by more than a century.

The "cut heads" motif falls within this figurative vein and had some success in Celtic art, both for decorating containers for the table and, beginning in the third century B.C., as a subject for great stone sculptures. We can cite as examples groups from Baux-de-Provence, Osuna (Spain), the "Tarasca" (whose stylistic and chronological classification is problematic) from Noves (Provence), and groups in which a feline creature seizes human heads in its teeth or claws. We may accept a proposed link to similar Etruscan groups found guarding tombs in the Vulcian *agger*, but with one qualification: in Etruscan examples, the severed head alluded to a defeated enemy, while in Celtic works the motif referred to Death overpowering the deceased. This figurative motif, therefore, even if its origins were Etruscan, took on a symbolic meaning that was specific to the environment and context in which it was being used.

An instructive comparison can also be made between the silenos heads that adorn the handles of Celtic pitcher with elongated spouts and those that adorn similar Etruscan pitcher handles or the handles of Etruscan *stamnoi.* For example, in the pitcher from Dürrnberg mentioned above or another similar one from Kleinaspergle (Baden-Württemberg), a silenos head is framed between volutes, palmettes, and leaves and features an exaggerated bulging of the eyes and cheekbones and an extreme stylization of the mustache and hair. The exaggeration of decorative expression is typical of environments in which figurative elements that had been developed elsewhere were primarily admired for their decorative value, rather than their original content. The new traits seen in the Celtic silenos heads may imply that new meanings had attached to these classical motifs. In any case, the cultural backgrounds of these two worlds—the transmitting (Etruscan) and the receiving (Celtic)—were quite different.

The reiteration of silenos heads on such pitchers was not accidental, since many Etruscan vases with this motif had reached central European locations, possibly influencing Nordic artisans. Keep in mind that among the grave goods of the tomb in Kleinaspergle, besides the locally made pitcher just mentioned, there was an Etruscan *stamnos* whose handles were decorated with silenos heads; it could have been the model for the local, reworked copy.

In the fourth century B.C.—the period when the Gauls descended into the Italian peninsula—Etruscan exports continued to continental Europe, although their cadence slowed. The most commonly found object was a *stamnos*-like *situla* in bronze with lion's-head spout. It was fitted with a filter and had a head of a silenos or divinity (Minerva, Herakles, or Helios) applied on its opposite side. Its distribution area was quite vast, from France to the Netherlands and Belgium, Germany, Bulgaria, and southern Russia.

Some examples from locations in eastern Europe may have originally arrived from Macedonia, where similar *situlae* were produced. The object was part of a wine service, and as a result it continued to be exported by Etruria to continental Europe and sped the European embrace of Etruscan culture.

A number of Etruscan mirrors from Transalpine locations date to the end of the fourth and the third centuries B.C. They belong to a more recent production that includes the sculptural groups of the Dioscuri, the Lasa, and the Crown of Leaves. Most have been found in France (Savoy, Lyon, Burgundy, Champagne, Île de France, and Loire). One was found in

the riverbed of the Saône near Lyon and was used, at least at its final destination, as an ex-voto. Another from the third century with a depiction of the Dioscuri was found in Paris in a tomb in the necropolis of Faubourg St. Jacques; its owners must have treasured it as a valued item since it was associated with material from the first century B.C.

Near the hills of Piccolo San Bernardo, a mold for a mirror was found that depicted the beheading of Medusa. This same iconography appears on a silver mirror with reliefs preserved at the Museo Archeologico in Florence. We may infer that Etruscan masters moved to the Transalpine region with molds (and tools) to work there. Etruscan mirrors from the Hellenistic period were also discovered at Olbia on the Black Sea and in the royal mausoleum of Neapolis (Scythia). However, it is difficult to say how these last pieces arrived at their respective findspots.

Many small bronzes depicting Herakles or Mars that fell within Etruscan and Italic production from the fourth and third centuries B.C. were found in various locations of Savoy, Jura, the Côte d'Or, and Burgundy. The figurines of Herakles, in particular, were common in areas where there were springs or hot springs. This connection derives from the Etruscan fondness for the scene of Herakles at the spring, and their probable worship of the hero as the god of springs.

Finally, we note that runes made their appearance toward the end of the Etruscan expansion into the European regions. These inscriptions may have been linked to magic and religion and were first seen in northern and central Europe between the late Imperial period and the first centuries of the second millennium A.D. Their language was Germanic in origin, and their alphabet northern Italic. Various runic letters came from the Lepontine alphabet, the Raetian alphabet (from Magré, Sondrio, and Bolzano), and the Venetian alphabet, and others from the Latin alphabet. In addition, these runes have some peculiar characteristics: there are no curvilinear elements, the verticals are much elongated, and the symbols are inscribed in a thin band, with letters touching the upper and lower edges. This last detail had a prior history in Etruscan epigraphs from the North, particularly the Volterran area, and in epigraphs from the Po Valley, such as an Etruscan inscription from Busca (Cuneo) in Piedmont and others that are Lepontine or Venetian.

It is difficult to say how the runic alphabets were formed, since the most recent epigraphic records in pre-Latin languages from northern Italy do not date beyond the first century B.C., and the oldest runes go back only to the second and third centuries A.D. (with the earliest examples being the farthest away from Italy). It is thought that this chronological gap could have been bridged by writings on wood that have been lost, but this is only a theory. This alphabet seems to have been deliberately crafted, and some have hypothesized that it could have been part of a conscious program whose nature was more than graphic: that it was a kind of resistance on the part of the peoples of northern and central Europe to Roman occupation.

Tiny bronze warrior with a runic inscription, of unknown provenance, second or third centuries A.D. Oslo, Universitat, Jahn Oldsaksamlingen

The Etruscans in Veneto

| LOREDANA CAPUIS

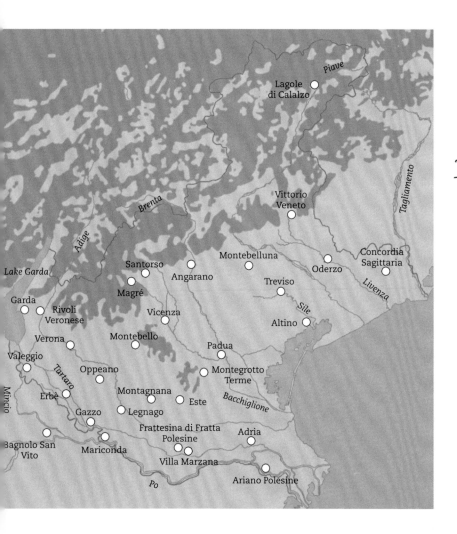

Various Greek and Latin authors (Polybius, Strabo, Diodorus Siculus, and Livy) speak quite specifically about Etruscan dominance north of the Po River. However, their references generally concern the great Celtic invasion of the fourth century B.C., which, in fact, marked the decline of the Etruscans in the Po Valley. Regarding the preceding period and the times and forms of an older Etruscan presence, we have but little written evidence (Virgil and his commentators). What little there is is not univocal and scholars have often attacked it as being mere mythohistoric legend. Today, however, these tales have gained a measure of credibility. Archaeological sources not only demonstrate an organized Etruscan presence in the Transpadane region—mostly commercial beginning in the seventh century, with permanent settlements by the middle of the sixth—but also enable us to reach further back in time by studying its cultural "forms of contact." The picture sketched by Titus Livius, the Patavian (Paduan) historian better known as Livy, who noted

On page 130, map of the main settlements in pre-Roman Veneto

On the preceding page, a tiny bronze warrior from the end of the eighth century B.C., uncovered at the Scolo di Lozzo in Este (Padua). It may have belonged to a tomb there. Este, Museo Nazionale

(5.33.7–10) that the Adriatic Sea owed its name to the Etruscan colony of Adria and that the Etruscans occupied the entire country beyond the Po "*excepto Venetorum angulo*" (except the angle belonging to the Veneti), has been entirely confirmed.

In fact, the territory of the Veneti never saw any precise form of Etruscan dominance. However, its geographic situation inevitably led it to become a hub of commercial traffic, and it undoubtedly functioned as an echo chamber for complex phenomena of cultural exchange between the Italic peninsula and the region of central Europe—an exchange hosted and led by the Etruscans.

The first visible connection between the Veneto and the mining region of Tuscany dates back to the end of the Bronze Age and it is well recorded at Frattesina di Fratta Polesine, a proto-Villanovan city that rose on one of the northern branches of the Po near an ancient coastline. It was an outlet for amber and metals, a place where the entire cultural dynamic of Italy in the upper Adriatic was concentrated. There, finished products were bartered for raw materials —bronze for amber, glass paste, bone and ivory, even ostrich eggs— in a scene that mingled the peoples of the Italian peninsula, continental Europe, and the eastern Mediterranean. Materials from the storerooms of Frattesina, and similar ones in other cities that were located along the Adige-Po watershed, also attest to direct contact between the Venetian area and the metalliferous region of Tuscany during the ninth and tenth centuries B.C.

The result of this lively exchange of goods, people, ideas, technological innovations, and culture was a common language—the so-called proto-Villanovan koine—that only between the end of the Bronze Age and the beginning of the Iron Age began to acquire specific regional traits. The future historical cities began to coalesce in Etruria. In Emilia rose the city of Bologna, which is now known to be Etruscan back to its founding. In northeastern Italy the culture of the Veneti, one of the most noteworthy in the multifaceted picture of pre-Roman Italy, began to take shape. Although it had its own specific identity, it owed much to the Etruscans, such as the production of manufactured goods and, above all, its ideology and institutions.

The new urban order in Veneto, which encompassed the large territory between the Po and the Alps and between the Adige and the Tagliamento Rivers, was marked by the birth of the dominant cities of Este and Padua between the end of the ninth and the beginning of the eighth centuries B.C. These cities nurtured their respective settlements with significantly different cultural outcomes. Este and its territory struck up a lively dialectic with the Villanovan-Etruscan, Bolognan, and Tyrrhenian worlds, gravitating toward the watershed system of the Adige, Mincio, and Po. Padua and its territory, on the other hand, were more receptive to stimuli from eastern Europe, thanks to the Brenta-Piave system. Recent discoveries in the area between the Sile and Tagliamento Rivers have also revealed the early nascence of cities such as Oderzo and Concordia, which predated Este and Padua and were characterized by a notably advanced urban organization. This seems to suggest that the area did not suffer from the "international" crisis triggered at the end of the Bronze Age by the collapse of the Aegean trade system; for a time Frattesina continued to act as a pole in the upper Adriatic for Mediterranean and Italic trade circuits.

Although there is a lot of information to digest, it seems clear that central Veneto, and especially Este, represents a fair sample for a discussion of the interaction between the Veneti and Etruscans.

From the eighth century B.C., a generic Villanovan *koine* is discernable in terracotta production (with its characteristic metopal bands and lamellar decorations) and in metallic works (with similar types of fibulae, spools, razors, and knives). But more important signs of a direct contact with the Etruscan world come in the form of individual objects that were closely linked to masculine and feminine power. These were imports heavy with "status symbol" value, the result of exchanges or gifts between leaders of different communities, according to a model that by now is unanimously recognized as a Homeric pattern of aristocratic reciprocity.

From the Vetulonian world we have the warrior statuette from Lozzo, a bronze that makes iconographic reference to the male roles of warrior and aristocrat. A number of swords uncovered mostly in Este and the Verona area refer to types once seen in Tarquinia and Veii. These finds are exceptional in that they were absolutely foreign to the Venetian funerary ideology, as was the inclusion of weapons in tombs. A model of a shield used as a lid for a bronze ossuary, taken from a very rich tomb of a Paduan man, is similar to examples known in Etruria itself and at Verucchio, and it may be said to have similar value. The transmission of specific symbols drawn from the feminine world is just as weighty from an

ideological point of view. Feminine items ranged from diamond-shaped belts of a Villanovan type, discovered in Este and the Verona area, to spindles that, together with the more common spools and loom weights, elevate the role of weavers in a ritual that was well documented from Verucchio to Bologna and from Etruria itself to Lazio. One immediately calls to mind the world of Homer and Penelope, who used her loom as an instrument—and a symbol—of aristocratic, political, and family bargaining. We think of Odysseus, too, the able carpenter who made their wedding bed from the trunk of a tree, when we see the carpenter's tools found in tombs at Este, often in complete sets that had their exact counterparts in Veii.

Thus the presence of objects or gifts in the emerging Venetian society was evidently not only a sign of sporadic aristocratic reciprocity, but of a much deeper form of ideological and cultural contact. In this sense, the Ricovero Tomb 236 in Este, which dates to the end of the eighth century B.C., is emblematic. It is one of the most ancient tombs, with ossuaries for a male and a female, a symbol of marital bonds and the dominance of family. As in the Etruscan world, the man had grave goods with warrior or artisan connotations (a sword and

Bronze antenna sword and bronze cannon-shaped axe-head, second half of the eighth century B.C. Both pieces were ritually broken and deposited in the situla-ossuary at Ricovero Tomb 236 in Este (Padua). Este, Museo Nazionale

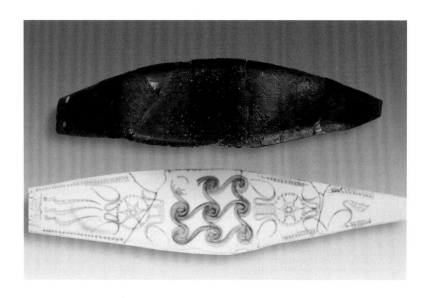

Villanovan-type bronze belt, end of the eighth century B.C., found in Pelà Tomb 8 in Este (Padua). Este, Museo Nazionale

for Orientalizing luxury. Imports or imitations from the world of men were less apparent, although these always reflected status. Villanovan-type horse bits identify the owners and breeders of the prized Venetian horses so often mentioned in sources; bronze tableware (including a tripod and fluted cup from Vetulonia) signifies the aristocracy's adoption of the banquet or symposium; and the double-edged axe is a symbol of power.

The Venetian aristocratic class demonstrated its sanction of the Etruscan ideology in other ways as well. Women were entrusted with advertising their family's economic stature through the richness, variety, exotic qualities, and sheer quantity of grave goods, while men were accorded the symbols of socioeconomic prestige: insignia. The circulation of Etruscan or Etruscanized materials reveals that during the entire seventh century B.C., Este and the territory around the Adige-Mincio-Po watershed maintained steady relations with the Etruscan region. The mediating role of Bologna, where "exotic" items comparable to those in Veneto have also been found, is apparent as well.

Along the same route, from coastal Etruria to its inland regions and thence to the Bologna region, the cultural climate saw a shift that led to one of the showiest artistic displays in the Venetian world: *situla* art, that is, the production of vases and other objects in sheet bronze with figurative decoration.

The most ancient non-Geometric decoration appeared in Este on a cup that was intentionally made without a handle and was used as a lid for a *situla*-ossuary. It dates between 650 and 625 B.C., and represents an interesting union between a

carpentry tools), and his bones were deposited in a bronze vase wrapped in a cloth, according to a ritual with Euboean and Homeric roots. The female grave goods are quite extensive, with objects that denote her social and economic role.

Over the course of the seventh century B.C., the relationship between Veneto and the Etruscan region changed noticeably. The horizon for imports widened to include not only occasional objects that were laden with symbolic value, but also a range of luxury goods that suited a general aristocratic lifestyle. Female burials most clearly reveal the exhibition of magnificence and wealth, a clear symptom that socioeconomic stratification was increasing and that power was being consolidated into the hands of a few emerging families. These grave goods featured rich personal ornaments, such as pendants in bone and faience, refined fibulae, necklaces, and containers for oil and perfume: all items exemplifying the fashion

shape from a central European tradition (a cup with a deep body and a raised handle) and a decoration of Corinthian Orientalizing descent (a grazing mountain goat). Its technical and formal characteristics (figures embedded in the background and thin outlines) find their precise match in contemporary products from Bologna. It is thus obvious that a complex network of cultural models and stimuli has built up between the Etruscan-Tyrrhenian world and central European Hallstatt circles. Bologna was the junction and Veneto the resonance box in this story, in which the transfer of skilled specialized artisans in both directions played a major role. We now know that the spread of a figurative language that could express ideological content common to the various local aristocracies was closely related to the mobility of artisans, a mobility favored by the easy river and land routes that— via the valleys of the Tiber, the Ombrone, and the Arno—facilitated contact between southern and inland Etruria, the Bolognan district, and the Po Plain.

How else could we explain the unexpected and nearly contemporary appearance of unique creations—a *tintinnabulum* from Bologna, a throne from Verucchio, a helmet from Pitino, and the Benvenuti *situla* from Este—that shared a common stylistic and iconographic language? Time and again this artistic vocabulary was applied to objects made according to local tradition, with themes that reflected local concerns. These were the fruits of common skilled workers, serving a diverse clientele.

The Benvenuti *situla*, an undisputed masterpiece of its genre, dates to around 600 B.C. and is often called the "poem of the Venetian people" for its scenes of

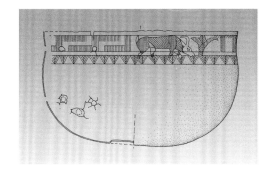

Bronze cup with a figure of a grazing mountain goat, seventh century B.C. It was used as the lid for the situla-ossuary from Benvenuti Tomb 122 in Este (Padua). Este, Museo Nazionale

Below, Vetulonian-type bronze tripod, seventh century B.C., found in Pelà Tomb 49 in Este (Padua). Este, Museo Nazionale

At *right*, schematic drawing of the Benvenuti situla decorations

Below, bronze *situla* with an embossed narrative representation, from the Benvenuti Tomb 126 in Este (Padua), about 600 B.C. This masterpiece of *situla* art contained a clay ossuary. Este, Museo Nazionale

hunts, games, banquets, battles, and farming. It certainly brings to life images of an aristocratic elite that adopted "established" figurative schemes in order to sanction the "message" of the Etruscan princes, just as individual motifs such as imaginary animals, vegetal backgrounds, and details of clothing and customs evoke the contemporary repertory of late Orientalizing. However, the language of the Etruscan matrix provided only a formal means of conveying scenes that were of local importance, even if we no longer know how to read them as their contemporaries did. With the coming of the sixth century B.C., a new historical cycle commenced in Veneto, as a pre-urban society gradually became truly urban. Evidence of the new "city ideology" included the acquisition and diffusion of writing, the transformation of the social structure, and the reorganization of residences, necropoleis, and land-holdings. We see the production of technologically innovative manufactured goods, exchanges that were decisively commercial, and the establishment of places of worship. All of these are familiar symptoms of the urban mentality that had already asserted itself in Etruria.

It was from Etruria, especially the inland regions, that the Veneti had acquired writing, along the same routes that had brought the introduction of the figurative and narrative language of *situla* art. Their writing was based on an Etruscan alphabet and adapted to their language. The most ancient Venetian

given us exceptional and unique evidence—bronze tablets and writing styli that were certainly derived from Etruscan handbooks—regarding the teaching and learning techniques of the alphabet in pre-Roman Italy, and the practice of writing based on syllables. These objects were dedicated as ex-votos at the Este sanctuary of Reitia, a divinity whose many attributes included the magical profession of writing.

inscription, incised on a *kantharos* from Lozzo, dates back to the first half of the sixth century B.C. It shows an early phase of writing that lacks punctuation, attributable to the influence of one of the northern Etruscan cities, probably Chiusi, via Bologna. In the course of one or two generations, a "reform" that originated in Caere and Veii brought the introduction of syllabic punctuation, which would remain in use until the transition to the Latin alphabet and language. Veneto has

Reflecting the locals' adoption of writing was the appearance of stone tomb-markings with the name of the deceased, including *cippi* with pyramidal bodies from Este and figured stelai and large bowls from Padua. Of particular interest is the oldest of the Paduan stelai, which joins an Etruscan form with the formal language of *situla* art.

The adoption of the double-name formula, in the manner of the nobility, is also a clear Etruscan influence. The social organization of the nobility was soon reflected in the necropoleis: wide, circular structures covered by small tumuli were built to accommodate future burials in an obvious hierarchical relationship. Noteworthy

Above, alphabetic tablet in bronze from the fifth or fourth centuries B.C., a reference guide for teaching writing. It and other similar items were found along with writing styli in the sanctuary of Reitia in Este (Padua). Este, Museo Nazionale

changes were also seen in residences, such as more permanent architecture and a uniform street layout. Recent excavations in the heart of Padua give proof of this change. There, among other things, a *cippus* with a value mark *X* (*decussis*) was discovered, similar to others in Marzabotto and Spina, suggesting that urban restructuring may have been under way. Some valuable furnishings, such as two figured terra-cottas from Oderzo, recall terra-cotta works from Capua and the inland regions of Etruria, just as the oldest residences and environments arranged around a central courtyard recall models from Etruria Padana, that is, the Etruscan presence in the Po Valley. The accelerated process of urban transformation and the new organization of the territory were clearly linked with the new economic and commercial systems that revolved around Etruria Padana. These changes were immediately echoed in Veneto.

In fact, the presence of the Etruscans in the Po delta region goes back to the second half of the sixth century B.C. The urban characteristics of Adria and the organization of the territory show their influence, with the population divided between the coastline as it was at that time (San Basilio, Taglio di Po, Contarina) and the hinterlands (Borsea, Gavello, Le Balone). In the same way, the opening of the first artificial canals—*fossae* that connected Adria to Spina through inner waterways—drew on the consummate hydraulic skill of the Etruscans. After being deserted for more than two centuries, the delta area took up the role that Frattesina had played in its time: as a meeting and transit point for different populations. The Veneti seem to have made every effort to facilitate the overland and maritime flow of Greek and

Etruscan products, which spread throughout Etruria Padana and into Lombardy, ultimately reaching the wealthy Celtic courts beyond the Alps. The cities along the Adige, from Este to Gazzo, from Oppeano to Rivoli, were particularly involved in these new commercial dynamics. However, important new evidence has been uncovered in eastern Veneto and above all in Altino, demonstrating that the latter was a significant emporium along the

On the facing page, below, a hypothetical reconstruction of a funerary enclosure in the Ricovero necropolis in Este (Padua), with little "tumulus" coverings for the tombs

Above, bronze vases from wine services for symposia, fifth or fourth centuries B.C., found in Capodaglio Tomb 31 in Este (Padua). Este, Museo Nazionale

Below, local copies of terra-cotta Schnabelkanne and skyphos from the fifth century B.C., which were uncovered without a context at the necropoleis at Este (Padua). Este, Museo Nazionale

inner waterways, a city that transshipped Greek and Etruscan-Padane products from Spina toward Padua and its territories.

Attic ceramics and bronze tableware, both imported and locally produced, found in the tombs of rich Venetian lords, demonstrate an increasingly wide diffusion of practices linked to symposia and banquets. Their ideology is reflected in a number of "indigenous" iconographies, such as a buckle from Carceri or a bronze offering bearer from Padua. In fact, a Schnabelkanne (a spouted pitcher) together with either a cup (*kylix*) or an umbilicated *patera* appeared in both places. In the same way, a terra-cotta Schnabelkanne, a local imitation of the precious Etruscan bronze pitchers used for mixing wine, was discovered at Este. The presence of typical pottery from the Po Valley and black-painted pottery (first Attic, and then Volterran) also underscores this new focus on the ritual banquet. Early imports were soon joined by locally produced imitations in semi-refined gray pottery. This once again highlights Venetian society's mature process of acculturation, which did not passively acquire new fashions and products but rather assimilated their ideological value in such a profound way that it discernibly changed the standards of manufactured goods.

The presence of *aes rude* has been linked to the trade of Attic pottery and wine. These were bronze fragments used for exchange before the minting of coins, according to a custom that became widespread wherever there were Etruscans. Right in Este, in a case that is so far unique in Veneto, an *aes signatum* (currency bar) was also found, stamped with the mark of a dried branch. It was similar to others in northern Tuscany, from Emilia to Forcello, an area that had close relations with cities between the Adige and Mincio Rivers.

Bronzes scattered generously along the Etruscan travel routes in the Po Valley give evidence of an early spread of religious

Small votive bronze sheet with an embossed figure of a warrior, from the fifth and fourth centuries B.C. Caldevigo sanctuary area in Este (Padua). Este, Museo Nazionale

On the facing page, bronze worshipers and offering bearers from the fifth or fourth centuries B.C., from the sanctuary of Reitia in Este (Padua). Este, Museo Nazionale

reflected the new climate of Etruscan-style religious practices. These sanctuaries were suburban, situated just outside the cities, and territorial, having a real or symbolic function as a border marker. Clear models for these have been found in the Italic world. No temple structures have survived, but we do have a number of *cippi*, primarily those that marked the borders of places dedicated to the gods, and a large crop of ex-votos that allow us to compare production in Etruria with that of northern Umbria. Certain ideological forms were held in common, such as rites of passage for girls and boys, the aforementioned practice of writing, and the prevailing use of bronze according to norms shared among all of the northern Etruscan, Umbrian, Apennine, and Adriatic cultures. It is evident that in the sacred sphere the Etruscans did not explicitly impose their beliefs and gods through their influence, but rather furnished models for behavior that the Veneti adapted to their needs.

Thus the process of acculturation that Veneto underwent at the hands of the Etruscans is varied and complex. Its effects would linger throughout the course of its history: a quite fertile interaction, inasmuch as Etruscan culture was not passively received but actively modified.

A recently discovered example shows how ideology could cross over through the simple transmission of objects and typologies. This is the incredibly rich tomb of Nerka Trostiaia, which was found in Este and dates to the first half of the third century B.C. Clearly inspired by the Etruscan chamber tombs, it is shaped like a large casket with a pitched roof, like those found in Bologna. Numerous grave goods from the tomb, although locally

articles not unlike those of northern and Apennine Etruria. Significant examples, such as the Herakles of Contarino and some bronzes from Adria and the Veronese territory, were joined by locally produced imitations. However, the blossoming of true sanctuaries during the sixth and fifth centuries B.C. in the dominant cities of Veneto was much more significant and

A tiny bronze worshiper engaged in prayer, known as the "goddess of Caldevigo," from the fifth century B.C. Caldevigo sanctuary area in Este (Padua). Este, Museo Nazionale

produced, recall the Etruscan world: a bronze *olpe* with the inscription *ego Trostiaiai*, a *flabellum* (fan), a candelabra, a bronze throne that was one of the last works of *situla* art, and granulated jewelry. Many of these items are "exotic" and probably arrived by way of Adria and Spina, such as black-painted pottery, a piece from Gnathia, and an Attic krater

by the Filottrano Painter. The tomb is practically a mirror of a rich mercantile class that continued to reap the benefits of trade. Great was their debt to the famous Venetian horses, but also to their country's favorable geographic position, which allowed them to control the transit routes and maintain the upper hand at the region's vital crossings.

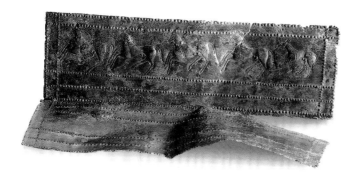

At left, bronze model of a seat with an embossed back, from the early decades of the third century B.C. The Nerka Tomb in Este (Padua). Este, Museo Nazionale

Below, parts of a necklace made of glass paste, amber, bone, gold, and silver, from the early decades of the third century B.C. The Nerka Tomb in Este (Padua). Note the ornaments decorated with granulation according to Etruscan tastes. Este, Museo Nazionale

The Etruscans in the Lepontine and Raetian Regions

| LUCIANA AIGNER FORESTI

The Lepontine Tribes

The Lombard-Piedmont region extends from the Adda River to the Sesia and from the Ticino to the Po. Geographically speaking, it is a passage from the Mediterranean to central Europe. As a result, it has been open to the exchange of cultural influences, religious images, and models for living since the thirteenth century B.C.

It was then that a new culture, the so-called Canegrate culture (Varese), broke with the artisan tradition of the preceding period and rejoined the urnfield culture of central Europe, adopting their rite of cremating their dead and burying the remains in an urn together with grave goods. The link between the two regions continued during the twelfth and especially during the tenth centuries B.C., as witnessed by weapons and ornamental objects, the first signs of relations between group leaders.

The artifacts of the Golasecca culture (Varese), which also extended to the Ticino Canton and the Graubünden, suggest cultural continuity in the territory up until the fourth century B.C. Thus, the earlier Canegrate phase represents the first exterior expression of a precocious and hardy ethnic unity in the region. These were the Lepontine tribes that lived at the sources of the Rhine (Caesar *Bellum Gallicum* 4.10) and the Rhone (Pliny *Naturalis Historia* 3.135), to the left of Como (Strabo 4.204), which ancient tradition considered Celtic (Cato in Pliny *Naturalis Historia* 3.134) or Raetian (Strabo 4.204).

These peoples tended to gravitate culturally toward the Celtic Transalpine region. Celtic linguistic characteristics permeated their language, which is conventionally called Lepontine, as seen in a series of inscriptions beginning in the sixth century B.C. The historical inhabitants of the Golasecca-culture region, therefore, seem to be locals who had come under Celtic influence early on, through groups that infiltrated the territory from central and southern Europe beginning in the twelfth century. In the course of time these groups were augmented through overlapping and mixing, first by outlying populations of neighboring tribes who were mostly of

Fluted bowl in sheet bronze, fifth century B.C., from the Carrettino Tomb at Cava Gini in Ca' Morta (Como). Como, Museo Civico Archeologico P. Giovio

Ligurian stock, and then, during the sixth century and especially beginning in the middle of the century that followed, by Celtic tribes who reached Italy through the Alps in successive waves of uneven demographic consistency. This last group gave the territory its Celtic cultural imprint and unified language, which lasted until Romanization.

Beginning in the tenth century B.C., the territory shows evidence of contact with other regions as well. A number of artisan forms were taken from Veneto, and we find highly valued objects that originated in Lunigiana and Versilia in Liguria, perhaps as gifts or a primitive form of payment. Objects of a chiefly military nature came

from Villanovan Etruria in the ninth century. Local shops quickly imitated these helmets and swords, and their copies were considered technically superior to traditional ones.

The Lombardy-Piedmont area displays a certain openness toward regions that in some cases were quite far away. Its inhabitants were able to capitalize on their strategic location as a transit area for goods moving toward the Transalpine world, especially toward central Europe and the Hallstatt culture, which had been in touch with the Etruscan-Villanovan world since the ninth century B.C. They eventually translated their advantageous geographic position into a drive to organize this traffic and, ultimately, those who were most involved in economic operations saw their status rise.

Malpensa (Milan) and Ca' Morta (Como) showed a strong demographic increase, as is evident in their tenth-century necropoleis. These two gathering points coalesced in a territory that was otherwise characterized by dispersed communities with mostly homogeneous social groupings and poor grave goods. There was a lapse in the ninth century, when Ca' Morta showed a decreasing number of tombs and residences, perhaps because of climatic changes. Then the district of Como, which had previously experienced a high population density, began to rise at the beginning of the eighth century. Como flourished noticeably between the end of that century and the beginning of the next, with an urban area forming out of previous settlements. There, highly skilled local artisans appeared, and grave goods simultaneously began to diversify. Social differentiations emerged in the necropoleis around Como,

with an aristocratic warrior class that took its direction and customs from the aristocratic warrior classes of more evolved areas. Veneto exported ornamental objects to Ca' Morta, and from Tyrrhenian Etruria and Etruscan Bologna came high-class items, such as a two-horse chariot with its related Villanovan-type horse bit and valuable furnishings associated with the symposium. These social customs may have taken on a political value.

However, the warriors of Como and its surrounding area also turned toward two Hallstatt areas. Once again they took up the Transalpine rite of cremating the dead, along with a chariot and a type of bit that were used by nomads in the Thracian-Cimmerian steppe. They also turned to the

inhabitants of the eastern Alps, with whom they shared specific assemblage of grave goods: a four-wheeled ritual handcart, weapons, and tableware for symposia.

Another early urban area took shape toward the end of the eighth century B.C., this one in the district of Sesto Calende Golasecca-Castelleto Ticino. It is a hilly

Strainer in sheet bronze, fifth century B.C., from Tomb 4-1926 in the Butti quarry at Ca' Morta (Como). Como, Museo Civico Archeologico P. Giovio

region, where the Ticino River flows out of Lake Maggiore on the fringe of the Lodigiano, and it boasted a genuinely local artisan class. The high demographic concentrations that we see in the necropoleis of Castelletto Ticino imply that provisions were being organized and local agriculture boosted, no doubt financed with profits from trade. The cultivation of grapes may have been introduced from Etruria during this time.

During the seventh century B.C., this area took the lead over the areas of Como and

closed, barring any upward mobility on the part of the lower classes.

The aristocratic warriors interred in two tombs in Sesto Calende had adopted Etruscan customs and ideologies, just as the warriors in the necropoleis of Como, and especially Ca' Morta, had done in the past. Sometime in the second half of the seventh or the beginning of the sixth centuries B.C., two Etruscan symbols of rank had been adopted: a two-wheeled chariot and part of the military uniform, which were found among the warriors' grave goods. Religious

Ca' Morta in the number and extent of its residences. The urban phenomenon in the district of Golasecca-Sesto Calende, unlike that in Comasco, came about through the amalgamation of older villages, which was stimulated by commercial interests linked to river navigation. However, the settlements in the Golasecca area did not develop beyond this pre-urban or proto-urban stage, with the sole exception of Como. This appears to be due to the persistence of aristocratic structures that were centralized and

beliefs and cultural customs may also have been taken up at Castelletto Ticino, in tandem with valuable Etruscan objects. It was in this period that the alphabet reached Sesto Calende, and with it the custom of inscribing objects with their owners' names. The intermediaries of this cultural transmission were either Etruscans or people of Celtic origin, such as a certain *Larθ Muθikus*, who had joined northern Etruscan society but eventually returned to his native land, perhaps Piedmont.

Still, the warrior aristocracy in Golasecca, which was open to Etruria and its culture either directly or via Bologna and Genoa, continued to turn toward the Hallstatt world with more conviction than in the previous century. Common ideologies, artistic tastes, and artisan traditions are reflected in *situlae* that were decorated with an Archaic technique, derived from the urnfield civilization and perhaps executed by traveling artisans. Wheeled incense-burners for rituals were used both in Sesto Calende and Styria (Austria), signaling a common religious orientation among those who purchased them. The kind of weapons and horse bits that were used by the nomads of the steppe, which had been imported from the western Hallstatt area, reveal the adoption of new equestrian techniques. The association of such heterogeneous materials tells us that the emerging classes of Golasecca, displaying an attitude that is universally familiar, admired and consumed precious foreign objects as well as imitations that encouraged the emergence of skilled local artisans.

The sixth century B.C. opened with an event of international significance: The Greeks founded Massalia and opened the valley of the Rhone, which became a trade route for the Celts and their merchants. A number of decades later, around 550 B.C., the Etruscans withdrew from southern France and simultaneously founded a number of colonies in northern Italy, including Spina, Adria, and Marzabotto. The Celts may have infiltrated this region, attracted there by a thriving Po Valley, as Livy thought, but for now the material evidence does not support any substantial changes to the more traditional view. From this time on, the two districts of the Golasecca area, Como and Sesto Calende, set off toward

different destinies. Como saw an expansion of its residential area and turned toward the Venetian and northern Etruscan regions, especially through Bologna, from which it drew most of its artisan techniques. In Golasecca, by contrast, the aristocracy continued to cultivate its ancient relationship with the southern Etruscan world. They continued to prefer its tableware for symposia, especially jugs, basins, *situlae*, and the famous spouted pitchers, which arrived from Volsinii and Vulci and then reached the Celts via age-old roads. As in Etruscan

Situla in sheet bronze with crescent-shaped handles, second half of the seventh century B.C., from the right bank of the Ticino River in Golasecca (Varese). Milan, Museo Archeologico del Castello Sforzesco

Stele with an Etruscan
inscription from the second
half of the sixth century B.C.
that was found on the left
bank of the Maira River,
from Busca (Cuneo). Turin,
Museo di Antichità

society, the women of Golasecca were the keepers of the family wealth and the guarantors of its continuity.

With the end of the sixth century B.C., the necropoleis of Golasecca peter out, a sign that the interests of its inhabitants had moved elsewhere. This fact must be connected to the flourishing of Como during the fifth century, when its material life was further enriched with Etruscan furnishings

for symposia from Vulci and Bologna. These were often found together with Attic and Rhodian pottery from Adria and Spina and were destined for the upper class, as were Greek oil and wine. A coin from Populonia that was uncovered in Prestino is a sign of the commercial prestige that this great mineral city of northern Etruria enjoyed.

The abandonment of Golasecca also ran in tandem with the emergence of other Po cities that were located at river junctions (Forcello and Mantua), at the mouth of valleys (Brescia), or along a connecting road that, having moved east with respect to the district of Lake Maggiore, crossed Bergamo and Brembate di Sotto (southwest of Bergamo) and reached Como and Lodi on the Adda plain, carrying goods from the Adriatic Sea or central Italy. During the fifth century, Como was the commercial hub of trade to and from the Celtic lands.

Even more important, however, is the fact that contacts with Etruria stimulated the development of local craftsmanship. Local workshops began to produce tableware for symposia by imitating and applying new technologies, such as the fast lathe, new chromatic schemes, and modified vase shapes imported from the Padana Etruscans. The alphabet was re-adapted to the needs of the Celtic language at this time and took on a national character. It was then used to write in Lepontine on a cup from Castelletto Ticino and on stelae from Prestino and Como, where numerous Celtic inscriptions tell us that knowledge of the alphabet must have been relatively widespread.

Beginning at the end of the fifth century B.C., Celtic tribes from southern and central Europe invaded northwest Italy. The distribution of their tombs and their belongings amid local grave goods demonstrate that they had followed commercial routes. At this stage the aristocracy of Golasecca conformed to their new circumstances and adopted Celtic armor. Tyrrhenian-Etruscan imports continued to flow without interruption, a sign that the ancient modes of life were not abandoned. Through Brembate, spouted pitchers reached Comasco, and

melded the old traditions with those of their recent conquerors.

Organized into tribes, the Cisalpine Celts who succeeded the Lepontine tribes lived in small cities during the third and second centuries B.C., of which at least one, Vercelli, took on urban form. (Ancient tradition considered that Como, Bergamo, Brescia, and Verona had been founded by Celts.) Their political struc-

Basin in double sheet bronze with embossed decorations, seventh century B.C., from the Tomb of the Basin in Motto Fontanile at Castelletto Ticino (Novara). Turin, Museo di Antichità

from there the upper stretch of the Ticino, or they were shipped up Lake Maggiore and entered the valley of the Toce.

At the beginning of the fourth century B.C., Comasco too was abandoned. The necropolis of Ca' Morta fell into disuse, the residences of Como were deserted, and craftsmanship suffered a recession. This slump was certainly linked to a collapse of the entire social system and the fact that the territory of Golasecca had become Celtic, as seen in local grave goods with Celtic materials or imitations. The imitations themselves show how the culture of Golasecca was still creating new and distinctive forms that

ture was more evolved than that of other Celtic territories in northern Italy and had roots in the Etruscan-Italic past; we know, for example, that it included the institution of a magistracy that represented a community of citizens (*civitas*), as was mentioned in an inscription from Briona. This early development would make things easier after 49 B.C., when the Romans entered Lepontine territory. Augustus gave it an entirely geographic name, Transpadane. In doing so, he hoped to distinguish it from other Italian regions that kept, and still carry, the names of their first inhabitants.

At *right*, bucchero kylix, sixth century B.C., Giani Krumm collection, Golasecca (Varese). Milan, Museo Archeologico del Castello Sforzesco

Below, tripod, end of the sixth century B.C., from the Tomb of the Tripod in Sesto Calende (Varese). Sesto Calende, Museo Civico Archeologico

At *right*, spouted pitcher of the Schnabelkanne type in sheet bronze with a mermaid handle, fifth century B.C., from Tomb 15 in the Pedemonte section of Gravellona Toce (Novara). Turin, Museo di Antichità

Fragment of a basin in sheet bronze with a beaded rim, sixth century B.C., from Tomb 1985 at Cascina Bonifica, Garlasco (Pavia)

Cista a cordoni (ropelike ornamentation) in sheet bronze, second half of the seventh century B.C., from the Tomb of the Basin at Motto Fontanile, Castelletto Ticino (Novara). Turin, Museo di Antichità

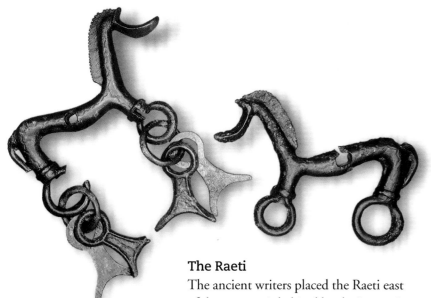

The Raeti

The ancient writers placed the Raeti east of the country inhabited by the Lepontine tribes. The appellation covered a number of Alpine peoples, including the Euganei from the Verona area, the Stoeni from the Valli Giudicarie, and the Camuni from the Val Camonica. The Raetian territory corresponds to the distribution area of Raetian inscriptions beginning at the end of the sixth century B.C., from western Lombardy to Trentino-Alto Adige and the Austrian Tirol. The Raeti shared their border to the north with the Transalpine Celts, to the east with the Veneti.

Our most important sources on the history of the Raeti—the Latin writers Livy (5.33) and Pliny the Elder (*Naturalis Historia* 3.103)—identify the Raeti as descendants of Etruscans who had taken shelter in the mountains at the arrival of the Celts, becoming barbarous in their customs and language due to the area's savage nature. Recent studies have demonstrated a genetic relationship between the Raeti and the Etruscans, confirmed by common place names. But Raetian personal names totally differ from Etruscan ones, which means there was little human contact in historical times.

The material culture of the Raeti demonstrates a general tendency to gravitate

Etruscan-type (Veii) horse bits, eighth century B.C., from the necropoleis of Vadena/Pfatten, Bolzano. Bolzano, Museo Archeologico dell'Alto Adige

toward the Transalpine areas, but only as far as the valley of the Inn. During the eighth century B.C., singular individuals began to emerge in the great river valleys of the Sarca, the Adige, the Isarco, and the Inn. These may have been warriors who adopted a social orientation and funerary images borrowed from Villanovan Etruria, including weapons, aspects of their clothing, and the use of horses. The latter were fitted with southern-Etruscan-type bits that had been made by local artisans. Despite this openness toward more evolved areas, the Raetian area did not see any local aristocratic class step forward to take on managerial responsibilities, nor any significant demographic concentrations that might have led to proto-urban development.

During the eighth century B.C., Val Camonica also took on a distinctive profile. Following ancient traditions of Neolithic origin, the Camuni decorated giant rock surfaces with many incised figures, a true mirror of their society and customs. This activity, evidently inseparable from their customs, was practiced until the Roman period. From the seventh through the sixth centuries, the valley of the Adige became part of a vast cultural environment encompassing Veneto and the eastern Alps. But relations with the Etruscan world did not entirely run dry, if the graffiti on axes from a storeroom in Caldaro (Bolzano) can be accepted. These constitute the only proof of an early knowledge of the alphabet in the region.

Only at the end of the sixth and beginning of the fifth centuries B.C. did the area in question truly begin to thrive. This prosperity coincided with the permanent establishment of the Etruscans in the eastern Po Valley and the shift of the commercial axis

from the course of the Ticino River to Lake Como. Close to one hundred inscriptions in the Raetian language are on record beginning in the sixth century, written in three local variants and adapted to the needs of the native language, which is proof that they consciously sought to set themselves apart from the Etruscan tradition.

During the fifth century B.C., Sanzeno in Anaunia opened shops for bronzeworking and others that created new styles of clothing and new forms of pottery. A close-knit local aristocracy emerged. Their affluence was based on agricultural production, particularly the cultivation of grapes, and the sale of manufactured goods. The most interesting phenomenon was that these cultural innovations in Sanzeno spread rapidly throughout the entire region up to the valley of the Inn, causing demographic concentrations at crucial points along the river valleys and their convergences. The Raeti from the Sanzeno culture once again drew on precious objects

that were typical of the Veneto area, although they created their own motifs and iconographies. Above all, they introduced Etruscan customs from the social, political, and religious spheres. Votive bronzes, which were partly imitations, were consistently of exquisite craftsmanship and came from local artisan workshops that were highly professional.

The Raeti of Sanzeno, therefore, already possessed proto-urban structures when, in the fourth century B.C., the Celts expanded into northern Italy through the territory of the Lepontine tribes. It was then that the Etruscan world in the Po Valley was snuffed out, and Sanzeno's main source of cultural mobility withered.

The Po Valley became Celtic, and the Raetian valleys were the avenue through which the Transalpine Celts rejoined the Cisalpine Celts, as Raetian Celtic-type helmets demonstrate. The culture of Sanzeno participated actively in developing a local Celtic style that can be seen in decorative objects. Despite some Mediterranean influence from the fourth to the second centuries B.C., the peoples of Raetian descent remained largely attached to Archaic traditions that slowed the formation of city structures until the Roman period.

At left, pitcher in sheet bronze, fifth century B.C., from the finds of March 1897 at Cassotta, Albate (Como). Como, Museo Civico Archeologico P. Giovio

Below, part of a fifth-century *situla* with vegetal motifs, from Tomb 13 in the necropoleis of San Maurizio/Moritzing, Bolzano. Bolzano, Museo Archeologico dell'Alto Adige

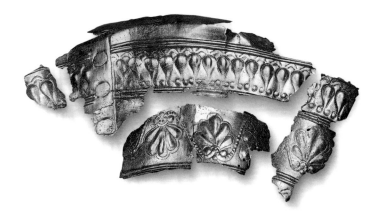

The Etruscans in Liguria

| ADRIANO MAGGIANI

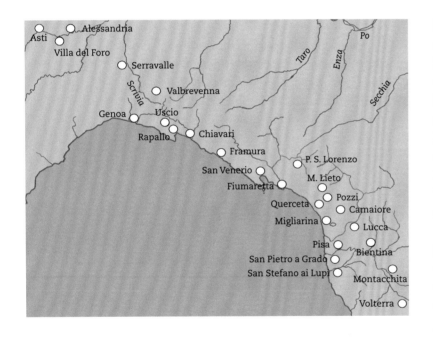

The coast of eastern Liguria and Versilia between the Bronze Age and the early Iron Age

The border area between Liguria and the extreme north of Etruria above the Arno River has seen a succession of different ethnic and cultural configurations. Before Luni was founded in 177 B.C., the hilly area that faces the coastline between the

Magra and the Arno River swarmed with small settlements of Ligurians, which we know today from their necropoleis. They were a warlike people at a rather primitive level of development. As Strabo recalls, they fought hard against the Etruscans of Pisa in the third and beginning of the second centuries and eventually fought the Romans who came to the Etruscans' aid. The sources seem justified in deeming this territory Ligurian.

The situation, however, had not always been thus. The Paduan historian Livy (41.13.4), writing during wars between the Ligurians and Romans, recalled how the *agger* of Luni "*Etruscorum antequam Ligurum fuerat,*" that is, had been in Etruscan hands before its current occupants settled there. Archaeological research in recent years has demonstrated that this pre-Ligurian Etruscan phase ended sometime during the fourth century B.C., perhaps as a result of the great migration of peoples provoked by the second Celtic descent into Italy during the late fifth century. Groups of people who had settled in

Two lids of impasto ash urns with white over-painted decorations, first half of the seventh century B.C., from a necropolis for cremations in Chiavari

the Apennines pushed south in this period, occupying the hills that the retreating Etruscans had vacated. The routes that penetrated toward the Po Valley, which had been kept open by the Etruscans, fell into disuse. Their traces can still be

discerned on the plain of Lucca and, above all, that of Pisa.

However, even the Etruscan presence in this region, whether on the coast or inland, dated back to a relatively recent era.

The arrival of the Etruscans, who at first came exclusively to trade, was first noticeable along the coast beginning in the late eighth century B.C. In the mountainous inland areas and the river valleys of the Secchia and its tributaries, however, archaeological finds demonstrate their presence beginning at least in the late seventh century. Works in bucchero have been found with stamps from settlements in the western Po Plain (Modena and Reggio), which had their precise counterparts in similar works that circulated on the Tyrrhenian Sea in the Pisa-Populonia district.

This commercial wave found cities of an indigenous culture in its path, cities that had developed locally from settlements dating back at least to the late Bronze Age. These populations could legitimately be called Ligurians, our designation for peoples who settled in the larger part (especially the eastern one) of what in historic time would become Liguria. The Etruscans interacted with this ethnic and cultural entity in a variety of ways. At times the foreign cultural structures were completely subdued, while at other times the two mingled in a complex relationship of (forced?) acculturation. In some cases, especially in the areas closest to Etruria proper, the interaction brought about a complete integration of the native populations into Etruria's sociopolitical structure and cultural environment.

Before examining in detail the characteristics of this major phenomenon—the Etruscan civilization's thrust into the northwest coast of the Italian peninsula—it is well to sketch the character of the culture that had blossomed in Liguria during the early Bronze Age.

The available records are relatively abundant for eastern Liguria and Versilia, where a local culture thrived between the Bronze Age and the Iron Age. Its features are well-defined, especially at the extremes of the chronological arc indicated above, although it remains more opaque during the first two centuries of the Iron Age (the ninth and eighth centuries B.C.). The cities that emerge as the most significant archaeologically, from the end of the eighth century, obviously resulted from a long period of demographic concentration at crucial points along the coast: at the mouths of rivers that deeply penetrate the mountainous hinterland.

The most important known sites are two, Chiavari and Baccatoio. The Chiavari necropolis, which was affiliated with a city that has yet to be precisely identified, was built on a sand dune that had already been intensely inhabited during the proto-historical era (the late Bronze Age). The situation at Baccatoio, near Pietrasanta, must have been fairly similar. There, necropoleis from the late eighth century B.C. form a sort of arrival point for a wave of cultural shifts, whose main stages took place during the late Bronze Age at Monte Lieto, at the end of the Bronze Age at Valdicastello, and in the early Iron Age at Colle alle Banche, where a mass of materials from the end of the Bronze Age was found together with others from later periods. These necropoleis, which served indigenous (that is, Ligurian) cities and not Etruscan suburbs, are distinguished by certain elements linked to funerary rites and personal clothing. The tombs contained only cremated remains, with ashes collected in ossuaries either shaped like ollas or vaguely biconic. They were always

standing, without handles, and were placed in boxes that were made from slabs of rock. The ossuaries were generally undecorated, or decorated with a plain engraving or relief. The characteristic types of female clothing among the grave goods included belts fastened with large rectangular plates furnished with hooks; these are not found in Etruscan contexts. The types of burial and clothing elements (and, as we will see, the warrior panoply as well) give a sense of a culture that was closely related to that of Golasecca, which flourished between the Bronze Age and the Iron Age in present-day Lombardy and southern Piedmont.

The settlements, which were concentrated mainly on the coast beginning in the late eighth century B.C., pursued an important line of commerce. The trade centered on local resources that were available even in that early age: metal (iron) was traded for lumber, animals, and leather. As the sources noted, this commerce was more or less the same one that the emporia of Genoa would later pursue. In a relatively short time, the local peoples began to acculturate to all things Etruscan, a process that began with the natives taking in a number of goods of Etruscan make. Although crescent-shaped razors and other elements from the grave goods of Baccatoio are known only through the descriptions of excavators from the last century (the finds themselves appear to be irrecoverably lost), those found in the Chiavari necropoleis can be evaluated scientifically, and without doubt they hearken back to Etruscan models. The same can be said for fibulae and some ceramic tableware, even though scientific studies from the necropoleis have yet to be

Statue-stele from Lunigiana portraying a warrior, with an incised inscription, sixth century B.C., from Bigliolo (Massa)

Above, left, fragment of an interior tondo of the Genucilia plate, showing a woman's face, second half of the fourth century B.C., from the Via XX Settembre necropolis in Genoa

Above, right, small olla made in Volterra with perforated handles in black glossy impasto and stamped decorations between the end of the eighth and the beginning of the seventh centuries B.C., from Tomb 9 in the Chiavari necropolis

published, and as a result we have only an incomplete picture. An extremely old crescent-shaped razor was found in Tomb 323; it is of the Sirolo-Numana type, which was found in Etruria at Veii, Tarquinia, outside of Terni, Caracupa, Sirolo, and Marino. Although the presence of so ancient an object—it can be dated at the latest to the beginning of the eighth century—remains problematic, the crescent-shaped razor from Tomb 43A has been classified as the Benacci type, which was widespread in Etruria during the entire eighth century. As far as fibulae are concerned, those that were largely in fashion in northern Italy in the Golasecca and early Veneto regions lie alongside many others that had their exact counterparts in northern Etruria, especially Volterra. In Chiavari, too, the ceramic tableware seems mostly imported.

An olla decorated with concentric circles from Tomb 9B recalls southernmost Etruria (but also the Tiber area in Falerii and Lazio) in the years around 700 B.C. At the same time, bowls with sunken rims and drawing vessels (*capeduncole*) in bucchero-like impasto that were found in a large number of necropoleis are clearly from the Pisa, Volterra, and Populonia area. The small olla from Tomb 9A came from the same area and had typical perforated handles and triangular decorations on its shoulder, which are comparable to a type of vase that had recently assumed a fixed form and became widespread at the end of the eighth century in Populonia and Volterra.

The bowl in bucchero-like impasto with an anthropomorphic stamp seems particularly noteworthy and had exact counterparts in Massaciuccoli, Pisa, and other places—the circulation area for this entire class of pottery, whose place of origin will probably be identified as Pisa. That city—the northernmost of the three mentioned above—had the most interaction with the northern coast. At one point it probably had a monopoly on trade to these areas; during the course of the seventh century, it shows no evidence of products from Vulci, for example. The Vulcians apparently sought more receptive markets along the coast of southern France.

Important coastal sites in the late Orientalizing period (between the late seventh and beginning of the sixth centuries B.C.) included Chiavari and nearby Rapallo, where grave goods from a tomb excavated in 1911 and published the following year by Arturo Issel included a typical olla with stepped shoulders. There

were comparable objects of its kind throughout the coast, from Pietrasanta (Querceta) to Massaciuccoli, and even Pisa and Lucca. A part of the Riviera di Versilia (the Seravezza and Pietrasanta areas) must have been inhabited by Ligurians, although records are quite scarce at the moment. Nevertheless, this theory is supported by the massive diffusion of burials within stone-slabs boxes, which had begun at the end of the seventh century.

At Massaciuccoli, we find evidence of an emporium, possibly dependent on Pisa, which distributed materials both northward and inland.

Alongside this massive Etruscan commercial penetration into Ligurian territory, we see evidence—not surprisingly—of the effects of acculturation. This is especially apparent because the people who had settled in the Magra basin adopted a type of funerary stele with a representation of a warrior chief. The recent discovery of a monument of this type, which had been reused as the edging for a well in Lerici (La Spezia), has allowed this argument to be placed on more solid foundations. This monument is modeled after a type of prehistoric stele that was connected to the great local megalithic tradition. It portrays a warrior with a small, round shield in the act of attacking with a javelin. It remains to be seen how much the model draws on the monumental typologies and ideological premises of the Volterra and Fiesole areas. Meanwhile, the warrior's armor, which includes a large antenna sword, decisively points to the Golasecca area, as is demonstrated by a royal specimen in iron that is quite similar and comes from Pietra Ligure.

Perhaps because of its proximity to coastal sites frequented by the Etruscan navy, the Lerici stela represents the oldest and most faithful transcription of this type of model. But local populations provided a wide series of variants of a curved stela portraying a high-ranking celebrity.

At an early stage, stelai from Lunigiana reused prehistoric monuments (from the late Neolithic and Aeneolithic eras) that had been used to mark the region's landscape and were still seen in significant numbers during the late Iron Age. Later, artisans developed a specific type of monument that, through a series of approximations, led to the creation of true statues; an example of the latter from Reusa probably already existed at the end of the sixth century B.C. Beyond monumental typology and ideological assumptions, we find indisputable evidence of the acculturation process on these recorded statue-stelai in the form of inscriptions in the Etruscan alphabet, although these spelled out an indigenous language and names. This extraordinary phenomenon, which in the course of about a century produced a dozen monuments, disappeared without a trace during the late Archaic period, a sign of the complete dismantling of local cultures. A bit farther south, in the heart of Versilia, numerous hemispheric- and column-shaped funerary *cippi* in marble, a type from Pisa, demonstrate a somewhat different trend: the complete cultural homogenization of native peoples. However, they continued for a time to use a traditional method of burying the dead in chests along with symposium wine services in bucchero, purely Etruscan in taste.

To the north, the necropolis of Chiavari was abandoned during the early decades of the sixth century B.C. This may have been due to a major upheaval in the northern Tyrrhenian Sea, linked to the foundation of Massalia (about 600 B.C.), or perhaps to the activation of new trade routes. Through these routes Etruscan trade reached indigenous (Ligurian?) settlements in Piedmont, where the stele of Busca marked the Etruscan presence in the fifth century.

Along the Versilia coast, the role of Pisa was certainly predominant and must have remained so to the end of the Classical period. From that time on, traces of the Ligurians become much more faded and seem to be limited to sites beyond the course of the Magra River, which were more protected. These included Ameglia, on the lower course of the Magra, where cube tombs within stone enclosures were used during the third century B.C. However, a number of grave goods included elements from the Archaic period that were clearly Etruscan (bucchero bowls and pyxides from throughout the sixth century, in Tomb 7 of the Cafaggio necropolis). The exceptional nature of these finds has yet to be conclusively explained. Still, it seems unlikely that these were remains of Ligurian chest burials from the Archaic period that had been reused in the early Hellenistic period; Ameglia in that period had once again begun to thrive.

Moreover, Etruscan works in bucchero were found with local impasto items near Pieve di San Venerio in the Gulf of Spezia. The Ligurians were certainly also among those who settled inside the ancient fortifications of Uscio and on Mount Dragnone; the former is a village not far from the sea, the latter is a prehistoric site well inland on the ridge between the valleys of the Vara and Magra Rivers. In the

sixth and fifth centuries B.C., both received materials that had been transported by sea, such as Etruscan amphorae.

After the Archaic period ended, the entire coast of northern Etruria and Liguria seemed to undergo a restructuring. The most important episode was certainly the opening of the Genoa emporium, which was destined for great prosperity.

In the climate of general withdrawal that characterized central Italy in general and southern Etruria in particular during the fifth century B.C., what has been called the "port facies" was an exception. This horizon featured remarkable imports of Attic pottery, which reached the main seaports of the Tyrrhenian, from Populonia to Pisa, and from Genoa to Aleria in Corsica.

Traces of a settlement in Genoa date back at least to the beginning of the sixth century B.C. Evidence of urban organization, however, only commences at the end of the sixth century. The areas of San Silvestro, Castello, and Chiostro di Santo saw the highest density of settlement, along with the area of Porta Soprana, which dominated the port area. The necropoleis extended to the areas of Via XX Settembre and Piazza de' Ferrari.

Strabo defined Genoa as the emporium of the Ligurians. Nevertheless, there were many Etruscan-speaking people here during the city's earliest stage, as a striking group of Etruscan inscriptions on vases (*laris*; *la plaisas*) attests. The city's ethnicity was certainly mixed, as indicated by stone epigraphs on a large bowl—and perhaps a border *cippus* signifying ownership—which belonged to a certain "*Nemetie.*" This person's name is clearly of Celtic origin (and thus perhaps Ligurian), but the structure of the phrase and the alphabet

are Etruscan. No names or letters appear in the necropoleis that might record local burial traditions, possibly indicating a massive population exchange. Chest tombs are completely absent, and the burials are in fact in pits, each with a smaller pit at the bottom, covered by a large stone slab, to contain grave goods. This type of burial had extremely old roots in Etruria and was seen, for example, during the early Orientalizing period in Artimino (Florence) and during a more recent period in Chiusi and Verucchio. The type seems, therefore, to recall the northern inland area of Etruria, but not, at least as far as records show, the coastal area or Pisa in particular, where the inhabitants buried the dead inside large jars in pits. The ash urn was almost always a precious Attic figured krater, usually decorated with scenes of a Dionysian nature. The other grave goods betrayed heavy Etruscan influence. They abounded in bronzes for symposia, very similar to products from the Etrurian workshops of Spina, Populonia, and even Vulci.

During the Hellenistic period, the situation appears to change yet again. With the descent of the Ligurians from the mountains—they had densely settled the entire area of Garfagnana and Versilia—even stronger commercial ties built up between the new arrivals and the northernmost Etruscan cities. Pisa and Volterra exported black-painted pottery, numerous examples of which have been found in the small Ligurian cube tombs of the third century B.C. However, in the most important cities of the territory such as Ameglia, we also find valuable painted and modeled pottery that came from southern Etruria and Lazio (pottery from *atelier des petites estampilles* and Genucilia plates). The necropolis of Ameglia, in Cafaggio, gives us an idea of how the new arrivals adopted Etruscan cultural elements during that period. The inscription *enistale* was discovered in a tomb there; the name is rooted in indigenous Ligurian tradition (it survived into the Roman period in the name *Entistalius*), though the alphabet used would also have served adequately for northern Etrurian writing.

Impressive metal weapons frequently appear among the grave goods of Ligurian necropoleis, especially "jockey cap" helmets in bronze and iron, mostly products of Arezzo, the most industrialized city of the northern district. According to Polybius, the remaining Ligurians pushed into this area. We have proof of a certain amount of mixing between these two territories (or at least the presence of both peoples). The typical conical plate in rough impasto, for example, an item commonly found in Ligurian fortifications during the mid-Hellenistic period, was also found in Massaciuccoli. That city must still have been a lively emporium even during this late period. Ligurian-type fibulae discovered in the smaller border cities, such as the one affiliated with the necropolis of San Miniato in the lower course of the Era River, are further proof. Another sign of this bicultural situation is in personal names, which seem to derive from the Volterran epigraphic tradition of the late Hellenistic period. We also find a number of tombs at the Castiglioncello necropolis, on the border between Pisa and Volterra, that clearly refer to Ligurian women who had come to Etruria as wives of Etruscan or Ligurian merchants: the funerary ritual is cremation, the ossuary has a characteristic biconic shape with a separate back, and the grave goods contain items such as beads used in weaving. In Genoa there was a jump in the number of imports that were brought by sea from the great cities of the peninsula, items such as pottery for the table and transport amphorae.

During the Hellenistic period, the Etruscan presence in the great Ligurian port gradually faded, while the Ligurian component became increasingly recognizable and characteristic, filling the late Classical and Hellenistic strata with its typical native pottery. This justifies Strabo's statement, which may have been based on Posidonius and referred in any case to a very late Hellenistic period, that the city was the emporium of the Ligurians.

Above, large bowl with the Etruscan inscription *mi nemeties* (I am of Nemetie) showing its ownership, fifth century B.C., from the San Silvestro necropolis in Genoa

Below, fifth-century bronze baking dish that was found in Tomb 10 in the Via XX Settembre necropolis

The Etruscans on the Po Plain

| GIUSEPPE SASSATELLI

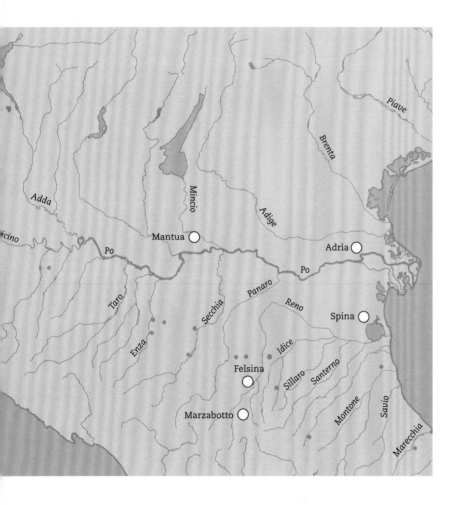

Many sources, both Greek or Latin—Cato, Livy, Pliny, Virgil, Strabo, but also Caecina, Silius Italicus, and Diodorus Siculus—agreed that the Etruscan dominion had once extended far beyond the borders of their latter-day motherland, which today corresponds to Tuscany and northern Lazio. In ancient times, the Etruscans pressed into southern Italy and reached Campania, while in the north they crossed the Apennines and establish themselves permanently on the Po Plain.

The sources mentioned accept as indisputable that the Etruscan expanded beyond their native land. They also show special interest in the conquest of the Po Plain and impart significant information as to how and when this conquest occurred. According to a tradition that began with Aulus Caecina and Verrius Flaccus, Tarchon, the eponymous hero of Tarquinia, was the author of this conquest and therefore it dated to the dawn of Etruscan civilization. Another tradition that began with Silius Italicus holds that the campaign was the brainchild of

Perugia—in the figure of its king, Ocnus, the son or brother of Aulestes—a city that has only recently yielded signs of an Etruscan presence.

These two traditions, which need not be interpreted as mutually contradictory, seem to suggest a chronological sequence; in other words, Tarchon led the first expansion and Ocnus followed up on it at a later date. Archaeological records in Bologna and its surrounding area seem to confirm this sequence. Thanks to this research, a succession of steps toward colonization becomes clear.

The older influx can be dated to the beginning of the Iron Age (ninth century B.C.); it seems above all to have been motivated by a desire for more land to cultivate. Meanwhile, the second, much more recent wave (middle of the sixth century) was directed at restructuring the Po region on a vast scale, and its goals appear to have been mostly commercial. This historic tradition, which is quite straightforward and consistent, emphasized the fact that the Etruscan expansion in the Po region created a series of autonomous cities, which in turn were united into confederations.

The historian Titus Livius, or Livy (5.33.9–10), relates how the Etruscans crossed the Apennines and occupied the Po Plain. They then organized themselves into a confederation of twelve cities, each derived from one of the twelve cities in their Tyrrhenian motherland. Pliny the Elder (*Naturalis Historia* 3.15.115–16) informs us that within the Etruscan confederation of Po cities, Bologna took on an important and directive role: *Bononia, Felsina vocitata tum cum princeps Etruriae esset* (Bologna, which was called Felsina when it was the chief place in Etruria).

The ancient historical tradition, therefore, clearly portrayed the Etrurian expansion in the Po Valley—or Etruria Padana—as an organized system of cities. A leadership role was given to Bologna (Felsina), the *princeps Etruriae*, an appellation that has recently been interpreted as synonymous with "metropolis," that is, a city with a decisive role in the birth and formation of the Etruscan *ethnos*. Consequently the city was recognized as having a prominent leadership role with respect to the surrounding territory, whose vast expanse was now firmly in Etruscan hands. It is essentially regarded as the "capital" of Etruria Padana.

These written accounts have but few items in concordance with one another and could not stand alone as evidence. But taken in conjunction with powerful archaeological evidence, we can reconstruct the main historical stages of the Po region during the Etruscan era in some detail, especially regarding its capital Felsina (Bologna).

Bologna, like most Etruscan cities in the Tyrrhenian area, saw an abrupt and consistent demographic increase at the beginning of the Iron Age (ninth century B.C.). In the past this population boom has generally been attributed to the influx of people from Tyrrhenian Etruria, who pushed north in search of new land for cultivation. Owing to a remarkable increase in the amount of evidence found at sites relating to the preceding Bronze Age (especially the end of the Bronze Age) in just the past few decades, we are able to hypothesize that the area was well organized, economically consolidated,

On page 168, map of Etruria in the Po Valley during the fourth and fifth centuries B.C. with the major cities marked

On page 169, terra-cotta askos in the shape of an animal with an armed rider, from the end of the eighth to the beginning of the seventh centuries B.C., from Tomb 525 in the Benacci necropolis in Bologna. Bologna, Museo Civico Archeologico

On the facing page, grave goods from the middle of the fifth century B.C., from the "Great Tomb" (Tomba Grande) of the Giardini Margherita necropolis in Bologna. The richness and high artistic quality of the objects makes these grave goods the most opulent from Bologna. Bologna, Museo Civico Archeologico

densely populated, and solidly established within large commercial circuits that ran on one side toward the Aegean Sea and on the other toward Tyrrhenian Etruria, which up to then had been primarily trading in metals. Significant finds from this period have included numerous storerooms of bronze objects, which indicate both hoarding and technically advanced metallurgy. The theory that the local population dropped at the end of the Bronze Age has become harder to substantiate, and therefore it no longer seems necessary to posit an influx of groups from outside to explain the sudden and intense demographic concentrations that are recorded in the Bologna area beginning in the ninth century. This change in density could mostly, though not exclusively, be accounted for by the peopling of the surrounding area during the preceding period, the end of the Bronze Age. This population moved from its native territory and then organized itself in new ways that coincided with the appearance and rise of Villanovan culture, which is certainly the oldest cultural sign of the Etruscans. The early settlement period saw the rise of many villages, built close together but nonetheless distinct from one another. Within this new demographic picture, a clear proto-urban organization progressively began to take shape. At this point one of the oldest villages, Villa Cassarini-Villa Bosi, which fell between the Aposa and the Ravone Rivers, seems to have assumed a dominant role within the entire system. It took on urban outlines and eventually gave rise to a historical city, coinciding with the progressive and rapid decline of the other villages that were its contemporaries.

At the beginning of the eighth century B.C., at the end of this settlement process, Bologna also became a city with clear proto-urban attributes: a complex economic organization and social structure, an embryonic political-institutional structure, and, above all, urban planning, which only later would take on the features of a true *urbs*. This proto-urban conglomeration extended from the Aposa River to the Ravone, which made up its eastern and western borders, respectively. To the north, the border of the inhabited area was defined precisely by the cemeteries, which built along its edges and more or less corresponded to Via Riva di Reno, Via Falegnami, and Via Righi. Toward the south, the inhabited area certainly extended as far as the first range of hills, but not beyond Villa Cassarini (the present-day Facoltà di Ingegneria); beyond that southern limit, the steep terrain of the mountains would hardly have been favorable to settlements.

Given these borders, the residential area could have comprised about three hundred hectares (750 acres), an expanse that was larger than even the great Tyrrhenian cities. Such figures should be weighed carefully, however, since archaeological evidence of the residential areas is mostly modest and erratic. Burial grounds were usually found around residential areas in a scheme that reflected deliberate urban (or at least proto-urban) planning but here they are entirely absent. On the one hand this demonstrates a clear break with the demographics of the preceding Bronze Age, in which the habitations were arranged in villages, and on the other it

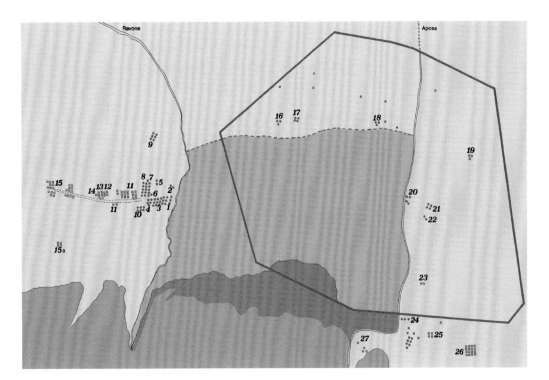

Map of the Etruscan city of Bologna. The residential area is shown in ochre, bordered by two important watercourses. Cemeteries, which developed outside the residential area, are numbered here and either marked with an asterisk (from both the Villanovan and Orientalizing periods) or a square (the Felsinian phase).

implies that the settlement had all the preconditions for the development of a true city.

The inhabited area, at least during its initial phase, seems to have been made up of individual residences or small groups of residences that were spaced without crowding in a regular and homogenous pattern that covered the entire area. Open spaces for agriculture and connected activities—the preparation and creation of foodstuffs, their conservation and stocking, harvesting, and the keeping of cattle—must naturally have remained around these small settlement cells, which however did not seem to achieve the autonomy of compact groups. Such settlements would explain the really remarkable extent of the area set aside for residences.

This kind of structure is often seen in early forms of individual landholding: a modest plot of cultivated land—often quite narrow—adjacent to a residence. They were similar to the *haeredia* of two *iugerum* that Romulus assigned to each head of the family (*herus*); the householder was also authorized to leave the property to his children as an inheritance (Varro *De Re Rustica* 1.10).

The allocation of land for agriculture and related activities within the residential area does not compromise the proto-urban character of this conglomerate, which was understood as a unified structure and not a mechanical sum of various villages. It is quite possible that, faced with an steep increase in the density of residences, some of these plots were taken out of agrarian production and put to other, more urban, uses. Consequently smaller residential areas would have been formed, in which farming had been abandoned or seriously curtailed within the larger settlement.

The proto-urban city that was built along these lines gradually encroached on the vast surrounding territory, whose qualities made it especially suitable for the intense cultivation of legumes and cereals. The rural structure of the territory was subject to the economic needs of the city. Although the city maintained control and command of the countryside, the hierarchical relationship between the two followed the traditional productive model in which the city is debtor to the surrounding country.

Bologna's occupation of this vast territory, particularly for agricultural purposes, was progressive and widespread. This is demonstrated in the chronological sequence of the outlying areas: nearby sites were older and generally just a step behind the city in terms of development, while those that were farther away were much more recent and their chronology indicates that expansion was still under way during the seventh century B.C. By the end of this long process, the territory of Bologna pushed north almost to the Po, as finds in Bondeno, Argenta, and San Martino Spino illustrate. To the south it penetrated the various Apennine valleys less extensively, with the exception of the Reno Valley: there, it held more extensive and firm control, since it was the route that connected Bologna to the Tyrrhenian region. To the west the territory must certainly have reached the valley of the Secchia River, and in all probability, it

even extended beyond it. To the east it halted near the valley of the Santerno River, beyond which we see a sort of demographic void, perhaps due to the early and persistent presence of the Umbri, at least in the Apennine belt.

Archaeological records for the residential area of Felsina include more than five hundred huts from a broad timespan that runs from the beginning of the eighth to the middle of the sixth centuries B.C. These huts were made of wood, with walls plastered with clay and straw roofs, and they were generally circular or elliptical in plan. There are few traces of quadrilateral or multiple huts, those with more than one room that were for high-ranking figures or functions.

Metallurgical activity is well documented here. Bronzeworking must have played a primary role in the city's economy, as the storeroom in Piazza San Francesco proves. It consisted of a huge vessel that contained almost 15,000 carefully stowed bronze objects. These were intended for remelting and would have yielded an overall mass of about 1,418 kilograms (3,126 lb.). This must certainly have been a deposit for scrap material from one or more workshops and demonstrates the presence of many tools that were linked to metallurgy, such as saws, files, hammers, and anvils. The picture we form is of a workshop that was quite diversified in its activities, where the workers may have been involved in repairing utensils or maintaining tools, as illustrated by a number of axes with sharpened blades. The container also held ingots of pure copper, which may have come from mines in Tyrrhenian Etruria, particularly Elba or the Vetulonia area.

Head of a marble kouros that was imported from Greece and uncovered in the residential area of Marzabotto (Bologna), beginning of the fifth century B.C. Marzabotto, Museo Nazionale Etrusco

Terra-cotta lid with knobs, second half of the fifth century B.C., from the kilns of Marzabotto (Bologna). At its center, a first name and that of a noble line, *Larisal Kraikaluś* (in the genitive case), are incised. The lid was made to cover a well located in the courtyard of a house, and the inscription indicates the name of its owner. Marzabotto, Museo Nazionale Etrusco

Only a consolidated division of labor could have led to such an accentuated specialization in craftsmanship; it sheds light on the complexity of society in Felsina between the end of the eighth and the beginning of the seventh centuries B.C. We do not know why this storeroom was closed and concealed during this interval.

This San Francesco deposit has been a goldmine of information on otherwise unknown artisan activities, due to the presence of many tools above and beyond those already mentioned. Saws, drills, rasps, chisels, gouges, and axes, for example, prove that woodworking was widely practiced, both carpentry and the making of utensils. The axes may have been used as weapons, but may also have been used mostly for woodcutting. The large scythes and sickles must have been related to cultivating and reaping. The billhooks, besides generically suggesting arboreal activities, could also have been used for cultivating grapevines. Hooks and harpoons, finally, show the prevalence of fishing, probably an important means of feeding the community in an area rich with watercourses.

In addition, productive activities such as spinning and weaving, and even ceramics, must have played a role in the economy of the city. However, we know almost nothing about how they were organized.

The cemeteries fanned out around the residential area. We know of more than four thousand tombs from the Villanovan (ninth and eighth centuries B.C.) and the Orientalizing (from the beginning of the seventh to the middle of the sixth centuries) periods and almost a thousand from the era that followed (from the middle of the sixth to the beginning of the fourth centuries). Their placement follows a sort of topographic sequence that proceeded from the city toward the countryside, coinciding with their chronological sequence.

Burials began in the areas closest to the residences and moved steadily outward. The even march of these burials across time and space, from the ninth to the beginning of the fourth centuries B.C., was mirrored in the continuity of the residential area, which also grew in predictable patterns over the same time period. Scholars in the nineteenth century thought that the area saw an ethnic shift over this time period. But the steady accretion of both cemeteries and residential areas over such a long period suggests rather that the city continued to develop in a linear and organic way without interruption or abrupt changes, even as the community itself experienced radical transformations.

The cemeteries, which are rich and vast, represent an indispensable source of information on Etruscan Bologna. The archaeological evidence they contain allows us to focus on the salient features of the various cultural stages and also to pinpoint the main moments of its economic and social evolution. An increasing inequality began to appear in grave goods, especially from the middle of the eighth century B.C., the clear result of radical structural changes. It is therefore easy to infer that the transformation of the residential structure was not merely a topographic effect, but was closely connected to changes in the economic and social order.

Attic red-figured kylix, 460–450 B.C., showing the exploits of Theseus as a young man (on the border) and his coronation (at center), from Tomb 18C in the Valle Pega necropolis at Spina (Ferrara). This unusually large cup is the work of the Penthesilea Painter. Ferrara, Museo Archeologico Nazionale

Individuals began to emerge from the mass of the community, forming groups that assumed a dominating position in society. They had wealth and political power—which was at times military as well—and took up leadership. This new order quickly assumed the same features as the aristocracies in the Tyrrhenian area. The possession of horses, as shown by deposits of horse bits and other harness trappings next to the deceased, was symptomatic. Besides being an indicator of wealth and an essential tool in connecting the remote sectors of the territory, horses may also have taken on social and political implications by expressing, for example, membership in a "knightly class." The presence of weapons in the tombs, on the other hand, evoked roles of a military character. However, these finds are rare in Bologna, where the rite of burial did not include the exhibition of weapons and connotations of the deceased as warrior— just the opposite of what had occurred in the Tyrrhenian area.

The commitment with which the aristocracy of Felsina proceeded to monumentalize sectors of the city, or at least those they were affiliated with, is a fact of great importance and can be interpreted as a sign that the transformation of the residential area into a fully urban entity was imminent. The high artistic level achieved and the obvious monumentality of a number of funerary sculptures, which may have been executed by foreign artisans (even those from the East, according to some theories), indicate strong economic development and an elevated artistic culture. Both of these are hallmarks of the close-knit aristocratic group that made Bologna in the seventh century B.C. a city of great prominence and indisputable importance.

No less important on a cultural level, and also linked to this group of *aristoi*, were the early acquisition of the alphabet and the consequent practice of writing. Just a few years ago it was thought that writing was a more recent (fifth century B.C.) acquisition, but today a number of important discoveries have shown that the alphabet and writing had already arrived among the Etruscans of Bologna at the beginning of the seventh century. An early and somewhat crude acquaintance with letters was followed by a long period in which writing was learned and mastered. At first letters were used to initial manufactured goods of every kind (bronzes and pottery). Perhaps the goal of the owners was to develop a number system that would improve counting operations in the agricultural and commercial environment (for example, to number a series of ceramic pieces, handmade goods, or metal ingots that were going to market).

The most sophisticated example of this long learning and development process known to date is an inscription on a small amphora in the Melenzani tomb, which dates to the end of the seventh century B.C. It is the longest in Bologna and one of the longest in all the Etruscanized areas.

The inscription contains the name of the vase in its diminutive form, *zavenuza* (*zavena* means "amphora"; therefore *zavenuza* means "small amphora"). It also bears the name of the individual it was given to, who is indicated as its owner, and perhaps his wife. A series of names is unfortunately incomplete and full of gaps, but it does tell us who gave the vase

Above, bronze model of a sheep's liver with the names of divinities incised on its upper face, late second to early first century B.C., uncovered in Settima di Gossolengo (Piacenza). The object has been interpreted as an instrument of a haruspex, a priest charged with reading the internal organs of animals. Piacenza, Museo Archeologico, Palazzo Farnese

(*turuke*). Other words are linked to a verb whose meaning is unknown, which may refer to the funerary ritual (*samake*). Finally we have the signature of the artisan who made the vase and wrote the inscription (*ana mini zinake remiru*, or "Ana Remiru made me"). The inscription definitively confirms the linguistic, and therefore ethnic, continuity between the Villanovan phase and the Felsinian culture that followed (both undoubtedly Etruscan). It is also an extraordinary record of the high cultural level achieved in Bologna during the course of the seventh century B.C., which paralleled other important artistic advances mentioned above.

Two *cippi* from Rubiera, in the valley of the Secchia River that marks the modern border between Modena and Reggio Emilia, confirm the acquisition of writing throughout the entire area controlled by the Etruscans. These two extraordinary monuments date between the end of the seventh and the beginning of the sixth centuries B.C. Their rich bas-relief decoration clearly shows Orientalizing influence. There are also two inscriptions, one of which contains the oldest known example of the term *zilath*. Here it probably indicated that one *Avile Amthura*, an Etruscan figure who is identified by his first name and lineage, held a military leadership position.

Besides Bologna, the other important Etruscan city in the region was Verucchio in Romagna, which was also active beginning in the ninth century B.C. We may guess that its development was similar to that of Bologna. Here, too, the population growth at the end of the Bronze Age, which was rapid and substantial

from its beginning, is not enough to explain the birth of the city in the ninth century. However, it certainly represented an attractive gathering point for outsiders who had the idea of establishing an outpost to control the valley of the Marecchia River and the Adriatic coast. This was probably part of a general plan to control the Po Plain through Felsina, and it may be that they even intended to expand along the central Adriatic coast from the Villanovan enclave of Fermo. The site chosen for the residential area of Verucchio was a relatively large plain (about 50 hectares, or 125 acres) that rises abruptly above the surrounding countryside with an average elevation of almost three hundred meters (1,000 ft.) above sea level. The rugged escarpment, which towers in some places more than one hundred meters (300 ft.), completely isolates the plain from the surrounding area; its geographic aspect closely resembles the typical landscapes of Tyrrhenian Etruria (consider the cliffs of Orvieto, which dominate the plain in the Paglia Valley below).

As in Orvieto, there are necropoleis at the foot of this steep hill and around it. Even the relationship with the sea harks back to the Tyrrhenian experience. The hill at Verucchio is about fifteen kilometers (9 miles) from the coast as the crow flies and enjoys an excellent view of it; conversely, the city can be seen quite readily from the sea. It is quite probable, therefore, that Verucchio had its port below, at the mouth of the Marecchia River at Rimini.

Regarding the residential area and its structure, we find evidence of a stage when the huts were mostly circular. This

was followed by another phase with dry-wall foundations of cobblestones, which are the remains of houses with tile roofs built using the same construction techniques found in Bologna and Marzabotto. In both stages we have a number of well-documented commercial installations, such as large ovens for firing pottery and bricks and smaller ones for melting bronze; the latter use is confirmed by considerable deposits of raw bronze (*aes rude*) and metallic dross.

and on the other reached the Adriatic Sea along the valley of the Marecchia. Verucchio looks more like a commercial outpost than a populated city. The necropoleis themselves, which were arrayed at the foot of the cliffs, seem to have linked up with the most important exit routes of the city.

These tombs have yielded materials of extraordinary importance and quality. Rough and cut amber from the Baltic (Verucchio became a center for amber

Compared to Bologna, whose territory stretches far into the plain, the area connected to Verucchio was not very extensive. No trace of a more extensive organization has been found, and in fact the city seems not to have been interested in putting its vast surrounding territory into agricultural production. Instead it focused on controlling the routes that on one side crossed the Viamaggio Pass into the Tiber Valley

working and distribution); horse bits; weapons, whose presence here contrasts with their absence in Bologna; fabric of rare technical refinement; an extraordinary variety and wealth of fibulae, necklaces, and earrings, in which amber was widely and delicately used; and ossuaries and tableware richly decorated with stamps: these are just a few of the most salient elements of this new archaeological evidence from Verucchio. However, the most unusual finds from the tombs are surely works in wood, which have been preserved in large quantities thanks to extremely unusual soil conditions. There are round tables with three shaped legs, thrones with a curved back that are often decorated with Geometric motifs in intaglio or complex figurative scenes, chair backs (some inlaid), footstools, vases with bronze knobs, small chests, knife holders, handles for tools and axes, and tiny sculptures with animal protomes

shared by groups that asserted influence within the community. The throne itself was a sign of royalty and the exercise of power.

The political and economic structure of Etruria in the Po Valley, which was anchored during this earliest period in the two cities of Bologna and Verucchio, underwent radical change beginning with the middle of the sixth century B.C. The international picture at this time altered substantially, especially in the western

Below, stone funerary *cippus* with a frieze of griffins and sphinxes in relief and inscriptions that contain the name of the deceased, Avile Amthura, 625–600 B.C., from Rubiera (Reggio Emilia). Together with another column *cippus* that was also illustrated and inscribed, this monument provides the most significant evidence of sculpture in the Po area. Reggio nell'Emilia, Civici Musei

or human figures meant to decorate furniture.

An extraordinary wooden throne was found in a princely tomb that is typologically quite similar to other examples in bronze from Tyrrhenian Etruria. Its back features intaglio decorations with figurative scenes that are quite complex and arrayed on two levels. These scenes are important evidence of aristocratic etiquette and the ideology

Mediterranean area. Reawakened conflicts between Etruscans, Greeks, and Carthaginians, no longer kept within the limits of commercial competition, resulted in a number of naval battles on the Tyrrhenian Sea and led to the progressive erosion of the Etruscans' previously uncontested dominance there. Traveling the routes of the northern Tyrrhenian became increasingly risky, as well as cumbersome, and consequently

A view of the eastern necropolis at Marzabotto-Bologna, which dates to the end of the sixth to the fifth centuries B.C. Cube tombs, which were originally filled with earth, were built with huge slabs of travertine. Marzabotto, archaeological area

trade with Celtic Europe was rerouted through Massalia and the Rhone Valley.

At this point the Po area took on new relevance. It underwent a radical restructuring aimed at plotting new commercial routes that would divert trade to Celtic Europe through the Alpine valleys. The *ex novo* foundation of the urban cities of Marzabotto in the

Bolognan Apennines, Spina on the Adriatic coast, and Mantua just north of the Po—not to mention the "refounding" of Bologna—established a network that was the basis of a revitalized economic system. It was well positioned to trade with Tyrrhenian Etruria, Greece, and Transalpine Europe.

This new structure of the Po territory no longer just catered to the needs of agricultural production (although agricul-

ture continued to be important). It was organized to suit the needs of itinerant traders, which led to the creation and strengthening of routes that were well supplied and secure. From this time on, it was the directors of commercial traffic who formed the backbone of a new system of settlements, which were essentially urban in form. The "second colonization" by inland Etruria (Chiusi and Volterra) has been unanimously attributed to a decision made at the provincial sanctuary of Volsinii (Orvieto).

Nevertheless, the newly founded cities, especially Marzabotto, were clearly dominated by the nobility from the Po area, whose names we can identify by a suffix that was only used in that region. This confirms that a substantial part of the population was of local origin. It calls into question the theory that a colonial movement was planned and put into effect by new people who came from the outside. The main promoters of this process of radical transformation were the Etruscans of the Po region themselves. Even if there were external stimuli on an organizational and economic level, the process primarily made use of local human resources.

Bologna was central to this economic effort. The city was strongly involved in transforming its old productive model, which for centuries had revolved around agriculture and which was suddenly outdated. The definitive evolution of Felsina-Bologna, a process that saw the old proto-urban center "refounded" as a city—urbanistically as well as architecturally—should be seen within this context. The city built a true Etruscan-type *arx*, a monumental sacred place for the entire community of citizens, fitted with

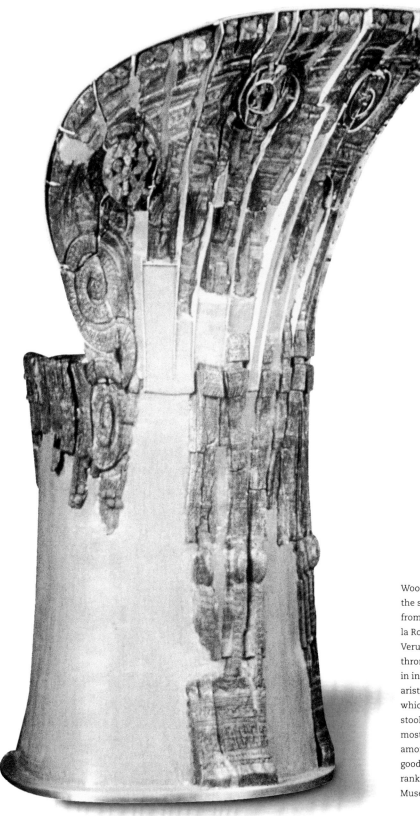

Wooden throne, middle of the seventh century B.C., from Tomb 89 in the Sotto la Rocca necropolis in Verucchio (Rimini). The throne's back is decorated in intaglio with scenes of aristocratic life. The throne, which has a matching footstool of inlaid wood, is the most significant element among extraordinary grave goods belonging to a high-ranking figure. Verucchio, Museo Archeologico

enduring furnishings. An acropolis was built in the Villa Cassarini area near the present-day Facoltà di Ingegneria, which stands on one of the very first spurs of the Apennines and therefore in a dominant and central position in relation to the inhabited area.

The area had at least one temple building with modeled *cippi* in travertine (and one in marble) destined to hold the offerings of the faithful. These offerings included bronze ex-votos of the highest quality and two images of divinities, Herakles and Apollo, who may have been the deities worshipped there. Its elevated position, about forty meters (130 ft.) above the residences below, corresponded exactly to the characteristics of the *arx*, which was typically placed at the edge of the urban area on a high point from which it could overlook the entire city, the necropoleis, and a large part of the *chora*, or surrounding territory. Among other things, its position played an

important role in the city's foundation ritual.

However, it was once again the necropoleis that provide the most important evidence of the new urban structure, especially its political and institutional implications.

Among the monumental operations that the city undertook in this period, the construction of the road through the entire western cemetery was one of the most important. This was an extremely old route, and tombs had already been placed near it during the Villanovan phase. At the time, the road had a cobblestone pavement and drainage channels on each side, similar to the great interurban roads of the Mediterranean world, such as those that joined Athens to Piraeus or Caere to Pyrgi. Tombs clustered around this road, which was the access route to the city for those traveling from the Reno Valley, and therefore from Etruria itself through the Apennines. The tombs added to the monumental air of the road, with elegant horseshoe stelai that were decorated in bas-relief, one of the distinctions of fifth-century Felsina.

These same stelai supply valuable information about the political and institutional organization of the cities. Court scenes, with standard-bearing figures paying homage to the deceased, and particularly solemn ceremonies, such as games in honor of the deceased, are both seen relatively frequently in pictorial decorations on stelai. (Games were held in honor of those who had held the post of magistrate, a prominent position both politically and institutionally within the urban community.) In some cases the inscriptions make explicit reference to the position of *zilath*,

A view of the eastern necropolis of Marzabotto (Bologna), which dates to the end of the sixth to the fifth centuries B.C. Marzabotto, archaeological area. In the background, the gate led to the burial area over a gravel road, which was originally fitted with a monumental facade

a supreme citizen-magistrate whose authority and functions were similar to those of a Latin praetor.

Just as older cities were restructured or refounded in this period (the middle of the sixth century B.C.), new cities were also founded: Marzabotto in the Reno valley, along the route that connected the Po plain to Tyrrhenian Etruria through the Apennines; Spina on the Adriatic, a port for Mediterranean traffic; and Mantua, just north of the Po, which was a crossroads for routes that ran from Etruria in the Po Valley toward Transalpine Europe. All of these cities, especially Marzabotto, featured a uniform and planned urban structure, in which large spaces were set aside for economic activities. In Marzabotto these mostly involved the transformation of primary materials, especially metals, while in Spina and Mantua they were more commercially oriented.

Marzabotto is especially renowned for its urban structure, which has been perfectly preserved. It was based on urban plans from the Greek world—especially Magna Graecia—in which individual monuments and structures are clearly identifiable. These were linked to a specific foundation ritual, such as the *auguraculum* on the acropolis or the *cippus* with a *crux* incised on top as a sur-

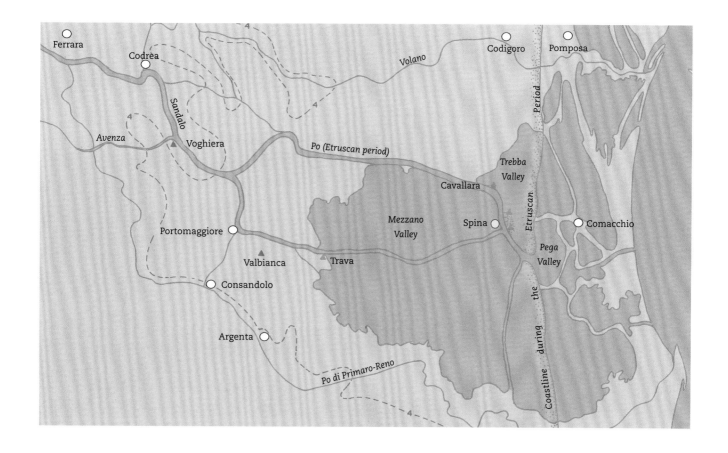

veying marker to be placed at the center of a street grid. This foundation ritual was often referred to in sources and was explicitly attributed to the Etruscans.

Something quite similar can be hypothesized for Spina, where a similar *cippus* was found with the added inscription *mi tular*, which means, "I am the benchmark." This obviously refers to operations for the city's founding and regularization. Further evidence of the latter could be found in the regularity of the channels and internal roads, which helped the city in its quest to become a great commercial port on the Adriatic, serving the entirety of Etruria Padana.

The urban and territorial organization that the Etruscans achieved in the Po area beginning at the middle of the sixth century B.C. was quite integrated economically. Cities could not afford rivalry or conflict among themselves; they had to be able to count on the others to maintain their economic roles and functions within the Etruscan system. A single major landing place on the Adriatic was vital for all these cities in order to guarantee efficient and enduring trade relations with the Mediterranean and Greece. Felsina counted on Marzabotto and Mantua in order to keep trade active with Tyrrhenian Etruria on one hand and with the

Map of the Po delta, showing the city of Spina. The coastline in the Etruscan era was well east of where it is now.

Transalpine region on the other; all three cities depended on Spina, both to acquire whatever sailed in from Greece (figurative pottery, oil, wine, marble statues, essential oils, and many other goods) and to help inland products flow out (grain and cereals, animal products, amber and tin from the north, and perhaps copper and iron from the Tyrrhenian area through Marzabotto and the Reno Valley as well). This interdependency demanded close coordination and firm integration on the economic and political levels.

Given the common need to safeguard the system of commercial trade in its entirety and complexity, one can imagine that there may have been some enduring kind of provincial organization. The system was the Etruscans' main economic resource in the Po region, especially after the old agricultural model, which was centered on Bologna, fell into crisis.

The solid territorial and political organization that the Etruscans achieved on the Po Plain was rudely disturbed at the beginning of the fourth century B.C. Gallic peoples from Europe and the territories north of the Po moved toward the south in great numbers, with a disruptive effect, at least initially, on the entire system of cities created by the Etruscans. Marzabotto suddenly lost its urban identity and became a sort of military outpost that the invading Gauls used to control the valley of the Reno.

Events seem to have been less traumatic in Bologna, although they were not very different. Only Mantua and Spina appear to have survived this upheaval. The first owed its survival to its strategic position. The second was surrounded by marshes and dunes and was also some-

what remote from the routes that the new Apennine masters favored. They preferred the eastern portion of the region, which reached the heart of the peninsula via Romagna rather than the Reno Valley.

Not only did Spina emerge untouched by the Gauls' invasion but it seems to have become a gathering point for many Etruscans of the Po region who had fled the inland regions as a result of the disturbances. Once uprooted from their rich and fertile inland region, these people had little choice but to dedicate their lives to piracy on the Adriatic Sea. The results can be called satisfactory, if one considers the economic vivacity that Spina and the entire band of coastline maintained until almost the end of the third century B.C.

With the Gallic invasion of the first half of the fourth century B.C., the urban model created by the Etruscans on the Po Plain was undermined to its foundations, with the consequent shattering of the territory's organization. There were rapid changes in routes and the distribution of settlements. The Gauls themselves decided to become the chief middlemen between the Mediterranean and continental Europe, and therefore replaced the Etruscans, ousting them from the role they had held firmly for a long time.

It was with this goal in mind that new commercial routes connecting to the Apennine passes were activated and reinforced. Livy (33.37.3–4) defines Gallic Bologna, which continued to be called Felsina, alternatively as *oppidum* or *urbs*. This is an extremely significant variation, since *urbs* would seem to honor its urban past, while *oppidum* seems to mirror its new situation as a dismantled urban

entity. The distinction is not just topographic and urbanistic but also institutional and political.

After this early period of adjustment, the two ethnic groups integrated. The new arrivals fully embraced the Etruscan lifestyle (the ideology of the symposium, the consumption of wine and meat, and athletic games), which actually provoked a gradual Etruscanization of the upper level of Gallic society. Nevertheless, the situation had changed. The organization of the territory was no longer by "city" as it had been in the preceding century, but by *vici* (agricultural settlements on plains) or by "castle" (hill settlements charged with the defense and control of the territory and its lines of communication). Both of these types of settlement had been profoundly changed in their structure and their economic role with respect to the previous Etruscan period.

The eastern necropolis of Marzabotto (Bologna) from the end of the sixth to the fifth centuries B.C. The funerary markers generally consisted of oval river cobblestones, and more rarely column-shaped or onion-shaped *cippi*. A variety of stelai decorated in low relief were discovered at Marzabotto. Marzabotto, archaeological area

The Etruscans in Umbria

| PAOLO BRUSCHETTI

Polygonal enclosure walls from the second half of the fourth century B.C. in Amelia (Terni)

On the facing page, the Etruscan necropolis of Crocifisso del Tufo from the middle of the sixth century B.C. in Orvieto

To understand how the Etruscans came to Umbria and what forms of their culture were introduced into the territory, a sense of the local geography is essential. Only a small part of the region corresponds to "Regio VI" in the Augustan order, and that in turn was based on an older order dating back to protohistory. Its borders then were the Tiber River to the west, which separated it from Etruria; the Nera River to the south, which divided it from the territory of the Sabini; the Esino River and Adriatic Sea to the east; and the terri-

tory of Ravenna to the north. It was a large, complex region that was rich in history and people who had manifold traditions and cultures.

Here we will limit our discussion to the area within present-day administrative borders of Umbria, which begin at the Tiber and reach the western slopes of the Apennine Mountains. The area south of the Nera will be excluded since it geographically belongs to Sabina, despite the fact that one of the most remarkable works of Etruscan artistic craftsmanship was found in that region. This is a wooden chariot, now preserved in New York, which is covered in sheet bronze embossed with scenes from the legend of Achilles. It was found in a chamber tomb at the Colle del Capitano necropolis in Monteleone di Spoleto and dates to the middle of the sixth century B.C. The geographic and demographic picture of this part of Umbria has been largely the same since antiquity. Hills and mountains take up much of the territory, with abundant vegetation (albeit considerably different

from that of the past), small and widely scattered cities, and lines of communication that, with the exception of few large motorways, follow natural routes and adapt to them.

The Umbri have a separate and interesting history with respect to the origins and extent of their lands and their relations with other peoples living on the peninsula. But they also shared profound cultural and traditional traits with the Etruscans and other peoples of central Italy. Their relations with the former were particularly steady and profound, because people of the Umbrian race lived within close reach of some of the major Etrurian cities that were located just beyond the border. Moreover the Tiber itself was more than a line of demarcation: It was also a means of communicating with the other peoples and cultures in the region, with whom the Umbri enjoyed favorable relations.

A continuous relationship developed between the populations on both sides of the river, with benefits for both communities in the economic sphere, in cultural and artistic exchange, and, above all, in political and administrative relations. The easier crossings of the Tiber and the areas along the borders gave rise to cities whose primary function was cultural and commercial exchange. Let us consider, for example, the territory along the upper course of the river. To the right, in Etruscan territory, was a system of Archaic settlements that were based on fortified *oppida* (towns); these had been set up at key points from which they could survey both the valley and the neighboring Umbrian lands that had relations with main cities, such as Perugia and Cortona.

Among the main forts was the *oppidum* of Monte Murlo, which was enclosed by a massive wall. To the left, in the area belonging to the Umbri of Gubbio and Tifernum, there were similar forts— Monte Civitella, for example—that kept watch over territorial borders and monitored the roads crossing into the interior.

In southern Umbria, the city of Terni enjoyed an enviable central position with respect to the lines of communication, whether these ran toward southern Etruria, the Tiber area in Sabina, or the interior valleys of the Apennines that led to the Adriatic coast. Unlike most of the Umbrian inhabited areas, which tended to be established on the flanks or peaks of hills, Terni was located on the plain. This location had favored the city in every respect ever since

On the facing page, Tomb 5 of the Crocifisso del Tufo necropolis in Orvieto

Below, Tomb 24 from the Etruscan necropolis of Crocifisso del Tufo

Oinochoe and basin in sheet bronze, late sixth to early fifth centuries B.C., from the Colfiorito necropolis in Foligno (Perugia). Perugia, Museo Archeologico Nazionale

the most ancient times: Terni emerged during the early Iron Age (tenth and ninth centuries B.C.), although there are remains of settlements that date back to the Neolithic and Aeneolithic periods.

The settlements, and especially the necropoleis, which for a long time were situated around the residential area, have yielded a large amount of material from the Villanovan culture, the Lazio culture, and even the traditions of the Umbria and Picenum areas. The form of the interment itself—burial of the dead in rectangular trenches that were sometimes covered with piles of stones—was a sign of a culture that was common to much of the

Italic environment. The continuity of Terni's city life—maintaining and guaranteeing the vitality and well-being of its people without interruption—demonstrates its important position.

The Colfiorito plateau had an entirely different geographic situation, but it shows a similar relationship among the peoples in the area. The plateau was the only passage linking the eastern and western territories of the peninsula. Here the various permanent settlements were occupied by Umbrian peoples of the Plestini tribe (known to us through literary sources), beginning in the ninth century B.C. The settlements were surrounded by necropoleis that were often rich with "princely" tombs, containing grave goods that flaunted an elevated social status and materials that had been imported from Etruria and Picenum. Among these finds are numerous bucchero vases from the cities of southern Etruria and bronzes from Volsinian workshops. One tomb that was excavated at Annifo, dating to the sixth century, included a large quantity of valuable objects imported from the Volsinian territory, which was evidently an intense trading partner. The tomb contained the rich grave goods of a buried male, including, among other things, a bucchero-like impasto olla; an Attic black-figured *kylix* (cup); a series of large bronze vases that were destined for banquet use, such as an *oinochoe* (pitcher), a cauldron, and some basins; andirons; skewers and javelins; and finally, a chariot of which only a fragment of an iron rim remains.

Besides an exchange of goods, relations between the Etruscan and Umbrian civilizations also brought a substantial integration of many features of Etruscan culture, including their political structure. Umbria's small cities were autonomous and often at war, with rare and fleeting moments of truce, though they almost always maintained reciprocal political ties. This pattern of behavior, which was also common among the Etruscan cities, meant that they only came together for sacred celebrations or games, and even then they were constantly battling one another: A sense of "nation" was never very strong among the Etruscans. The economy was fundamentally based on agriculture and sheep farming, often accompanied by control over traffic that

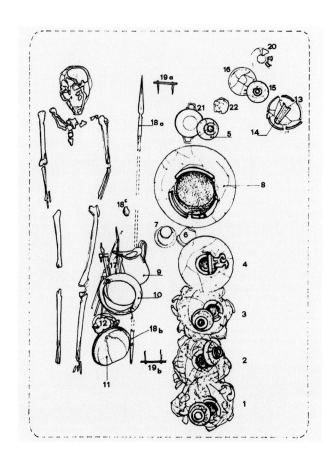

flowed through the narrow river valleys and could be dominated from settlements above, which represented another opportunity for enrichment. Forms of worship were often organized according to the same principles, with strong ties to nature and everyday life. Sanctuaries were generally placed at high points along the main lines of communication. Votive offerings were often the same sort of *koine* common to all the peoples of the Italian peninsula; we have found masses of these modest offerings, as well as a few rare gifts that give evidence of a significant social diversity. All over the Umbrian territory we find small places of worship, only

Diagram of Tomb 6 in the Colfiorito necropolis, dating to the beginning of the fifth century B.C., in Foligno (Perugia)

At right, oinochoe in sheet bronze, late sixth to fifth centuries B.C., from Tomb 3 in the Colfiorito necropolis in Foligno (Perugia). Perugia, Museo Archeologico Nazionale

Below, cauldron in sheet bronze, late sixth to fifth centuries B.C., from Tomb 6 in the Colfiorito necropolis in Foligno (Perugia). Perugia, Museo Archeologico Nazionale

On the facing page, chamber tomb with a barrel vault, late second to early first centuries B.C., at Colle in Bettona (Perugia)

was mostly agricultural or pastoral; the economic level was therefore modest and relatively uniform across the territory.

The Tiber River and its valley bear traces of intense and continuous relationships between the local populations. In the middle section of the river, Orvieto (ancient Velzina) stands at the top of a cliff a short distance from where the Tiber joins the Paglia. It may have been the site of Fanum Voltumnae, one of the most significant sites of worship and political gathering, a symbol of all Etruria. From that renowned city, the troops of Fulvius Flaccus brought more than two thousand statues to Rome after their triumph in 264 B.C. (Metrodorus of Scepsis in Pliny *Naturalis Historiae* 34.16.7). Although it stood at the edge of Etruscan territory, the city's political and cultural influence was also strong on the other side of the river. The Archaic necropoleis of Montecchio and Baschi, which may have been connected to an urban outpost in the Umbrian-Italic environment near Etruria, were filled with evidence of the Orvieto civilization. The same kinds of tombs were built: chamber tombs excavated in the tufaceous bedrock, with benches on each side and in back for the deposition of the deceased, and grave goods generally piled on the rear bench. Moreover, the quantity of grave goods offers proof of elevated social status and affluence among the local families. Next to works in bucchero made in Orvieto were Vulcian bronzes and Attic and Etruscan pottery that was imported via the city on the cliff.

Among the cities on both banks of the river, however, it is probably Todi that experienced the deepest economic, political, and cultural relationship with

identifiable today by the presence of votive cabinets or occasional finds of schematic bronzes, which are directly comparable to what we find west of the Tiber, both in the form of religious practice and the divinities celebrated. The prevalence of statuettes representing offering bearers and, more importantly, domestic animals (oxen, swine, and generic quadrupeds) implies that work

The Etruscan necropolis of Crocifisso del Tufo in Orvieto. The "urban" structure of the necropolis is a sign of a substantial and equal distribution of rights and privileges within the social sphere. There was one tomb for each family, with well-defined features that were identical for everyone.

the other side. The name itself (*tular* in Etruscan means "border," as confirmed by the inscription *tutere* on coins minted in Todi) indicated that it was a place where civilizations met. Located on the left bank of the Tiber, beside an easy crossing that naturally gave rise to a river port (hence the place-name Pian di Porto in Todi), the city has been recorded in literary sources as both an Umbrian and Etruscan city. After an early Archaic stage during which its Italic traits were dominant, it underwent a gradual Etruscanization, together with a process of urbanization that quickly spread from the neighboring Etruscan world. Located just a short distance from Orvieto, and connected to it both by river and by the Via Amerina that ran along the hills along the right bank, Todi became a clearinghouse and a link between the inland Apennine area and the Etruscan world. The necropoleis on the slopes of the hills, which were common from the sixth century on, held the grave goods of small groups of aristocrats who gathered around a *principes*, exploiting the city's geographic position and controlling the commercial routes. The tombs—of which there are no traces left—were mostly pit tombs or rectangular tombs lined with stone slabs (*cassone*) and only rarely chamber tombs, which linked them to a common Italic-Umbrian tradition. One of the most important tombs is in a Peschiera style; there researchers found a set of jewelry and a bronze helmet that must have certainly belonged to a warrior, or at least a prominent citizen. A tomb, possibly a chamber tomb, from Le Logge, preserved the remains of a chariot decorated with embossed sheet bronze, which originated from the inland Etruscan

Architrave with an inscription, from Tomb 20 in the Etruscan necropolis of Crocifisso del Tufo

On the facing page, Etruscan urn from the Hellenistic period that originated in Perugian territory. Perugia, Museo Archeologico Nazionale

culture. A pit burial in San Raffaele was reserved for a male figure whose elevated social status was displayed through iron banquet implements (skewers and andirons), sheet bronze vases, and Attic pottery that had come through Orvieto. At the city's peak, between the fifth and fourth centuries and coinciding with its

definitive urban structuring, an absolutely remarkable quantity of Attic pottery appears, associated with the more socially elevated classes who must have grown wealthy through trade and control over commerce. The great bronze votive offering found in a sanctuary at the edges of the urban center—the so-called *Mars*

that was produced in workshops in Orvieto and offered by a person of Celtic origin, whose name is inscribed on the cuirass—demonstrates the cosmopolitan character of the city, which was open to influences from other areas on the peninsula and enjoyed a general affluence. Among other things, Todi heroically managed its pivotal but structurally unstable site, which was subject to landslides, via soil stabilization and water drainage projects.

Todi was transected by the Via Amerina, which had been plotted about 240 B.C. over older routes as an interior artery to connect the territories of Lazio and Perugia. Together with the Tiber whose valley it shared, the road constituted an important axis in the relationship between the Umbrian and Etruscan peoples. Ancient itineraries recall the city of Bettona (Vettona) as a stop on the stretch between Todi and Perugia. This city was located on a hill not far from the Tiber in Umbrian territory, although it was strongly influenced by the nearby powerful Perugia and may even have been an Etruscan political outpost. Surrounded by an enclosure wall in *opus quadratum* that dates to the fourth century, the city included a necropolis from the same time and a temple from the Hellenistic period. The tombs of the necropolis had architectural features and types of grave goods that were typically Etruscan, mediated by Perugia. The most well known tomb of the Bettona necropolis, a chamber tomb with a barrel vault and a series of benches for the deposition of ash urns, dates back to the end of the second and beginning of the first centuries, when Romanization had already permeated most of central

Italy. However, its forms recall an architectural model that was common in the northern Etruscan interior, with examples in the territories of Perugia, Cortona, and Orvieto. Directly related to Perugia was Assisi, one of the most important cities of the Umbrian world, which was located on a road that led toward the Apennines. Its contacts with the Etruscan world, however, have only been recorded through the work of the Latin poet Sextus Propertius, a native of the city. Many passages in his

On the facing page, terrace wall, third to first centuries B.C., above Via Santa Maria in Camuccia, Todi (Perugia)

At left, drainage tunnels with *alla cappuccina* (hooded) coverings, second or first centuries B.C.

At right, Etruscan urn from the Hellenistic period in Perugia. Perugia, Antiquarium at the Palazzone necropolis

work recall the vicinity and the steady relationship between his homeland and Etruria. Nevertheless, traces of this relationship are practically nonexistent, perhaps only because the evidence has not survived. Near Bettona, the city linked to the Civitella d'Arna necropolis played a

similar role as an Etruscan stronghold in Umbrian lands. The necropolis was made up of tombs that date between the fifth and second centuries. Some Etruscan epigraphic evidence, which documents forms of Perugian personal names, has remained alongside grave goods and bronze funerary beds that were produced in Etruscan shops. The tombs here show signs of inhumation, despite the fact that the area

was dominated by Perugian culture where cremation was heavily favored.

Another important keystone of the relationship between the Umbri and Etruscans dates back to this same historical era. Etruscan graphical expressions were introduced, superimposed, and integrated with Umbrian modes (though at the moment we know them only from inscriptions of a public or religious nature). The largest and best-known example of this tradition is a group of seven bronze tablets known as the Iguvine Tables, which were written in the Umbrian language. They were discovered at Gubbio in 1444 and give an exact account of the political and administrative organization of one of the principal city-states of the Italic world, a religious leader among the Umbrian peoples. The first of the four tablets and part of a fifth, which date between 200 and 120 B.C., are written in a national alphabet derived from Etruscan, a sign that they fell within an Etruscan sphere of influence. However, the others, which date between 150 and 70 B.C., are written in a Latin alphabet, proof of an increasingly marked Roman influence over the city and its territory. Among the most interesting details in the "tablets" is the use of the sign "Λ" as an *M*, a typical usage in the territory of Cortona that spread from there to other neighboring Etruscan areas. Its presence in Gubbio may indicate a similarly strong relationship, whether economic, political, or cultural. Moreover, we see signs of contact with the Etruscan world already between the fourth and second centuries, first in imports from Arezzo and Volterra, then in an autonomous production of black-painted pottery and an influx of Attic and Etruscan painted pottery.

A final note should be added regarding Via Flaminia, one of the major roadways that the Romans coveted in order to accelerate and strengthen their control over the territories they set out to conquer. This artery, which was built over a preexisting route during the last quarter of the third century B.C., entered Umbria in the area of Otricoli and crossed the entire territory. Together with its side roads, it formed a formidable instrument for the spread of economy and culture among all the cities it reached. Thanks to this road, the Umbrian communities were able to take a leap forward, despite their inexorable absorption into the Roman political body. This destiny was shared by all the peoples of central Italy, whether Etruscan or Italic. While at least formally they maintained their own autonomous traits (see the Augustan division of Italy), they saw their cultures progressively extinguished by the conquering Roman civilization.

On the facing page, above, Tablet 4 of the Iguvine Tables, which describes a sacrifice, from Gubbio (Perugia). Gubbio, Museo Civico in Palazzo dei Consoli

At right, above, border *cippus* in sandstone with the Etruscan inscription *tular larna,* late third to early second centuries B.C., Bettona (Perugia). Bettona, Museo Civico. *Below,* detail of an architrave in Tomb 7 of the Crocifisso del Tufo necropolis (Orvieto)

The Etruscans in Picenum

| MAURIZIO LANDOLFI

Above, the hilly landscape of the valley of the Chienti in upper Macerata. *On the facing page*, the medieval village in the upper part of Cupra Marittima (Ascoli Piceno)

Easily accessible by sea, and connected via the Apennine valleys to the inland areas of central Italy, Picenum was always a region vulnerable to foreign incursions by land and sea. This vulnerability was also due to its position at the center of the western Adriatic coast and its hydrographic

profile: carved by almost parallel rivers that descend from the Apennine range. It also inclined the area toward a wide range of commercial contacts and trade.

Trade in this area during a protohistorical period followed two distinct commercial currents, one by land and the other by sea. Land traffic came primarily from Etruria and Lazio, while the sea trade flowed from areas oriented toward the upper Adriatic, from the Balkan Peninsula and the eastern Mediterranean.

The Picentes had intense and frequent contacts with the Etruscans, whether from the Tyrrhenian area or the Po Plain, along both routes. The economic prosperity that the Picentes enjoyed, especially during the Archaic period and over the course of the fifth century B.C., was due to the intermediary role their cities played in connecting the Mediterranean world with the Transalpine environment. The dock at Conero, for example, was responsible for the significance and wealth of nearby Numana. Conero was both a terminal for a trans-Apennine route and a stop on a

Below, a view of the medieval village of Cupra Alta. Cupra Marittima, Ascoli Piceno

At *right*, the highest point of Cupra Marittima (Ascoli Piceno)

maritime circuit that involved the entire Adriatic Sea, connecting the countries north of the Alps to the vast Mediterranean.

The Etruscans, especially those from the Po Plain, had a strong interest in this port, as we see from the remarkable importance that Cupra Marittima achieved between the seventh and sixth centuries B.C. During this period it became the main emporium for the mid-Adriatic area and erected a sanctuary to

the goddess Cupra; Strabo (5.4.2) claimed that it had been founded by the Etruscans, even though it was dedicated to a goddess whose name was originally Sabine. G. Colonna has interpreted this passage as a parody of Spina's interest in these areas during the period of their

supremacy on the Adriatic. This interpretation follows from the abandonment of the idea that the Villanovan Etruscans of Fermo founded Cupra Marittima, which was based primarily on the distance between the two cities. Fermo itself seems to not have had any sort of direct expres-

sions from Etruscan groups of the Villanovan culture, although, unusually for the Picenum area, it has two necropoleis from the ninth and eighth centuries B.C. with numerous cremation burials. The proto-urban settlement structure that began to form at Fermo was undermined by the rise of new forms of habitation made up of numerous dispersed settlements, and it was soon reabsorbed into the local structure of Picenum. These scattered settlements did not have much demographic consistency and were dotted along the highlands of the river valleys, from which they controlled the passages toward the Adriatic coast and the Tiber Valley below. The settlements, which were ruled by warrior aristocracies, were sensitive to the migratory currents that moved via the Apennine passes from Sabina and the district on the left bank of the middle and lower Tiber. These non-urban entities—dedicated to raising herds and controlled by a combative aristocracy—prevented central-Adriatic Italy from becoming an Etruscan territory or Etruscanized area.

We see faint signs of a possible Etruscan presence east of the Apennines in a number of place names at Visso (Macerata) and Numana (Ancona), where there are, respectively, signs for a location named "Rasenna" (the name the Etruscans called themselves), and a *fundus Rasenanus* (the "land" or "field" of the Rasenna people). But in any case the Etruscans must have frequented Picenum for commercial purposes. Etruscan objects were imported to the mid-Adriatic continuously over an extended period of time, to such a degree

that their presence actually distinguishes the civilization of Picenum.

Specific aspects and particular connotations within this commercial flow can be isolated and identified at various times. Although we know that Picenum had links to a number of individual Etruscan cities—Vulci, Vetulonia, Populonia, Chiusi, and above all Orvieto, together with cities in Lazio (Praeneste) and Falerii—as shown by the importation of their respective products, we know lit-

tle about the dynamics, conditions, and methods of this trade.

During the early Iron Age the importation of typical Villanovan objects, from both the Bologna and Tuscany-Lazio areas, were linked to the Villanovan cities of Fermo and Verucchio, which lay in the valley of the Marecchia. It was through this line of exchange that the censer of Novilara, the crested helmets, the Tarquinian-type antenna swords, and the rhombus-shaped bronze belts from Fermo

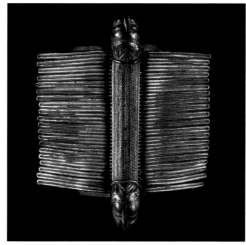

Silver "comb" fibula, end of the seventh century B.C., from Tomb 3 in Santa Maria in Campo in Fabriano (Ancona). Ancona, Museo Archeologico Nazionale

arrived in Picenum, together with other materials found in the necropoleis there.

From the late seventh century B.C. on, the "princely" culture that had distinguished a number of aristocratic generations in Etruria and Lazio on the Tyrrhenian side began to penetrate inland along the peninsula, reaching Bologna and Verucchio beyond the Apennines. It would also affect the Sabini, the Umbri, and Picentes during different periods and in their own ways.

In Picenum, the penetration and acquisition of the social model that had established itself on the Tyrrhenian side took its own path, with expressions primarily related to the birth and rise of local aristocracies. Power and wealth were above all attained by military valor and, in the interior areas, by the ownership of livestock.

The goods collected in the tombs of these "princes," besides displaying opulence, demonstrate that they were in contact with aristocracies of other cultures; they were part of a network of high-status individuals who exchanged valuable gifts. The "princely" tombs of Fabriano, Pitino in San Severino Marche, Tolentino, and Matelica show strong similarities with those of the Tyrrhenian environment: They are composed of rich furnishings and decorations that allude to the symposium and the consumption of meat, combined with the display of parade weapons in warrior tombs and a remarkable richness of personal objects in female burials. Objects related to decoration as well as their accompanying furnishings can be ascribed to Etruscan craftsmanship. These include a silver "comb" fibula from Fabriano and armor such as skullcap helmets and large parade shields, which can be attributed to groups BI (Fabriano) and BII (Tolentino) of the Strøm classification scheme. The furnishings include silver *skyphoi* from Fabriano; Massalia-type tripods seen in Pitino, Tolentino, and other locations of Picenum; the bronze Chiusian-type amphora whose handles have three horse protomes; and the valuable *oinochoe* from Tomb 14 in Pitino, whose mouth and handle are formed in the shape of a female head and chest, in ivory with gold decorations, and whose body is made from an ostrich egg with incised figurative friezes. This type of *oinochoe* had its exact counterpart in an example from Quinto Fiorentino, while the ostrich egg recalls Vulci.

Among the objects uncovered in these "princely" tombs in Picenum, the extremely rich grave goods from the tomb of the "princess" of Sirolo, containing two carriages, are especially noteworthy and can be placed at the end of the sixth century B.C. Here we find a bronze tripod of a type similar to seventh-century examples from Cerveteri, Orvieto, and Auxerre. The tripod and the tomb's other contents, such as a *kline* and a silver *phiale chrysomphalos* produced in Rhodes, are worthy of being compared to the most precious *keimelia* of the Homeric poems. They demonstrate the penetration into Picenum of the Homeric model of conserving and exhibiting luxury goods as status symbols.

The importation of valuable objects of prestige from the eastern Mediterranean, Greece, and the eastern Greek area (Rhodes) helped compensate for the paucity of worthy offerings from the Picenum area itself. These imports included Attic pottery, the silver *phiale chrysomphalos*, the eastern Greek *lekythos* with decorated bands, the *kline*, and perhaps a number of bronzes as well, such as a group of Rhodian pitchers (*oinochoai*) and some from Etruria. Among the latter, a group of bronzes stands out, including an *infundibulum* with a lyre-shaped handle, the aforementioned tripod, and a pair

Third-century Etruscan *thymiaterion* in bronze, from Tomb 8 in Montefortino in Arcevia (Ancona). Ancona, Museo Archeologico Nazionale

of sandals articulated with a bronze and wooden hinge. These were either directly imported through the Adriatic or bought through intermediaries in Etruria. Picenum in general, and Numana in particular, benefited from being both terminals for trans-Apennine routes and stopping points for ships crossing the Adriatic on the way from Greece.

The distribution of Rhodian pitchers in the mid-Adriatic area demonstrates once again that it is not easy to establish how certain products arrived in the Picenum area. There were examples of eastern Greek origin—Type A Shefton (Numana-Sirolo, Belmonte, Montedinove, and Campovalano)—and of Etruscan-Italic origin—Type C Shefton (Numana, Sirolo, Fabriano, Tolentino, Belmonte, Acquaviva Picena, Ascoli Piceno (?), Offida, Campli, and Campovalano—together with local imitations in bucchero-like impasto.

Picenum also acted as a pivot between the Faliscan territory with southern Tyrrhenian Etruria and the mid-Adriatic world, as seen in examples from Falerii, Trestina, Cerveteri, and Castro.

This inter-Apennine land-sea role is also confirmed by the appearance of the above-mentioned Etruscan sandals in the grave of the princess of Sirolo. These were articulated and nailed together, with a wooden interior and decoration in bone on the exterior. Similar sandals could be found in Etruria (Cerveteri, Praeneste, Bisenzio, and Falerii); in the mid-Adriatic area, sometimes in different styles (Campovalano, Capestrano, and Loreto Aprutino); and in Picenum itself (Belmonte and Recanati).

Contact with these Etruscan imports helped to spur the Picenum workshops to improve their own products. These were not simply imitations, but true originals in local style. It was above all in metalworking that this lively and stimulating relationship with Etruria—both Tyrrhenian Etruria and Etruria Padana—is manifest, particularly between the sixth and fourth centuries B.C. The spread of pitchers with elongated spouts (Schnabelkannen), funnel-shaped strainers (*infundibula* from Belmonte and Sirolo), ladles (*simpula* from Castelbellino), *stamnoi* (Sirolo-Numana, Moie di Pollenza, Monterolo di San Vito, Montefortino di Arcevia, Serra San Quirico, Moscano di Fabriano, San Filippo di Osimo, San Ginesio, Offida, and Ascoli Piceno), candelabras (Sirolo-Numana, San Filippo di Osimo, Santa Paolina di Filottrano, Montefortino di Arcevia), mirrors (Montefortino, Filottrano, Montesampietro Morico, Matelica, and Pieve Torina), censers (*thymiateria* from Montefortino di Arcevia, Servigliano), and *situlae* and *cistae* from Praeneste (Moscano, Servigliano, and Montesampietro Morico) all attest to the intensity and continuity of Etruscan commercial relations with central Adriatic Italy. Picenum's exchanges and contacts with Etruria were vitally important to its role as a bridge between the Transalpine world and the Mediterranean environment.

Picenum had frequent contacts with the Po-Romagna region, as we know from the array of objects, especially in bronze and amber, that are thought to have been produced in northern Etruria or in the Po Valley. Of particular interest in this group are: votive bronzes, such as the deity of Apiro from the final decades of the fifth century B.C., today preserved in Kansas

Bronze head of a youth,
fourth century B.C., from
Cagli (Pesaro). Ancona,
Museo Archeologico
Nazionale

City; candelabras, such as an example from Paterno in Ancona; the *sima* with a young man and a pig from Sirolo that is now in New York; and amber ornaments, such as pendants fashioned with a protome of a ram from Belmonte and Montegiorgio (we may add two new examples from the tomb of the princess of Sirolo).

The influence that Etruria exercised over Picenum in the area of religious ideology was quite strong, as shown by the deposit of Etruscan votive bronzes in places of worship in Picenum. These were produced in various cities and dated between the sixth and fourth centuries B.C. They included the kouros of Corinaldo, the "priest" from the Isola di Fano, and the head of a youth with a diadem from Cagli, which dated to the sec-ond quarter of the fourth century and which was based on Attic prototypes.

Other than bronzeworking, Picenum also drew stimuli and cues from the Etruscan world in the field of pottery. Beside the local terra-cotta imitations of both pitchers with elongated spouts and basins with beaded rims, we find imports of Etruscan-Geometric (the small olla of "Metopengattung" style) and Etruscan-Corinthian pottery from the seventh century B.C. (a *stamnos* with a silhouette frieze of running dogs from the area of Cupra Marittima) and the end of the seventh and sixth centuries (a *kotyle* from Pitino in San Severino Marche; pitchers from Belmonte Piceno, Cupra Marittima, and Fabriano; and a spherical *aryballos* from Grottazzolina). A three-lobed *oinochoe* from the latter period in

Numana was probably produced locally. In a rich grave of the Circle of the Fibula in Sirolo-Numana, next to an Italic-Geometric cup, there were a number of notable Etruscan works in bucchero (*kantharos*). Etruscan pottery from the fourth and third centuries was imported to Tolentino (a Faliscan red-figured *stamnos* from the so-called Fluido Group and an *oinochoe* from the so-called Barbarano Group), to Pieve Torina (*oinochoai* from the Barbarano Group, Toronto, and Phanton), and to Carpignano in San Severino Marche (*pocula* from the Roselle 1889 Group).

In the late Classical and Hellenistic eras, southern Etruscan goldwork and bronzes produced in Etruria, Falerii (*kyathoi*), Lazio (Praeneste), and Campania reached the mid-western side of the Adriatic. This was partly, if not completely, due to the great mobility of the Senones, a Gaulish tribe. The relationship that the latter had with Praeneste and Tivoli between 361 and 348 B.C., during the course of their raids and establishment in Lazio, surely played a determining role not only in circulating products from Etruria and Lazio to Picenum but perhaps also in shaping local craftsmanship, which can be generically defined as Celtic-Italic. Some theorize that metalworkers in the workshops of the eastern Italians made bronzes such as the basin of Santa Paolina in Filottrano, with a pair of modeled handles representing a pair of battling warriors. A roughly similar example was found in Borsdorf (Germany) and today is at the museum of Darmstadt, while another is at the Boston Museum of Fine Arts and came from Picenum.

The *situla* from Offida, the *cistae* from Servigliano and Montesampietro Morico, the censer (*thymiaterion*) from Servigliano, and the bronze strigils that were found in these southern Picenum cities have significant counterparts in bronzes from Gallic graves in Moscano di Fabriano, Santa Paolina in Filottrano, and Montefortino in Arcevia. In addition, the spread of strigils with the mark ΑΑΠΟΛΛΩΡΩ confirms these privileged relationships with Praeneste and the areas of Lazio and Campania.

From Livy we learn that the Gauls carried out various raids in Lazio, where they stayed for a long period, with moves on Campania and Puglia after the episode of Valerius Corvinus. Livy (7.9.1–2) and Polybius (2.18) agree that in 361 B.C. the Gauls, particularly the Senones, followed the Via Salaria and got within three miles of Rome, camping near the Aniene River. It may be possible to find tangible signs of their stay in the Lazio area and their contact with Tivoli and Praeneste—which had anti-Roman politics and did not refuse the Gauls' help—in the necropoleis of the Picentes and Gauls in central Italy on the Adriatic.

The Etruscans in Lazio

| ALESSANDRO NASO

A small model of a building from Velletri (Rome). Rome, Museo di Villa Giulia. *On the facing page,* the back wall of the Tomb of the Bulls, about 540 B.C., Tarquinia (Viterbo)

The Geographic Picture

According to the ancients, the name Lazio (*Latium* in Latin) derived from the Latin term *latus*, which means "wide." The Lazio territory is made up, in effect, of an ample fertile plain bordered by the Tiber River to the north, the Tyrrhenian Sea to the west, and the pre-Apennine ridge to the east. It includes the Colli Albani (Alban Hills) and the Lepini, Ausoni, and Aurunci Mountains, which reach into Campania to the south. The mountain ranges form the borders of wide valleys carved by rivers of various sizes. In addition to those that run north to south, numerous smaller watercourses lead to the Tyrrhenian coast. The river valleys constituted natural communication routes. Toward Campania and southern Italy, the corridor formed by the successive valleys of the Sacco, the Liri, and the Garigliano were particularly significant. Its northern entrance was controlled by the city of Palestrina, ancient Praeneste. The lesser watercourses were utilized to penetrate inland from the coast.

Geographic features of this type tended to cause the formation of similar yet distinct cultures that claimed their fortunes from the fertility of their soil. Alongside the ancient Latini, other groups settled in the region, such as the Ernici and the Volsci, who had gathered around Anagni and Palestrina, respectively; the Sabini, who

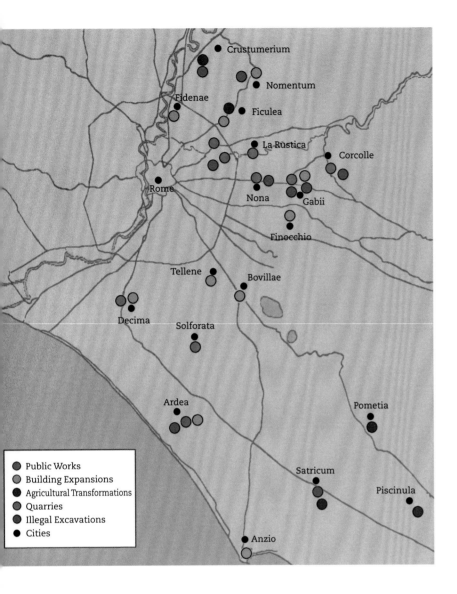

- ● Public Works
- ● Building Expansions
- ● Agricultural Transformations
- ● Quarries
- ● Illegal Excavations
- ● Cities

Map indicating the peoples
and cities of pre-Roman
Lazio

lived in the inaccessible mountainous area of the east; and the Aurunci, who dwelt in the south. Historians and archaeologists agree in placing the northern border of Lazio at the course of the Tiber, not only because of cultural subdivisions during the pre-Roman era but also because of the administrative partitioning by Augustus in the first century B.C. To the north lay Etruria, whose inhabitants were distinct from the Latini because of their distinct origins, which implied that their language, customs, and history were clearly different from those of all the other peoples of pre-Roman Italy (see G. Camporeale's contributions to this volume, above). In an environment with such a varied ethnic mosaic as the Italian Peninsula during the first millennium B.C., the Etruscans were undoubtedly the most dynamic and original experiment. Among the peoples of Italy with whom the Etruscans established relations, the people of Lazio took on a prominent role, not only because of the region's geographic contiguity with Etruria but also, and above all, because of the development of Rome. Rising along the Tiber near the natural ford provided by Tiberina Island, the city had intense and fruitful relations with Etruscan cities from the most ancient times onward.

The Iron Age
(Ninth and Eighth Centuries B.C.)

The geographic shape of Etruria and Lazio, and their natural projection onto the sea, favored a sort of commonality between the two regions, which were united in their inclination to make and keep contact with non-Italic cultures, especially the Greeks. It is no accident that common forms of aggregation and territorial organization were widespread in the mid-Tyrrhenian area from the early centuries of the first millennium B.C. onward. Scholars defined these forms as proto-urban and urban, and for the most part the rest of the Italian peninsula would not achieve them until the end of the millennium, following the unification brought about by the Roman conquest. Etruria and Lazio were also united by the early spread of writing, which resulted from the adoption of an alphabet that the Greeks used on the island of Euboea. This was due to the foundation of the oldest Greek colonies in Italy: the emporia of Pithecusae on the island of Ischia and Cumae on the mainland. A recent discovery at Tomb 482 in the necropolis of Osteria dell'Osa in Lazio, near ancient Gabii, has contributed something new to our understanding of this subject. The grave goods from a female burial that date to around 770 B.C. include a flask-type vase that was produced locally, upon which the word *eulin* is written in the Euboean alphabet. Although we do not yet know how to interpret it, it is the oldest inscription known in Lazio, and perhaps on the entire Italian peninsula. Even its findspot is significant, since during the period of the Roman Republic, Gabii was considered a city of culture, so much so that according to scholarly tradition, Romulus and Remus learned their letters there.

In addition to this extremely interesting relic, the cemetery of Osteria dell'Osa has yielded other treasures that are closely related to our area of inquiry. Worship of the deceased mandated the deposition in tombs not only of goods and furnishings that had been owned and used in life but also of objects that were used in the funerary rituals. As a result the necropoleis became true archives overflowing with cultural information. For example, the contents of Tomb 600, which was discovered by accident outside the regular excavation area, match characteristics of Etruscan grave goods, despite their being deposited in a Latini necropolis.

Based on current knowledge, Tomb 600 was more or less isolated and therefore distinct from the necropolis. In Etruria this feature marked the tombs of those who held the status of royalty. The terra-cotta tableware from this grave was lost after agricultural work disturbed the area. But the association of metal materials, which were reduced to minute fragments, remains of great interest, since they are comparable to a series of male grave goods from southern Etruria that date to the third quarter of the eighth century B.C. and belonged to warriors of high social status. What Tomb 600 contained, in fact, was the remains of a bronze panoply, including defensive weapons (a crested helmet, two shields, and a quadrangular breastplate), offensive weapons (a sword and sheath, spear, javelin, and battle-ax), and tableware in sheet bronze (a biconic amphora, four fluted *paterae*, and basins with beaded rims). The weapons, which are of Etruscan make, seem therefore to identify the origin of the warrior: He may have been a prince from Veii buried in the necropolis of Osteria dell'Osa in Lazio, where he had possibly integrated into that community.

The Orientalizing Period (Seventh Century B.C.)

The deceased buried in Tomb 600 at Osteria dell'Osa, then, may represent a case of geographic mobility. During the course of his life, this individual changed the community he resided in, making himself a home within the group at his destination. This picture is corroborated by Etruscan names that can be found in epigraphic records from the seventh century B.C., which reveal an influx of people of various origins into central Italy. The onomastic formula of one *Rutile Hipukrates*, buried in Tarquinia in a monumental tumulus, has a first name that derives from the Latin *Rutilus* (red), while the last name, an indicator of a person's origins, is a copy of the Greek *Hippokrates* (thus, "Hippocrates the Red").

The general picture includes not only sensational examples like the grave goods from Osteria dell'Osa but also other isolated finds, objects that were produced in Etruria and reached Lazio through contacts of various types. Besides commercial activities, the exchange of gifts between individuals of equal social status should also be mentioned, a phenomenon attested on the Italian peninsula by pre-Roman epigraphic records. A relationship of this kind could, for example, be understood from a bronze tripod from the first half of the seventh century B.C., which was made in an Etruscan shop, perhaps in Veii, but excavated in the La Rustica necropolis in the southern outskirts of Rome.

The gift-exchange circuit, which is explicitly referred to in inscriptions—the objects themselves give firsthand testimony that they were given from one person to another—helped intensify the relationships between noble families, which were primarily economic in nature. The concentration of goods seen in a number of tombs in Praeneste from the first half of the seventh century B.C. was undoubtedly due to the strong strategic position of the city, which controlled the natural route between Lazio and Campania as well as the direct itinerary toward the Apennine valleys and the Adriatic shore. These tombs belonged to people who owed their wealth to the imposition of tolls and compulsory levies for transit along these routes.

The set of jewelry in the Galeassi Tomb, which was made up of gold and amber fibulae and necklaces, can be indisputably attributed to a workshop located in

At left, bucchero chalice, dated between 625 and 550 B.C., from the votive deposit at Satricum. Rome, Museo di Villa Giulia

At right, oinochoe (wine pitcher) in bucchero, dated between 625 and 550 B.C., from a votive deposit at Satricum. Rome, Museo di Villa Giulia

On the facing page, above left, Etruscan-Corinthian aryballos (ointment container), from a votive deposit at Satricum, about 550 B.C. Rome, Museo di Villa Giulia. Below left, Etruscan-Corinthian alabastron (ointment container), first half of the sixth century B.C., from a votive deposit at Satricum. Rome, Museo di Villa Giulia. At right, Etruscan-Corinthian oinochoe from a votive deposit at Satricum, dated between 625 and 550 B.C. Rome, Museo di Villa Giulia

Cerveteri—ancient Caere—whose necropoleis turned up similar jewels.

What is also astounding is the heap of extravagant goods that accumulated in the Bernardini and Barberini tombs in Praeneste. In addition to vases in bronze, silver, and gilt-silver from remote regions of the eastern Mediterranean, such as northern Syria, Phoenicia, and the island of Cyprus, the grave goods in the Bernardini Tomb contain valuable intaglio works in ivory, such as a chalice supported by caryatids of Eastern make (possibly Syrian). The metal tableware includes silver cups decorated with scenes that reproduce the occupations of the Eastern aristocracies (hunting and court life), with

whom the princes of Etruria and Praeneste liked to identify themselves. There were also huge cauldrons on bronze supports. Here the heads of real and imaginary animals (lions and griffons) that surmount the cauldrons allude to their destiny as grave goods. The intermediary role played by the Etruscans, who brought these objects to Praeneste, is made clear not only by the occurrence of similar cemeteries in Caere and Vetulonia but also by the discovery of a complete table service in silver at the Bernardini Tomb itself. This was a product that in all likelihood came from the workshops of Caere. A spherical cup with an incised frieze beneath its rim holds the name *Vetusia*, which indicates the cup's

owner, who has been identified as the deceased. The scientific community has been divided over how to attribute this name, since some scholars thought it to be Etruscan, while others considered it Latin. The theory that the dead man is an Etruscan aristocrat, which seems to be substantiated by Etruscan inscriptions that were recently discovered, would appear to indicate a situation similar to that of the older grave goods in Tomb 600 at Osteria dell'Osa. The opposite case, on the other hand, would demonstrate the deep passion that the princes of Praeneste had for Etruscan culture of the Orientalizing era. This phenomenon is confirmed in other graves of the highest social standing at both Praeneste and in other locations in Lazio, such as Tombs 15 and 21 at the Castel di Decima necropolis and Number 70 at Acqua Acetosa Laurentina, both of which stand at the gates of Rome.

The landing at the mouth of the Tiber and the presence of materials from the first half of the seventh century B.C. in necropoleis in Lazio—materials such as Phoenician or Phoenician-type wine amphorae that up to that point had rarely been seen in Etruria—indicate that the community in Lazio cultivated autonomous relationships with Eastern seafarers without passing through Etruscan mediation.

The distribution of Greek pottery from Corinth during the first half of the seventh century B.C., however, seems to have been an initiative of the Etruscans. These objects are called Protocorinthian in order to distinguish the initial stage of their production and were found at various locations on the Lazio coast, including Lavinium and Satricum, beginning in the second quarter of the seventh century: tableware in bucchero and a refined sort of Subgeometric

painted pottery that was typical of workshops active in Caere. Such products indicate not only Lazio's high level of interest in the Etruscan metropoleis but also that goods from Caere followed a marine route for small-scale coastal trade. The most frequent stopping points were the mouths of watercourses, as seen at Lavinium, Ardea, and Satricum, and at natural inlets, as was the case with Anzio. For example, it was from this last location that a direct route inland toward the site of Satricum must have begun, near present-day Borgo Le Ferriere, where there was an important city.

Beginning in the last century, a variety of archaeological sites have been investigated at Satricum, which, in addition to graves, include the remains of buildings from different eras and with different purposes (from huts to temple buildings), not to mention votive deposits. Among the foundations of huts, which were made of perishable materials such as wooden poles and clay, those marked Numbers 6 and 7 particularly stand out. It was there that drinking services of painted pottery, either Protocorinthian or Etruscan imitations, were found. These were distributed via Caere and Satricum, perhaps by sea.

Votive deposits at Satricum, found together with buildings that were used as temples, were collections of gifts from the faithful to the divine. The offerings—vases of various shapes whose functions depended on their contents—were periodically gathered from the temple and deposited in pits that had been dug in the ground. This cleared enough space to allow the worshippers to dedicate new gifts at the temple. The votive deposit at Satricum brought to light a wide range of votive pottery, both locally produced and Etrurian. The identities of the offering bearers are revealed through inscriptions on the vases. On a number of bucchero fragments, shards of a cup dating to the final quarter of the seventh century B.C., the name "*[Laris] Velchaina*" was written in Etruscan. This figure was already known from an inscription on a bucchero cup that was found at Caere, whose text allows us to reconstruct the epigraph in Satricum. The inscription on the complete vase says *mi mulu larisale velχainas*, or, "I (am) given from/for Laris Velchaina." Meanwhile, on the fragment uncovered at Satricum, only the final part, *-le velχainas*, remains. The similar shape of the two vases, which are quite rare and easily recognizable, supports the completion of this last sentence fragment. The cups are divided in two by an internal baffle and were made to contain two liquids that were evidently supposed to remain separate, poured out through two different small spouts. The presence of dedications to the same person in two distant places such as Caere and Satricum is not unique in central Italy during the Orientalizing period, but it is certainly uncommon and emphasizes that Laris Velchaina had interests in Satricum during the final years of the seventh century, though he may have been a native of Caere.

A similar case came to light during recent discoveries at the necropoleis of Lavinium. A chamber tomb that had been used for a number of generations held a bucchero amphora with the inscription *mini m[ulu]vanice mamar.ce a.puniie*, or, "Mamarce Apunie gave me." This was an individual who was already known from an *olpe* (pitcher) in bucchero that was given at the sanctuary of Portonaccio at Veii. The two vases, with almost identical inscriptions, date back to about 570 B.C.

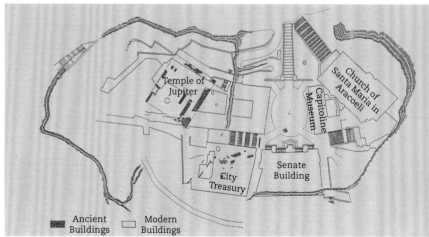

Temple of Jupiter

Church of Santa Maria in Aracoeli

Capitoline Museum

City Treasury

Senate Building

Ancient Buildings   Modern Buildings

The Great Rome of the Tarquins

This survey has so far excluded Rome, Lazio's most important city, which deserves special attention because of its central role. Up to now, Rome has not yielded any particular concentrations of Etruscan finds from the periods examined thus far, other than the known bronzes and tableware that were imported from Etruria. The group found under the Apostolico Lateranense

building stands out; these date back to the second half of the seventh century B.C. and can perhaps be connected to a settlement of Etruscan artisans in the nearby area between Palatino and Velabro, which is traditionally known as *vicus Tuscus* (the Etruscan quarter). At the end of the seventh century, the climax of a period of serious social tensions, the city saw the arrival of the Etruscan dynasty of the Tarquins, which according to the chronicles was made up of Tarquinius Priscus (616–578 B.C.), Servius Tullius (578–536 B.C.) and Tarquinius Superbus (535–509 B.C.). Tarquinius Priscus was the son of a Greek noble named Demaratos, who fled Corinth for Tarquinia about 657 B.C. Although the identification of the individual figures and their historical reality are still debated by scholars, it is nevertheless probable that representatives of newly formed classes caused the kings of Etruscan origin to take power in Rome. Thus Cato tells us that "almost all of Italy was under Etruscan dominance" (Cato fr. 62 Peter: *in Tuscorum iure paene omnis Italia fuerat*).

The second half of the seventh century B.C. coincided with a period of innovation in the city. For example, burials ceased in the valley where the Roman Forum was to rise. The valley was drained thanks to intense land reclamation efforts such as the creation of the Cloaca Maxima, which literary sources ascribe to Tarquinius Priscus. Other important initiatives in the field of urban planning are credited to this first Tarquin, such as the construction of the Circus Maximus in the hollow between the Palatine and Aventine Hills and the start of construction on the magnificent temple to Jupiter on the Capitoline Hill, which ever

since has been a sacred rock reserved for buildings of worship.

The literary sources report the colossal dimensions of this temple, which was dedicated by Tarquinius Priscus but finished by Superbus, and these can be compared with the ruins of walls that are still visible at the site. The interpretation of these remains, those of a building 62 meters long by 53.5 wide (203 by 176 ft.), is equivocal, however. The immense weight of the roof would have been beyond what wooden columns could support; this fact has led some to presume the use of stone columns, and others to hypothesize that such measurements correspond not to the temple itself but to its base, upon which a *cella* of lesser size must have stood. Discoveries during recent archaeological excavations, undertaken in connection with construction work on the Campidoglio, have provided new information, especially regarding the Temple of Jupiter, which has been covered in the daily press. It is preferable at this point to leave

open the interpretation of these ruins, pending the publication of scientific results.

The model followed, at any rate, was within the tradition of buildings with three *cellae* that was characteristic of Etruscan architecture, of which there are numerous monumental remains. It also follows the theoretic formula developed by Vitruvius during the first century B.C. in his architectural manual.

Such buildings were endowed with a complex covering system made of a wooden framework, upon which heavy decorations in terra-cotta were nailed to protect the beams from the elements. In addition, terra-cotta statues called akroteria were fastened onto the roof. Plutarch reports that the akroteria of the Temple of Jupiter on the Capitoline Hill portrayed a quadriga— a team of four horses—that had been commissioned by Tarquinius Superbus from a workshop in Veii.

Construction work carried out on the hill over the course of time has turned up a

At *left*, antefix of a female head, end of the sixth century B.C., from the garden of Aracoeli at the Campidoglio. Rome, Antiquarium Comunale

At *right*, bucchero bowl with an Etruscan inscription, second half of the sixth century B.C., from Clivo Capitolino. Rome, Antiquarium Comunale

The Archaic Period
(Sixth and Fifth Centuries B.C.)

The influence of Etruscan architecture can be seen in other Roman works as well, such as the Regia in the Roman Forum. This building, whose existence is known through literary tradition, has been identified with the remains of a residence that was reconstructed three times between the end of the seventh and the end of the sixth centuries B.C. In its most recent incarnation, its floor plan was enriched with two rectangular spaces in the interior, reflecting an architectural tradition that was widespread in Etruscan building. A bucchero bowl dating to this period had the inscription of ownership *rex*, in Latin, referring to a priest titled *rex sacrorum*, rather than the last of the kings.

A temple with a three-part floor plan, dating back to between 540 and 530 B.C., was also located near the church of Sant'Omobono and corresponded to an ancient river-landing along the Tiber. It is the oldest known three-celled temple. Its cult, whose foundation can be attributed to Servius Tullius, paid homage to an extremely ancient divinity called Mater Matuta and had the features of an emporium; this was in keeping with the nature of the place, which was designated for trade. It held rich votive deposits containing earthenware in bucchero and Etruscan-Corinthian pottery. It is not always easy to distinguish local products from those imported from Etruria. Among the finds in the votive deposit, which has only been partly explored, an ivory lion cub stands out. On its rear side the name of its owner,

Ivory *tessera hospitalis* in the shape of a lion cub (seen here from both sides), second half of the sixth century B.C., from the sacred area of Sant'Omobono. Rome, Antiquarium Comunale

number of archaeological finds, mostly without context. A fragment of a huge eave tile, with painted meanders on its visible part, has been linked to the Temple of Jupiter, while an antefix of a female head from the final decades of the sixth century B.C. has been attributed to the ornamentation of an unknown building. On the slopes of the hill, in a pit near the temple dedicated to Saturn, a bucchero bowl was recovered with an Etruscan inscription of possession—*ni Araziia Larania*, or "I (am)

Araz Silquetenas Spurianas, is incised in Etruscan. The plaque has been recognized as a *tessera hospitalis* and was paired with another of similar shape, a witness to the ties that bound their two owners. The onomastic formula includes a first name (*Araz*), a last name (*Silquetenas*), and a third element (*Spurianas*), which scholars have identified as either an appositive or patronymic.

Thanks to the tight network of relations that existed between cities on the mid-Tyrrhenian side, which favored the circulation of artisans and products, cultural characteristics that were markedly Etruscan did not stay concentrated in Rome but also spread to other cities of Lazio. Among the vast quantity of material records, we may cite the bronze male figure found at Gabii. Its typical curved staff leads the statue to be identified as an augur, a priest who interpreted the flight of birds. The tiny terra-cotta model of a building from Colle Ottone near Velletri should also be mentioned; it may be the sole remains of a place of worship. The model reproduces an internal partition of two *cellae*, following a plan recorded in Etruscan funerary architecture since the second half of the sixth century B.C., and the composition may have been completed by a mobile figure that portrayed the worshipped deity, which has since been lost. The contacts that linked the small town of Colli Albani with Etruscan workmanship are not limited to this find, but include the remains of the temple incorporated into the church of Santa Maria della Neve, which also had three *cellae* and yielded a series of large architectural terra-cotta roof decorations dated to the third quarter of the sixth century. These stamped plaques were placed on the facade, on the sloping sides of the pediment. One particu-

larly well-preserved example was cut on a slant, which means that it was once located at the top of the left angle of the pediment. The motifs, which were repeated in an almost frantic succession of friezes along the pediment slopes, accord with Tyrrhenian characteristics that can be attributed to the era of the second Tarquin king, when the cultural climate encouraged the sporting contests between high-ranking figures that were reproduced on these plaques.

Beyond the institutional and social changes that surrounded the collapse of the Tarquin monarchy and the introduction of republican institutions, which are traditionally dated to 509 B.C., archaeological evidence asserts the wide diffusion and enduring vitality of the planimetric scheme of three *cellae*. The temple erected in the Roman Forum in 484 B.C., whose ruins dominate its central area, shows this same interior subdivision. It was built in honor of the Dioscuri, Castor and Pollux, whom Roman sources call the Castors. The partition is not easily recognizable since it is incorporated within later reconstructions of the building, including a final one put into

Terra-cotta revetment plaque from a pediment dating to about 530 B.C., from Velletri (Rome). Naples, Museo Nazionale

effect during the early years of the first century A.D. Worship of the Dioscuri, which was originally Greek, also spread to Etruria and other places in Lazio, such as Lavinium, perhaps through the influence of Taranto.

The Middle-Republican Period (Fourth and Third Centuries B.C.)

The cities of southern Etruria, having fallen into decline beginning with the fifth century B.C., met the growing power of Rome in the fourth, when it began to conquer central Italy. The individual Etruscan cities were treated in various ways. While Caere had always cultivated a special relationship with the city, to such an extent that the Roman youth went there to study (Livy 9.36.3), Tarquinia was a number of times on the opposite side of the Latin city in bloody wars. For its part, Vulci has preserved an extremely interesting monument that dates back to the second half of the fourth century, an extravagant noble tomb, named François after the archaeologist Alessandro François, which displays painted friezes on its walls. At their center are two figures fighting. The decisive moments of a war between Etruscan cities are shown, each one represented by a hero. The onomastic formulas here, shown in inscriptions, include an appellative of the city of origin. One of them is "*Cneve Tarχunies Rumaχ*," or Cnaeus Tarquinius Romanus, whom scholars have recognized as a member of the ruling dynasty of Rome. Beyond the allusions to historical events that the frieze may contain—events linked to Etruscan history during the Archaic period—what matters here is that in the era when Etruria began to be dominated, ancient moments of glory were

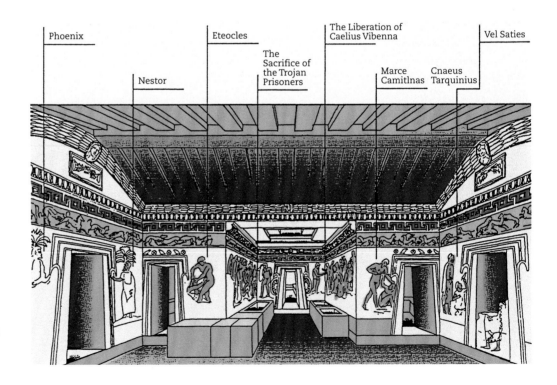

Perspective sketch of the atrium in the François Tomb at Vulci, which dates to the third quarter of the sixth century B.C.

recalled within a noble tomb. They were moments that had witnessed the supremacy of the Etruscan cities, even over Rome.

The presence of the Etruscans in Lazio did not fade out in the fourth century B.C. but continued in various forms until the late Imperial period, manifested in robust cultural contributions and linguistic loans from Etruria to Rome. That, however, would be another chapter in the long history of the Etruscans.

Combat scene from the François Tomb in Vulci (Viterbo), about 340 B.C., from the Ponte Rotto necropolis. Rome, Torlonia Collection

The Etruscans in Campania

| BRUNO D'AGOSTINO

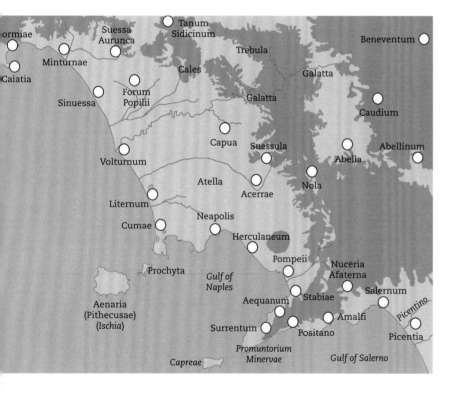

Above, map of ancient Campania. *On the facing page*, a lid of an ash urn surmounted by two human figures, ninth century B.C., from Pontecagnano (Salerno). Pontecagnano, Museo dell'Agro Picentino

The creation of Etruscan settlements in Campania was one consequence of a great transformation that swept over south coastal Etruria at the dawn of the first millennium B.C. In this period, in a number of particularly thriving districts, the tiny settlements that had been the norm during the end of the Bronze Age disappeared, and the population gathered in vast, proto-urban built-up areas, which could already be identified as the future historical cities of Veii, Caere, Tarquinia, and Vulci. This crucial change, which was driven by the need for more political cohesion, coincided with a powerful expansion that advanced in two main directions: into Emilia in the Po Valley and into Campania.

In the latter region, the two most important settlements that were born from this expansion, Capua and Pontecagnano, were in fact contemporaries of the rising proto-cities of coastal Etruria. The situation in Campania during this time is difficult to determine. For the moment the most ancient known tombs of the indigenous people, which ancient historians

designated as either Oscans or Opici, do not date back further than the middle of the ninth century B.C.

For their settlements in Campania, the Etruscans selected two areas that responded to different requirements. The first and most important requirement was ample and fertile land. Thus two great coastal plains north of Naples and south of Salerno were chosen. At the same time, the habitations also needed access to the sea and to trade with inland regions. Both Capua and Pontecagnano, in fact, rose a safe distance from the coast, on riverways that afforded good landings at the seaward end.

Capua's position was especially favorable, standing at the center of a plain proverbially known for its fertility. The river that feeds it, the Volturno, is the terminus of a inland river system that—through the Liri, the Tiber, and the

Chiana—opened Campania to the ports of Lazio and inland Etruria and even ran up as far as Orvieto and Chiusi.

Recent publications regarding a new group of tombs from the early Iron Age allow us to reconsider Capua's origins. In the light of these new facts, the case of Capua seems similar to that of Pontecagnano. Both were Etruscan foundations that were created by one of the great cities of southern coastal Etruria. The tombs of Capua, at least during the first half of the ninth century, show the essential traits of the Villanovan culture, such as the rite of cremation, the use of biconic ossuaries, and incised Geometric decorations that were often executed with a comblike instrument.

But while these features persisted at Pontecagnano for all of the ninth century B.C. and most of the following century, at

Capua typical forms of Villanovan funerary rituals were renounced and the people began to show a preference for a local culture that was shared among native settlements of the plain, such as Suessula. This process reveals that Capua was striving to position itself at the center of an important unification process on the Campanian plain. It is probable that this cultural shift is also a sign of weakening connections with coastal Etruria in favor of a more intense relationship with the Faliscan world and with Etruria along the Tiber.

When Pontecagnano was formed, the hills surrounding the coastal plain were controlled by small native settlements, about whose inhabitants little is known. The Picentino River certainly did not offer the same opportunities as the Volturno. Nevertheless, starting not far from Pontecagnano, this great river artery connected the Tyrrhenian and Adriatic coasts through the Sele and the Ofanto Rivers. From the early Iron Age until the Orientalizing period, the populations of the Oliveto Citra-Cairano culture, located along this artery, cultivated a relationship with Pontecagnano, which was the most attractive city in terms of economic potential and cultural openness.

Judging by the displacement of the necropoleis, the settlement in the early Iron Age—of which unfortunately no trace has yet been found—must have occupied the same area between the Picentino and the Frestola Rivers that was later to be built up during the historical period. This main built-up area was paired with a smaller settlement located in Pagliarone, which guarded the southern border.

This modest inhabitation rose on a small hill that is now occupied by the military airport (the site was further devastated by the airport's recent expansion). It was located at the confluence of two watercourses that flowed into a small lagoon. As Patrizia Gastaldi has noted, the primitive port of Pontecagnano was located in this lagoon, which among other things gave their ships the element of surprise that was so important for carrying out piracy.

In the vast necropolis at Pagliarone, and in the eastern one at Pontecagnano, tombs reveal frequent contacts with partners who had arrived by sea just after the middle of the ninth century B.C. Objects from distant places are included among grave goods, such as small ornamental bronzes from Sardinia or the typical pottery of Sicily with "plumed" decorations. Finally, the presence of iron swords that originated in Calabria leads one to suppose that the "right of burial" was accorded to a group of warriors who probably came from Torre Galli, an important site near Tropea.

The existence of these early contacts shows the advanced development of local society, which must also have played an important part in spreading southern cultural elements to coastal Etruria. Toward the end of the ninth century B.C., the appearance of graves containing numerous status symbols suggests the establishment of a social hierarchy. In addition, these tombs are distinguished by their "monumental" features and are grouped within special areas of the necropolis. The most significant example is Tomb 2145, which is situated below a horseshoe-shaped platform. A provisional dwelling for the dead must have been built here, where the deceased could wait for a definitive transfer to the afterlife.

During this period the prominent figures of the community began to promote a more complex ideology. As generally happens in simple societies, these figures tended to be free adult males who carried weapons, especially swords. Now, however, they also became an element of cohesion and continuity for their family group. Helmets that became the lids of ossuaries in these tombs suggest the emergence of this new role. Through the adoption of a new decorative system, the features of these ossuaries became more like those of a hut. The development of the society into groups seems to be suggested by another aspect in helmet decoration: animal figurines, seen on some helmets, may represent the animal totems of various clans.

This period of rapid development led to the need to rebalance the territory. It is probable that the settlement of Pagliarone, created to serve the lagoon port, tended to act autonomously and eventually became an obstacle to the full development of the principal city. This caused it to be abandoned. The landing at the mouth of the Picentino was improved, and trade activity returned to the city, moving the axis of territorial development toward the river.

During this time, new foreign partners appeared on the horizon of the middle Tyrrhenian Sea. As at Capua and Veii, the first Greek-made bowls appeared at Pontecagnano. Thus the relationship with Euboea began, which would contribute in a determining and defining way to the rise of the Etruscan world.

We do not know exactly what these Greek visitors were seeking in the territory. In the economy at that time, metal was certainly an object of great interest. From this point of view, the Tyrrhenian coast was a favorable spot, both for the resources of the Tolfa Mountains, between Caere and Tarquinia, and for those of the island of Elba and the metalliferous mountains behind Populonia, which were even more considerable. Nevertheless, as the Phoenician example illustrates, it is also true that in a world where the economy still had a very tenuous structure, proceeds from smaller-scale commerce were also of interest.

The Etruscan cities, however, already enjoyed a considerable level of internal cohesion, which made foreign contact more difficult. It may have been easier to approach areas on the margins of Etruria, which explains the roles played by the Etruscan cities of Campania and Veii. The essential problem for the Greeks was establishing contact with people who were locally influential. To this end, a typical custom of the Greek aristocratic world took on an important role: the consumption of wine according to a ceremony that established or consolidated links of solidarity between people of similar status. This was the vehicle that opened the gates of the Tyrrhenian cities to Euboean merchants. In fact, the Greek vases that were imported during this time are either cups (with semicircular pendants, chevrons, birds, meanders, and other decorative motifs) or pitchers for pouring wine (*oinochoai*).

This custom, which may already have been taking the shape of the symposium, was quickly embraced by the Tyrrhenian elites, who also introduced these types of vases in their grave goods. Demand for these vessels helped spark a local industry in their manufacture, which picked up techniques from Greek potters and adapted

the typical Geometric ornamentation of the Greek repertory to forms from the local repertory. These contacts, together with the wine ceremony, quickly spread to Etruria as well.

This stage, which featured rather ceremonial relations between the Greeks and Etruscans, ended with the foundation of the first Greek settlement at Pithecusae (Ischia). This small settlement of Euboean merchants and artisans was decisively important in transmitting important innovations in the technical and cultural fields and in changing the face of Etruscan society. Of course, it was only one aspect of a much larger shift that resulted from new cultural fermentations in the Near East, which affected all of the Greek Mediterranean over the course of the eighth century B.C. Within this picture, which corresponds with the beginnings of the polis, the custom of writing spread throughout Greece. The Homeric poems and the *Theogony* of Hesiod were drafted, establishing myths and models that were

destined to influence forms of collective imagery for a long time to come.

For the Tyrrhenian region, Pithecusae, the western terminus for Euboean crossings, was chiefly responsible for spreading these innovations, which began in the East at the emporium of Al Mina at the mouth of the Orontes ('Asi) River. Knowledge of the alphabet was transmitted to Etruria through Pithecusae. The first traces of Homeric poems can be found in inscriptions on vases, such as the famous Nestor Cup, and in aspects of the funerary rite of cremation, which was inspired by the model of the funeral of Patroclus. Euboean artisans helped to spread new techniques for working jewelry and metals and for making pottery. Although the Greeks were the main players in the process of acculturation, it nevertheless ran in both directions, creating a mixed culture. This phenomenon took on particular relevance in the field of personal clothing, where new types of fibulae, which were reworked from forms that were in use from the indigenous world, spread throughout the peninsula and Sicily with little deference to the local ethnic and cultural differences.

The tendency for society to develop along the lines of large kinship groups had already begun in this period. During the Orientalizing period that followed, it led to the birth of an aristocratic structure in Campania as well. The systematic examination of the necropoleis of Pontecagnano, led in recent years by M. A. Cuozzo, has helped us recognize that the behavior of aristocratic groups was imprinted by a strong partiality, even in selecting which outside communities might enter into social relations and marriages with their clan. Some groups were connected to the

Lazio area, and in that case, the grave goods included the typical vases of thin brown impasto, particularly *skyphoi* and small amphorae decorated with spirals or incised herons. Other groups maintained close relations with the valleys of the Sele and Ofanto Rivers, as can be seen in the complex feminine jewelry sets composed of personal objects in bronze.

This partiality was displayed not only in grave goods but in funerary customs as well. There seem to have been two main models. In the first, which can be compared to indigenous cultures in Campania and Lazio, the task of representing the status of the group was entrusted to women. A number of female burials are marked by extraordinarily rich grave goods, with numerous metal objects of personal adornment; these form a sort of "traditional costume" that often allows the deceased to be identified as native to another community. In Pontecagnano these were generally women who came from the valley of the Sele, from the area of the Oliveto-Cairano culture.

The other model, which we could call innovative, was inspired by the Greek conception of heroism, as represented by princely tombs not only at Pontecagnano but also in the great cities of Lazio (Praeneste), coastal Etruria (Caere and Vetulonia), and in Greek Cumae. This choice was the prerogative of adult males

At left, silver *oinochoe*, seventh century B.C., from Tomb 928 in Pontecagnano (Salerno). Pontecagnano, Museo dell'Agro Picentino

At right, silver *kotyle*, seventh century B.C., from Tomb 928 in Pontecagnano (Salerno). Pontecagnano, Museo dell'Agro Picentino

who, in homage to tradition, presented themselves as warriors. Nevertheless, the placement of the weapons within the graves tended to deemphasize their importance, while the image of the deceased was primarily communicated through grave goods of luxurious, exotic-looking objects. Although inhumation was predominantly used at this point, cremation was reserved for these celebrities.

Among the "princely" tombs uncovered at Pontecagnano, the oldest, dating to about 700 B.C., features an entirely unusual treatment of the corpse. The bones do not seem to have been cremated, although they were gathered in a large bronze *lebetes*, as was typical only in cremation tombs. As in other princely tombs, the deceased was accompanied by a chariot, whose presence in this tomb is demonstrated by two extraordinary pieces of armor for a horse's head, made of sheet bronze with embossed decorations of hunting scenes with people and animals. These were made in northern Etruria.

The presence of chariots is also demonstrated in the contemporary Tomb 104 in Cumae (Fondo Artiaco) and in Tombs 926 and 928 in Pontecagnano, which were twin tombs that can be dated to the second quarter of the seventh century B.C. Here the tomb has been divided into two spaces: a *thalamos* and an enclosure. The *thalamos*, a *cista* made from slabs of local travertine, is located in a pit at the center of the enclosure. It contained a bronze *lebes*, in which the cremated body of the deceased was preserved together with rather valuable objects. Andirons, skewers, and other objects connected to the domestic hearth (*hestia*)—which was also a symbol of the group's continuity—took their places within the enclosure.

The objects that make up the grave goods, especially *lebetes* and other vases made of bronze and other precious metals, are partly of exotic origins, having been imported from northern Syria and Cyprus. The rest were produced locally or in Greece. The same assortment of objects can be found in other princely tombs on the Tyrrhenian coast and it seems to represent a sort of funerary custom that was adapted to the needs of "princes," independent of their ethnic origin. This demonstrates how local elites, whether Greek or

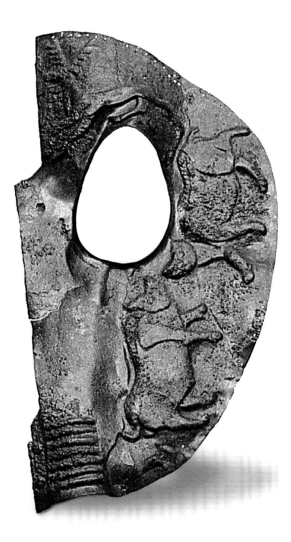

Etruscan artisans and merchants. It also facilitated the spread of luxury goods, bronze tableware, and weapons along the inland valleys of Basilicata and the Melfese River.

Relations with Etruria experienced a strong resurgence starting in the last quarter of that century. For about thirty years, thin bucchero imported from Caere became an important component in rich grave goods, along with Corinthian pottery. This renewed interest foreshadowed a sort of refounding of Campanian Etruria. Nevertheless, certain aspects of this quickening of Etruscan-Campanian relations—both political and cultural—bear further scrutiny.

The extension of Etruscan political dominance over Campania can essentially be demonstrated by the spread of language. Inscriptions on vases chart this spread, in Etruscan cities such as Pontecagnano and Capua—and the new settlement of Fratte di Salerno—and in cities of Italic origin, such as Stabiae, Pompeii, Suessula, and Nola.

Etruscan expansion met elements of resistance. It is no accident that precisely during the course of the sixth century B.C. an attempt was made to give a local language—an Italic, pre-Samnitic language that was akin to Latin and Umbrian—its written form. This experiment, which led to the development of an alphabet of the southern-Picenum type, was destined to fail. Italic inscriptions, although created over the course of the fifth century, use the southern Etruscan alphabet, with the exception of the language of Salerno, where the alphabet of Achaean Poseidonia prevailed. This gives the impression that, although the Etruscans had a dominant

Bronze armor for a horse's head, about 700 B.C., from Tomb 4461 in Pontecagnano (Salerno). Pontecagnano, Museo dell'Agro Picentino

Latin, had already formed a solid class that shared common cultural and ideological expressions.

Despite the intense relations described here, for Campania the seventh century B.C. represents a time of relative autonomy from Etruria. Even in Pontecagnano and Capua, which remained firmly anchored in their Etruscan tradition, a repertory of typically local vases was developed at this time. During this period Pontecagnano became an important emporium, which favored the influx of Greek, Phoenician, and

role, they were dealing with people of Italic descent who could express themselves in writing.

The involvement of the Greeks is also consistent with this picture. During the course of the sixth century B.C. the sanctuary of Apollo was created, looking out to sea at the edge of the inhabited area in Pontecagnano. Dedications in the Achaean alphabet with the name of the god, which date from the sixth to the fourth centuries, lead one to think that the sanctuary preserved its Greek character throughout this period. As Colonna suggests, it is also probable that, as in Pompeii, Pyrgi, Gravisca, and Adria, the divinity there had the role of protector over a small community of Greek artisans and merchants. It is also true, however, that especially during the sixth century the cities of the Tyrrhenian demonstrated a deep interest in Delphic Apollo for the political meaning of this worship. As L. Cerchiai has shown, in the case of Pompeii this took on features of a true civic cult. For individuals, the consumption of wine helped to overcome problems of linguistic and cultural diversity. Greek convivial inscriptions are found on vases from Fratte and Pontecagnano; here, Etruscan, Italic, and Greek elements are mixed together in complex relationships, some of them erotic, which well suited the atmosphere of the symposium.

Campania, therefore, appears to have been a world in which different peoples and cultures lived together and confronted one another. The assertion of Etruscan dominance, which also had a determining role in the forging of a new "citizen" culture, does not seem to have been in the nature of a colonial conquest. The refounding of a number of preexisting Italic settlements and the creation of a number of new settlements, such as Fratte di Salerno or Marcina near Vietri, seem to have been the initiatives of individual members of the Etruscan elite, who had come south to seek their own political space. The significance of their undertakings, which led to the cultural unification of Campania, was boosted by the role of Capua, Campanian "Etruscan-ness," and by the intense cultural relations that existed between Campania and Etruria.

At this point we see an Etruscan "coloring" in cultural material, which united all cities in Campania regardless of their political position. Bucchero, which at the close of the seventh century had been a sign of trade relations with Etruria, was now routinely produced in Campania, both in cities of ancient Etruscan tradition, such as Capua and Pontecagnano, and in those of Italic origin, such as Nocera and Caudium. The repertory that Etruria had acquired was enriched with either local forms or others that imitated the Greek repertory, such as a tasteful series of kraters with floral incised decorations from Caudium.

Next to this running production of pottery for the table, more demanding enterprises came and went. For example, the production of figured vases asserted itself for a brief period during the first half of the sixth century, imitating Corinthian-type pottery produced in Etruria. As L. Cerchiai has recognized, there were two schools that imitated the Etruscan-Corinthian workshops of Vulci and Tarquinia, respectively. Works from these two circles were found in tombs located in various funerary areas. This demonstrates once more that each group entertained preferential relations with one or another of the Etrurian cities.

In addition to typical motifs of Etruscan-Corinthian pottery, there were original subjects, such as the extraordinary *alabastron* with a Gorgon, or in the now-famous *kotyle* by the Wolf's Head Painter. The formation of a "Campanian architectural style," which was developed between Cumae and Capua and led to the building of the first monumental sanctuaries, had a different significance. This phenomenon has allowed us to discern important features of the active political process that played out on the Campanian plain over the course of the sixth century. As already mentioned, Capua had quickly achieved a sort of cultural convergence with preexisting Italic cities even by the early Iron Age. This reality is reflected in a passage from Strabo (5.4.3), who defines Capua as the capital of the twelve Etruscan cities.

Ever since the foundation of Cumae by Euboean colonists during the second half of the eighth century B.C., Capua had had to divide its territory with this important neighbor. An analysis of the historical tradition relating to Aristodemus, a tyrant at Cumae at the close of the sixth century, confirms that the Etruscan dominant class at Capua had strong political ties to the aristocrats of Cumae. Aside from brief periods of crisis, such as one caused by the tyranny of Aristodemus, the two cities seem to have lived harmoniously. This may explain why, in 525 B.C., Capua remained neutral in a terrible battle that pitted a coalition of Etruscans, Umbri, and Dauni against the Cumaeans.

A lasting harmony between the dominating classes, which disrupts the simple categorization of ethnic history, explains the rise of a coherent architectural style that Capua and its dependent cities on the

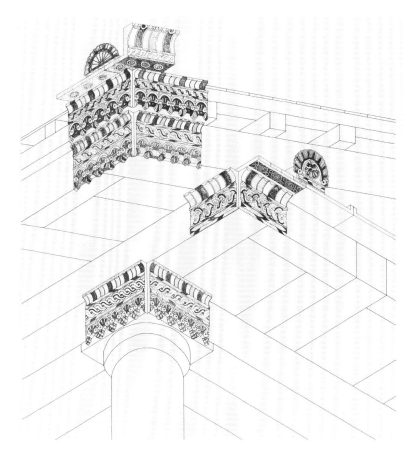

Below, Etruscan-Corinthian *kotyle* with a Gorgon, sixth century B.C., from Tomb 856 in Pontecagnano (Salerno). Pontecagnano, Museo dell'Agro Picentino

On the facing page, clay figure holding a piglet from Teano (Caserta), Santuario del Fondo Ruozzo

Campanian plain had in common with Cumae and Pithecusae itself.

The full development of a system of architectural terra-cottas known as Etruscan-Campanian—although they would be better defined as Greek-Campanian—can be dated to the third quarter of the sixth century B.C., although one can see the style beginning to form during an earlier period in materials uncovered in a lucky excavation during the last century in the sanctuary of Fondo Patturelli in Capua.

M. Bonghi Jovino has recently theorized the existence of a phase parallel to that of Murlo's early buildings, therefore dating to the beginning of the sixth century B.C., based on a number of problematic fragments. The oldest antefixae, a type with a completely round head, date to the same period and are in the Daedalic tradi-

tion. These are similar to ones from the Corinthian colony of Kerkyra (Corfu). In addition, other antefixae from the first half of the century—the simplest types with palmettes, Gorgoneion, or more complex images taken from mythology—can all be ascribed to the Corinthian tradition.

As L. Cerchiai has well observed, a fragment of a revetment plaque with lyre players also demonstrates the presence in Capua of facings similar to those on Etruscan buildings in Murlo and Acquarossa. Taking into account the fact that these Etruscan plaques were based on models from Magna Graecia, specifically Poseidonia and Metaponto, one must ask whether the example of Capua should be considered a contribution that was isolated from Etruria, or if rather Campania must be recognized as the path for the transmission of models from Magna Graecia to Etruria.

By the third quarter of the sixth century, the Campanian roof was already well defined. On its sides it showed a line of antefixes within a nimbus of leaves in the shape of reversed palmettes, with Gorgoneion or female heads, enlivened by polychromy and decorative motifs painted on the bottom of the fillets. Facings with simple or double-braided motifs and *anthemia* (florals) covered the beams. A bipartite *sima* was located on the sloping edge of the roof, with a strigil-shaped crown.

The sheer quantity and variety of types of architectural terra-cottas uncovered at Capua in the Fondo Patturelli sanctuary give an idea of the building fervor that characterized the Campanian city during the second half of the sixth century B.C. The prevalence of Campanian roofs in their canonical form imprinted a sign of

Capua's political hegemony upon all the cities of the surrounding plain, as far as the sanctuary of Marica at the mouth of the Garigliano. The harmonizing effects of this model were felt as far as Lazio (Satricum) and Etruria (Caere). Here, as at Satricum and Veii and in at least one case in Capua as well, the beam at the top of the temple must have been surmounted by sculptures in full relief, as the only surviving figure attests.

Capua's extraordinary development was promoted by a gradual change in equilibrium in the Salerno area. Already during the course of the seventh century B.C., Capua had surpassed Pontecagnano in controlling traffic toward Mezzogiorno. During the sixth century its ascent was favored by the new settlement of Fratte, perhaps ancient Irnum, which was in a favorable position with respect to the inland route despite its proximity to the sea. It should be no surprise, therefore, that Fratte immediately placed itself under Capua's protection, as demonstrated by architectural terra-cottas of a Campanian type that decorate the only sanctuary known to date. Through Fratte, Capua consolidated its relations with Poseidonia. As Kästner has recognized, during the last quarter of the century, the influence of terra-cottas from Poseidonia was evident in antefixae from Capua, with feminine heads in lotus flowers. It is also probable that Poseidonia stimulated the creation of the great Etruscan clay statues of the Archaic period.

The flourishing of Capua during the late Archaic period can be seen in other fields of artisanship. Bronzework reached new levels, as we see from the great spherical vases (*dinoi*) with lids holding a forest of figurines in full relief. So did terra-cottas and the art of pottery decoration, with various workshops producing black-figured vases between the end of the sixth and the first decades of the fifth centuries B.C.

The development of the arts and trades attracted a large number of workers from the countryside into Capua, and these individuals provided a distinctive contribution not only in the most humble work but also in the most prestigious artisan activities. This consistent group of rural Italic peoples must have increasingly felt like true participants in the fortunes of the city, despite being excluded from every political activity. The same phenomenon could be seen at Cumae, which in this period underwent a harsh oligarchic "restructuring" after the slaying of Aristodemus and his family.

In both cities, the dominating class did not have the farsightedness of the Greek governors of Neapolis, who knew well enough to progressively integrate the Italic peoples into city government. Instead, the artisan class was penalized by a strong downturn in public building. As an almost tangible expression of this turning point, the city was enclosed within a circle of walls that obliterated one of the most significant artisan neighborhoods.

As L. Cerchiai points out, the oligarchy considered this turning point as its true refounding, and perhaps it was this same ideology that lay behind the tradition transmitted by Cato (in Velleius Paterculus 1.71), which dates the foundation of Capua to 471 B.C. The ideology connected to these events is eloquently expressed in two tombs that were discovered just outside the city during the nineteenth century. One of these tombs had a cup by the Brygos

Painter, one of the masters of Attic ceramic decoration, which shows Herakles defending Hera from the assault of the Sileni.

The choice of this myth, and those portrayed on other Attic vases that make up the grave goods, responds to an iconographic program aimed at making a strong political statement: legitimizing an aristocracy that claimed to be the original inhabitants of the area, and at the same time reaffirming its proximity to the Greek world.

The other tomb, from around the same period, was a chamber tomb with painted decorations. The only figurative scene was on the back wall, where two cloaked figures focused on playing checkers in the presence of two boys. As Cerchiai shrewdly points out, this scene is firmly linked to the ideology of the oligarchy. In fact, the game of checkers evokes political activity, "which plans the city and the roles of the citizens with the same severity with which a player moves the piece on the ordered field of the checkerboard."

The blindness of the oligarchies contributed to growing tensions that exploded between 423 and 421 B.C., when the Campani, who had already become part of Capua and Cumae as a subordinate class, took control over the two cities.

This political restructuring, which the ancient sources considered a true conquest because of the sudden and traumatic manner of its coming, in reality had a long gestation period over the course of the fifth century B.C. The Italic world had matured culturally, thanks to the continual relations with the Etruscans and the Greek. In this process, the circulation of Attic figurative pottery had played an important role, with its representations of myths and the civic world.

The acquisition of these objects for houses and tombs was not motivated purely by the desire for social prestige. Above all, it was a reaffirmation that the local elites participated fully in Greek culture, even in everyday life. Stories that told of the Greek roots of the peoples and cities of the West, which had developed from Greek colonies mingling with local populations, now helped the locals to claim the "Greekness" of their origins.

These instances seem to have even influenced the faraway workshop of the Ceramicus Painter in Athens. In fact, a number of myths that were less well known in his homeland appear on highly prized vases that were exported to Campania. This is especially evident at Caudium, where two Attic kraters bear representations of Epeus and Philoctetes, two of the heroes most active in founding the cities of the West.

The "Campanian conquest" of Capua and Cumae did not signal a sharp break in the lives of these cities. Nevertheless it ended the Etruscan presence in Campania. It was just one aspect of a more general phenomenon, which saw Etruria close itself off during the fourth century, in the face of the impending Roman expansionism.

The Etruscans in Lucania

| ANGELO BOTTINI

An area inhabited between the sixth and the fourth centuries B.C. on top of the plateau in Serra di Vaglio (Potenza)

While preserving the modern form of the name established in the Augustan era for the huge "Regio III" (*Lucania et Bruttii*), the small modern region that today is called Basilicata represents only part of the territory of that Italic people. Lucania once extended on the Tyrrhenian Sea from Poseidonia (Paestum) to Laos and on the Ionian Sea from Sybaris (Thourioi) to Metaponto. It even included a large strip of land to the east, from the plateaus around Mount Vulture to Murgia in Matera, which was originally Apulian.

This geographically heterogeneous land has no clear natural borders. It was, however, blessed with a network of watercourses that, reaching the area's three marine frontiers, guaranteed access into and passage through a territory that, not coincidentally, had been the home of various ethnic groups long before the Lucani arrived.

Beginning with the first decades of the seventh century B.C., this patchwork of ethnic groups was forced to compete with the developed phenomenon of Greek col-onization. To the original presence of Ionians was added the aggressive activity of the Achaeans of the Peloponnese. The Ionian colonization culminated in the foundation of Siris (Polieion) by the people of Colophon, who had abandoned their city when King Gyges of Lydia threatened it about 680–650 B.C.

In the last third of the century, their dominion over this part of Magna Graecia was supported by the parallel rise of Metaponto on the Ionian side, between the Bradano and the Basento Rivers, and of Poseidonia just south of the mouth of the Sele River on the Tyrrhenian Sea. It was this organic political system, centered at Sybaris, that Strabo (6.1.13) credited with control over four *ethne* (tribal enti-ties) and twenty-five poleis ("urban" communities).

These Hellenic clusters were more interested in defining relationships of dependence than in physically occupying the inland regions. At the same time, they caused vast coastal "village communities" (linked to the Illyric culture of Salento) to

disappear and spurred the development of more remote sites that up to that time had been of very modest importance. Those benefiting most from this change were the Oenotrii in the wide southwest valleys, who had inherited the Tyrrhenian culture of pit tombs, as well as the inhabitants of the central and northern areas.

At any rate, everyone seems to have been affected by the population growth, which coincided with forms of accentuated social development related to the organization of the nobility. In some cases, this organization resulted in the rise of "royal" figures, individuals who were known to Greek historians. Signs of this social change can be found in the phenomenon of "emergent" tombs, to which we owe most of our knowledge about relationship of the locals with the Etruscans and other even more ancient peoples. Our understanding to date points not to a direct Etruscan presence but rather to a wide range of trade activity that included an Etruscan component. On the one hand, we know that the southernmost outpost of Etruscan culture during this period was Pontecagnano, just a few miles north of Poseidonia. On the other hand, there was also an obvious interest in trade goods (above all metals) that were furnished by the various poleis of Magna Graecia. These communities certainly joined in the prevailing (Etruscan) fashion for acquiring things that ruled the entire Archaic economy. At the same time, Sybaris, the center of the local territorial system, was one of the most celebrated hubs of trade in the entire Mediterranean.

Finds from the native environment, which were sometimes part of a deliberate ritual concealment, represent just a fraction of the goods that the Etruscan people brought to the Greek cities. Most of these goods were used and exchanged, and they were rarely preserved, even before the destructive upheaval that almost completely wiped them out. Still, the presence of these goods at the heart of the Lucanian valleys in itself merits special attention. From the moment that the natural land routes began to be exploited (the sea route would have required navigating around the Calabrian peninsula and passing through the treacherous strait), collaborative relationships with the Italic peoples began. One can imagine merchant caravans in seasonal transit and—more likely—a series of "consecutive" exchanges from one community to another. A certain balance of power was necessary to gain a foothold in this trade circuit (the line between "physical control" of the traffic channels and outright extortion was extremely thin; piracy was a common practice as a result), and one of the most efficient tools that the Greeks adopted was a gradual process of acculturation, whose aim was to curry favor with the dominant groups and win them over on both the ideological and material levels. The adoption of certain customs, such as sacred and profane conviviality based on meat and wine, which came quite early, led to the acquisition of cooking and banqueting accoutrements. New modes of self-representation and the mythological protection of elites imply that forms of religiosity and value systems were shared. Residential structures were built (and perhaps sacred ones as well, which were decorated with figured friezes) that subverted the traditional urban plan of the inhabited areas. We also see the development and enrichment of women's ornamental jewelry and of religious and sacred symbols that were typical of Italic tradition, such as the acquisition of Hoplite defensive armor for display purposes.

The custom of bestowing valued goods on the deceased allows us to establish certain facts. A significant portion of manufactured goods during the Archaic period that were imported for this purpose, especially metal plate, were produced in the Tyrrhenian region and in some cases Etruria itself, perhaps more frequently than in the Campanian area. We have as proof an Etruscan inscription written on the rim of a *lebetes* from Tomb 106 in Braida di Vaglio; and the bronze flask from Tomb 110 in Chiaromonte, one of the most important cities of the Oenotrii, which is most comparable to Tarquinian materials from the late eighth century B.C. It confirms that contacts were quite early.

For the entire sixth century B.C., basins (some with beaded rims) and *lebetes* prevailed in terms of their number. Somewhat less popular were umbilicated *paterae* (*phialai*) and *kotylai*. Among the vessels for pouring were pitchers (*oinochoai*), especially the Rhodian type; their complex variants make it difficult to pinpoint their origins, but those that were less developed technically are certainly Etruscan. Curiously, works in bucchero appear not to have been very widespread, but mostly rare or in series.

The most striking funerary contexts show additional pieces of a peculiar nature and purpose, some of which are even unique: among them is the bronze barrel with a pair of spouts and female protomes in sheet bronze that had been worked with a hammer, from Tomb 76 in Chiaromonte. Its Tyrrhenian origin, while probable, can only be presumed for the moment.

This situation obscures somewhat the local dynasties' role in commissioning

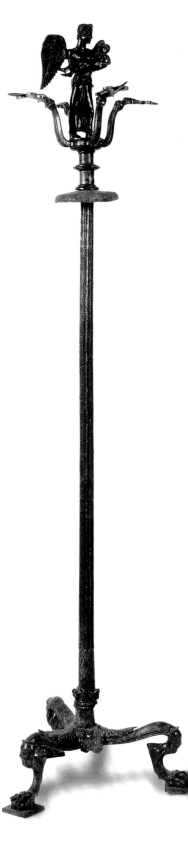

these objects; the Tyrrhenian influences are manifest in certain shapes of Sub-geometric Oenotrian pottery from the late seventh century B.C. The Etruscans' role may have run deeper than simply acting as suppliers of handmade goods. Greek culture did not prevail on every level. The high profile afforded to Italic women is evident in the banquet environment (among other things, their jewelry contains an impressive quantity of amber, which certainly must have arrived through the trade routes). This certainly does not derive from a Greek concept; indeed, the Greeks excluded women from their activities whenever possible. In the field of architecture, the introduction of "palatial" structures during the course of the sixth century B.C. can be directly connected to models that were Etruscan, in their attitude even more than in their architecture. And with all due deference to an *argumentum ex silentio,* it must be observed that while the locals imported decorative elements from Metaponto, such as terracotta figurative friezes (at Braida di Vaglio, but elsewhere in the area as well), they did not adopt a Greek temple structure along with them.

In the central area of the region, Etruscan and Etruscan-Campanian products also reached cities belonging to the Dauni of Melfi. In this case, the people who exchanged these goods were not looking to gain Greek partners. Cases such as the insertion of biconic ollas into a pair of "princely" tombs in Pontecagnano, 926 and 928 (sealed in the second quarter of the seventh century B.C.), show that the partners in these exchanges could have been the same indigenous communities that settled on the border between the Apennines and the first Apulian terraces. The ollas have "curtain" decorations (*a tenda*) and are traceable to the Ofanto area at the foot of Mount Vulture, immediately adjacent to Daunia.

The Archaic period was marked by extraordinary "princely" grave goods such as Tomb 279 in Lavello, but it is the fifth century B.C. that will dominate our discussion here. Once again the products of Etruscan experimentation in bronzeworking found ready customers from Ruvo Del Monte in Melfi, from Pisciolo, and from Lavello itself at Banzi. These items were often acquired in complete "services." Alongside the usual containers, the great candelabras with figured curves made their appearance in female burials. These types had originated in Vulcian factories that were oriented toward large-scale production. There were other valuable objects among these as well, such as the embossed strainer from Melfi (Tomb 64 in Ruvo Del Monte; Tomb 955 in Lavello).

From the point of view of social attitudes, these objects highlight both the introduction of the symposium (understood as a social event founded on drinking after a banquet) and the definitive establishment of the special role attributed to women of high status. Some of the largest and most beautiful carved works in amber belonged to these ladies and their companions in Melfi and Braida. These amber pieces were cut by artisans who may have had some relationship with Etruscan figurative culture, as is also the case for parallel works in other precious materials such as ivory (which were also found in the Apulian area).

Above, Tomb 76 at the Sotto la Croce necropolis in Chiaromonte (Potenza). Policoro, Museo Archeologico Nazionale della Siritide

Below, bronze basin, sixth century B.C., from Tomb 76 in Chiaromonte (Potenza). Policoro, Museo Archeologico Nazionale della Siritide

On the facing page, aerial view of the plateau of Serra di Vaglio (Potenza). *Above, at left*, the area inhabited from the sixth to the fourth centuries B.C. *Below, at right*, the fortification from the fourth century

In this fifth-century landscape, the cities of the Oenotrii are nowhere to be found. At the time, they were almost entirely reduced to silence by the sudden destruction of Sybaris (which occurred in 510 B.C. at the hands of their nearby rival Croton), which had tremendous consequences for the region. This crisis continued to be felt some decades later, around the transition between the fifth and fourth

centuries: groups of Oscan-speakers who originated from the southern Apennine area would spread into much of the rest of the indigenous world, to the point of becoming the *ethnos* of the Lucani.

The consequent phenomena of radical transformation and rearrangement also weighed heavily upon trade relations with the Etruscan world, which do not seem to have picked up again even during the period that followed. Finds from the same southern valleys that once hosted the Oenotrii and then the Lucani show a much more modest cultural impact: a past filled with metal goods and a tendency to preserve the most valuable items. The great tomb of Roccanova thus includes among its materials another Vulcian candelabra, produced back at the end of the fifth century B.C. It had been kept for at least two generations before being buried.

The Etruscans in Apulia

| ETTORE M. DE JULIIS

Above, bronze basin with a beaded rim, second half of the seventh century B.C., from Tomb 1/1982 in the Cupola quarter in Manfredonia (Foggia). Taranto, Museo Nazionale

Apulia never had a permanent or organized presence of Etruscans within its territory. Nevertheless, there are many important Etruscan objects that either reached Apulia from the Etruscan region or were imitated locally by artisans who were either native or had immigrated. Despite being less apparent than elsewhere, we can nevertheless discern the Etruscan civilization's cultural loans to Apulia and its consistent and lasting influences over it.

First, it may be useful to recall the categories and classes of Etruscan goods or their close imitations that have been discovered on Apulian soil. These fall within a wide chronological arc between the end of the seventh and the end of the fifth centuries B.C. Among the categories of objects are bronzes, pottery, jewelry, and works in ivory and amber. Among the bronzes, a certain basin with a beaded rim that was found in northern and central Apulia, from Canosa di Puglia to Rutigliano, deserves mention. Fibulae of the "proto-Certosa" type can be placed alongside these (from the late seventh to the middle of the sixth centuries), as can those of the "Certosa" type (from the final decades of the sixth to the middle of the fifth centuries). The latter spread exclusively in Daunia, where they were imported or transferred from Etruscanized Campania. Another significant class of Etruscan bronzes, even though only a few examples have been seen in Apulia, is the *cistae a cordoni,* which were Etruscan in origin and created in Felsina or the Po region in general. It was not by

Amber pendant sculpted in
the form of a woman's
face, from the early
decades of the fifth cen-
tury B.C., from the Tomb
of the Amber in Ruvo di
Puglia (Bari). Naples, Museo
Archeologico

chance, therefore, that "Apulian" examples were found in southern coastal cities (Gnathia, Brindisi, Rudiae, Cavallino, and Taranto) that were connected to the ports of Picenum and Spina by a sea route.

A tripod with supports that are twisted into an S also seems to be from the Adriatic. It was found in Oria and can be dated to the final quarter of the seventh century B.C. Its entire class of objects can be attributed to workshops in Vetulonia, although one example was attested in Bologna. Two strainers with wavy rod handles and rounded shapes, which were among the grave goods of two rich tombs in central Apulia (Ginosa and Rutigliano), are also signs of long-term relationships between the Etruscan world and Apulia. These can be dated to the fifth century. A candelabra found in a tomb in Ruvo di Puglia, which had until recently been ignored, is preserved

at the Museo di Napoli and rounds out the picture of Etruscan works in bronze. It can be dated to the second half of the fifth century and is linked to two other well-known examples that were discovered in Ruvo del Monte and at Melfi. Together these confirm that a trans-Apennine connection, from Campania to Melfi and central Apulia, was already established at an early period.

Moving on to pottery, a good number of bucchero vases are present throughout Apulia, especially in the north. Two fragments of *bucchero sottile*, which belonged respectively to a pitcher (*oinochoe*) and a cup (*kylix*), were found in Tomb 104/1979 in Rutigliano; as a result, the tomb was attributed to a foreigner. Tomb 3/1965 in San Severo (Guadone) also must have belonged to a foreigner. It contained just one skeleton that was lying on its back, which contrasts with Apulian customs that

called for the deceased to be buried in the fetal position. Two vases in *bucchero pesante* were also preserved in this tomb. Other vases in *bucchero pesante* were found in cities of northern Daunia, such as San Severo, San Paolo Civitate, Bovino, Carlantino, and Arpi. These were the outcome of relationships forged over the course of the sixth century B.C. between inland Daunia and Etruscan Campania.

The works in bucchero found in the Taranto area (Taranto Satùro and Faggiano) can be attributed to an entirely different route, a sea route from the Tyrrhenian to the Ionian Sea. These items were probably brought back on trading voyages between Greece and Etruria. In the pottery realm, we must not overlook a group of black-figured vases, especially column kraters that were of such high quality that they are easily distinguished from local figurative products and more closely resemble Attic works.

These vases have been attributed to artisans who came from Etruscan Campania along the Ofanto route, or, preferably, Etruscan artisans from the circle of the Micali Painter who came from Vulci, a city that was in a crisis of transformation between the late sixth and the early fifth centuries B.C. The findspots for these vases are in central and southern Apulia (Ruvo,

Rutigliano, Bari, Egnazia, Rocavecchia,
Cavallino, and Vaste).

The area of jewelry and other luxury
goods is another that demonstrates a
significant presence of either imported
Etruscan objects or imitations that were
probably by artisans of Etruscan culture.
The former can be found in Peucezia,
especially in Ruvo and other cities of the
inland area of Bari, such as Noicattaro and
Rutigliano. One gold necklace, of extremely
high quality and surely of Etrurian origin,
shows sileni heads, garlands, and lotus
flowers; it was found in Ruvo and is preserved at the Museo Nazionale in Naples.
It can be dated to the decade between 490
and 480 B.C. Numerous pieces of earlier
Etruscan and Magna Graecian jewelry, from
the second half of the sixth century, were

found at Ruvo, mixed together in the same
tomb contexts.

This phenomenon can be explained
through the strong demand on the part
of rich local aristocracies for expert goldsmiths, who came from both Magna
Graecia and Etruria and moved to the
indigenous cities of Peucezia. There these
artists established workshops, which were
then commissioned to produce handmade
goods of a local type, though with a technique that was clearly of foreign origin.

Among these objects were the so-called
"Apulian circles," which at one time were
thought to be "supports for ointment vases"
and today are better interpreted as hair ornaments worn at the temples. In the same category of locally commissioned works are the
great fibulae, with inflated arches and long
clasps ending with conical buttons, which
were later changed for a tiny ram's head.

Two small ivory revetment plaques that
must have adorned a jewel box either of
Etruscan make or from Etruria belong to
this same category of luxury product, which
was aimed at satisfying the needs of the
emerging aristocracy of Peucezia. These
were decorated with a banquet scene and a
biga pulled by winged horses, respectively.
They were discovered at a tomb in Ruvo,
date between 540 and 525 B.C., and have
been attributed, along with their entire type,
to shops in Vulci, from which they were
imported through Etruscanized Campania.

Finally, we must not overlook amber that
was cut into figures, although these deserve
further investigation. Substantial groups of
amber in the shape of human figures were
uncovered both in Canosa and Ruvo. The
Archaic characteristics of these works seem
due to the products they were modeled
after, which go back to the end of the sixth

century and are close to the Ionic style. Later, during the course of the fifth century, specialized artisans left the Campanian area of their origins to settle in Lucania and Puglia, where they continued a faithful adherence to their initial patterns.

The close cultural relations between Etruscan Campania and Daunia during the second half of the sixth and fifth centuries B.C. were also demonstrated in the area of architectural decoration. In fact, with the late passage from straw huts to more solid structures of stone, wood, and unfired brick, the use of terra-cotta antefixae with feminine heads in nimbi, which were typi-cal of the Etruscan region and widespread in Capua, was adopted in Daunia.

This type of ornamentation spread in northern Daunia between the end of the sixth century B.C. and the early decades of the century that followed, while the south-ern part of the region acquired a type of Greek "Gorgoneion" antefix. The distribu-tion area of the antefixae with nimbi (San Severo, San Paolo Civitate, Lucera, and Arpi) coincided, substantially, with that of bucchero vases, demonstrating a long and uninterrupted relationship between Campania and central and northern Daunia.

Gold pendant, second half of the sixth century B.C., from a tomb in Canosa di Puglia (Bari). Taranto, Museo Nazionale

In addition to the arrival of Etruscan manufactured goods in Apulia and their imitation, and the influence of immigrant artisans on local craftsmanship, a number of the Etruscan world's significant loans to and influences on central and northern Apulian culture deserve our consideration.

The first is recognizable in the introduction of underground tombs, the so-called little cave tombs (*grotticella*) that first appeared in Apennine and Murgian sites (Ascoli Satriano, Lucera, and Gravina). These appeared only in the second half of the fifth century B.C. and then spread densely in Daunia and Peucezia in the century that followed. The passage from a simple pit or *cassone* tomb to an underground tomb was not accidental and implies an alteration, albeit partial, in funerary ideology. Excluding the Magna Graecian model for obvious reasons—as being typologically, geographically, and culturally alien—the origins of such contributions must have gone back to the Etruscanized Tyrrhenian

area, with whom inland central and northern Apulia still preserved close relations at that time.

A second, fundamental loan on the part of the Etruscan world to the central and northern Apulian culture can be recognized in the use of funerary figurative painting. This, too, like the underground tombs, first appeared at an inland site in central Apulia; it later spread, but only to central and northern Apulia and not further south. There, by contrast, the inhabitants used a type of decorative painting that originated in Taranto. The latter was made up of Geometric and floral elements with tiny representations of objects and animals. The oldest examples of figurative painting in Apulia on record are in a chamber tomb in Gravina (a frieze of riders) and in the famous Tomb of the Dancers in Ruvo, both from the end of the fifth century B.C. There are other tombs from later in the fourth century with painted human figures that were discovered in Arpi, Canosa, and Egnazia.

The Etruscans in Calabria

| CLAUDIO SABBIONE

Above, the Calabrian coast at the Strait of Messina, north of Reggio Calabria. *In the background, at right,* the Tyrrhenian Sea; *at left,* Messina

On the facing page, the rock of Scilla, seen from the south

Within the picture of relationships between Magna Graecia and the Etruscan world—both central Italy and Campania—the role of the Greek cities in present-day Calabria has largely remained in the dark. The Calabrian poleis have yielded relatively few pieces of evidence in comparison to other regions of southern Italy, and their study has not been especially in-depth. In recent summaries relating to the interaction between

Etruria and Magna Graecia, facts concerning Calabria have been neglected, and the 1993 study convention on Magna Graecia, dedicated to relations between the Phoenicians and the Etruscans, saw specific reports on Campania, Basilicata, and Apulia, but not on Calabria. In effect, the difficulties in attempting a summary originate from a lack of systematic and homogeneous fact-finding from the various Calabrian cities. The ancient literary sources offer little help. Strabo (6.1.5) recalls how Anaxilas fortified the rock of Scilla (Skyllaion) against Etruscan pirates. This information, which is often discussed in studies on Etruscan piracy, is not accompanied by archaeological or monumental facts that might specify the nature and substance of such a settlement or help define a precise chronology.

The ancient sources do not support modern theories that Sybaris played at special role as a commercial and cultural link between Ionia and Etruria. These theories became obsolete when it was established that the isthmian routes had only local or regional uses, ones that did not lend

Two bone plaques. *Above*, a fish, late sixth to fifth centuries B.C. *Below*, two banqueters, 530–500 B.C., from Locri (Reggio Calabria). Reggio Calabria, Museo Nazionale

themselves to trade with distant places, and that the archaeological physiognomy of Sybaris was not qualitatively any different from other main poleis on the Ionic coast of southern Italy.

Archaeological evidence of Etruscan contributions to the Greek cities of Calabria becomes more frequent around the sixth century B.C. From Sybaris only few fragments in bucchero are known, almost all *kantharoi*, the most common and characteristic form of Etruscan exports in the entire Mediterranean basin.

There have been no finds of Etruscan pottery fragments in Croton from excavations of the city area. It may be impossible to ascertain if the extremely rare Nuraghic bronze boat recently uncovered in the sanctuary of Hera Lacinia at Capo Colonna is a sign of a direct contact between Greeks and Sardinians, or if such an extraordinary and valuable find passed from Sardinia to Etruria, as did other known examples of its kind (one was found in the port sanctuary of Gravisca), and whether it then reached Croton from Etruria through other hands. Among the collections of the former Museo

Civico di Crotone—established in 1911 from private collections formed between the late 1800s and early 1900s, then joined to the Museo Archeological Statale in 1967—is a fragmentary *oinochoe* handle in bronze of a Rhodian type often seen in Etruscan works. We know neither the exact location nor the circumstances of the handle's discovery, but it probably can be traced to Croton and its territory. Its fragmentary state and hard crust lead one to rule out the possibility that it reached Croton through the modern antiquities trade.

The discovery of a bucchero *kantharos* fragment in the territory north of Croton should be noted, among excavation evidence from Serra Sanguigna, the site of an indigenous settlement on a rise immediately adjacent to Cirò Superiore. A beaded rim fragment of a bronze basin came from another settlement in Murge di Strongoli, from a disturbed funerary context. Its diameter is reduced; it is quite deformed. Its seemingly concise size and working once again pose the question of the possible presence, among other examples of this kind uncovered in Magna Graecia, of imitations that were realized in the cities of southern Italy beside imports from Etruria.

In Locri Epizefiri, the recent (1998) discovery of a small bucchero fragment (probably of a *kantharos*) from a temple dig in Marasà stands out. Small bone plaques produced at Vulci, decorated with either reclining figures or a smooth surface, belong to facings of a jewelry box. Probably they come from the sanctuary of Persephone in Mannella, as did most materials from the Candida Collection (to which these belonged). The collection, formed at Locri at the turn of the twentieth century, was acquired by the state in 1908.

Certain materials in the collections of the former Museo Civico in Reggio Calabria (which merged with the Museo Nazionale in 1954) give indications that their provenance is "from Locri," and nothing more specific. This makes their interpretation problematic. Such is the case with a Campanian black-figured amphora by the Pittore delle Code Bianche (White Tails Painter) with female figures turned toward the right, and also with a group of Faliscan Genucilia-type plates. Although black-figure pottery produced in Capua circulated in areas that were not much larger than the regional environment where it had been produced, and therefore far from Calabria, Genucilia-type plates had a much larger diffusion. The latter, however, still did not reach the Calabrian area. Their asserted provenance from Locri is an exception for both classes and leads to extremely strong doubts as to the trustworthiness of the attribution. Unfortunately, any kind of documentation on how the amphora and the plates were acquired by the Museo Civico in Reggio Calabria are long gone, as are any regarding when this acquisition occurred (although in all probability it preceded the earthquake of 1908). It does seem possible that antiquities merchants, who would have no scruples about selling materials that were foreign to Calabria to the museum of Reggio Calabria, created a false provenance of Locri. The directors of the museum between the end of the 1800s and the early 1900s were not equipped to recognize the true origins of these materials (Capua and Falerii), which were offered as being from Locri; their acquisition can thus be set down to the somewhat frantic accumulation of civic collections during that period.

Above, at left, black-figured amphora from the early decades of the fifth century B.C. by the Pittore delle Code Bianche (White Tails Painter), provenance unknown. Reggio Calabria, Museo Nazionale

Below, a single and group of Faliscan Genucilia-type plates from the fourth century B.C., provenance unknown. Reggio Calabria, Museo Nazionale

For Reggio, a great basin with a beaded rim is especially memorable. It is fragmentary, with part of an incised Greek inscription, and it was found among votive materials at the Griso-Laboccetta sanctuary.

The group of thick-walled bucchero vases studied by M. Cristofani, who recognized them as having been produced in Campania, has been given a general provenance of "Reggio" by the inventory of the Museo Civico (they were once a part of its collections), without any other geographic indications. These, too, lack any helpful documentation. Cristofani, while accepting that they originated in Reggio, prudently marked some doubts that remained, since these were materials from collections rather than from scientific excavations. It is difficult for whole vases such as these to survive a residential context, and it would be more convincing to link them to a tomb context. Nevertheless, in Reggio no Archaic urban necropoleis are known that could be linked to finds of this kind. The suspicion arises that the Campanian works in bucchero attributed to Reggio entered the Museo Civico with Faliscan and Campanian vases assigned to Locri, or at least conveyed there in a similar manner by merchants who tended to falsify their provenance to induce a sale.

The presence of Campanian works in bucchero in Reggio is certainly historically more plausible than that of the vases falsely attributed to Locri. (In fact, these did not arouse particular suspicion among researchers who came into contact with them, from Vallet to Cristofani, despite their location in an area of the Strait of Messina on routes that brought many Etruscan materials to eastern Sicily.) However, it pays to exercise caution in considering the Reggian prove-

nance of such works in bucchero. Similar considerations are possible for an Etruscan-Corinthian *aryballos* and *alabastron*, which were also in civic collections and had an asserted (although not specified or provable) provenance of Reggio. The entire subject of imitations of Corinthian pottery in Reggio (like that of most of Magna Graecia) requires further research to identify and isolate local products from the Etruscan-Corinthian ones.

The Tyrrhenian side of Calabria provides other facts of notable interest.

In Matauros an extremely small number of bucchero *kantharoi* fragments were sporadically uncovered in the area of the Archaic necropolis, where there were also some Etruscan commercial amphorae that could be traced to the *EM A* group. These had been reused as ash urns.

In Hipponion, rich votive deposits in the Scrimbia quarter yielded important bronze vases—probably Etruscan imports—such as the great basins with beaded rims (at least six examples, mostly Type C) and a strainer with a handle ending in a duck head. Among the pottery at Scrimbia was an *aryballos* in bucchero with incised Geometric motifs, and in the indigenous cities on the Tyrrhenian coast, in the province of Cosenza, an Etruscan commercial amphora was found among the votive deposits of the Imbelli sanctuary near Amantea. The latter is like those found in Matauros. Fragments of another Etruscan amphora came from the inhabited area of Petrosa near Scalea.

This brief survey is by no means exhaustive, but it offers a view of the Etruscan presence in Calabria that was poorer than in other areas of Magna Graecia with which it integrated. A few other observations are in order. The picture here is similar to what has been discovered in Sicily: The presence of works in bucchero and commercial amphorae seems in some way parallel and was primarily concentrated during the first half of the sixth century B.C.

Nevertheless in Calabria, the commercial amphorae seem to be spread only (yet never intensely) along the Tyrrhenian coast. Up to now, these objects have not been found in the great poleis of the Ionic coast, where works in bucchero (mostly *kantharoi*) were probably more widespread than current records would suggest (for example, an in-depth inspection of materials from the urban areas of Croton or Caulonia has yet to be carried out). This signals a probable sea route along the Ionic coast that could be connected to the presence of works in bucchero at Taranto and the more far-away regions of the Aegean. The above-mentioned vases were used either for containing wine (amphorae) or drinking it (*kantharoi*), and this leads one to conclude that the commercial movement in Etruria toward Campania was essentially based on wine, with all the implications that such a product brings (i.e., the symposium and its connotations of the elevated social status of its participants).

The distribution of more valuable materials, such as basins with beaded rims or jewelry boxes decorated with bone plaques (and perhaps the Nuraghic small boat from Capo Colonna as well), may have somewhat different features. The influx of such precious objects began chronologically with the second half of the sixth century B.C., and it is not coincidental that they were essentially destined for the prestigious votive offerings in some of the major sanctuaries of the Greek poleis.

Within the relations between Etruria and the Greek cities of Calabria, the unusual phenomenon of the wide diffusion of Chalkidian figurative pottery in Etruria cannot be forgotten. Its production in Reggio (or at least in the environment of the poleis on the Strait of Messina) has been validated by discoveries—some quite recent—of black-painted pottery or other vases with simple vegetal decorations in the cities of southern Calabria (Matauros, Hipponion, and even Locri). These were surely connected to workshops producing Chalkidian pottery, although they only spread to the regional environment. By contrast, the more valuable products from these shops, such as black-figured vases, were widely exported. Etruria represented a privileged outlet for Chalkidian vases, the only class of products from Magna Graecia that was widespread in the Etruscan world. They would influence contemporary Etruscan pottery and paintings.

On the facing page, vases in Campanian bucchero, 600–570 B.C., possibly from Reggio Calabria. Reggio Calabria, Museo Nazionale

Below, Etruscan transport amphora of the EM A group, first half of the sixth century B.C., from the Matauros necropolis at Gioia Tauro (Reggio Calabria). Reggio Calabria, Museo Nazionale

The Etruscans on Corsica

| LUIGI DONATI

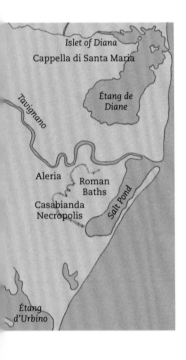

Above, map of the territory of Aleria on the Tyrrhenian coast of Corsica

The Greek mythological tradition tells that Herakles passed by Corsica on his return from the Garden of the Hesperides. He left his son Kyrnos there to become its king, and the island took his Greek name: *Kyrnos*. According to a tradition of Roman origin, on the other hand, the island was named for a girl named Corsa, who arrived there by boat from Liguria, following a bull from her herd after it dove into the sea. These traditions probably reflect the central role that the island played in the history of the northern Mediterranean in antiquity; modern etymological research suggests that the ancient name of the island can be traced to a pre-Indo-European root that means "cape" or "headland."

To those who approach the island by sea, it appears to be a single ponderous mass crowned by the peak of Mount Cinto, which is more than 2,700 meters (8,800 ft.) high. Because of its extremely rugged coast, Strabo (5.2.7) declared it to be largely inaccessible. It is a land of strong contrasts, however. Corsica includes a narrow strip of plain on its eastern side that is more than a hun-dred kilometers (60 miles) long and widens visibly in the middle area that corresponds to the Tavignano River. At the confluence of the Tavignano with the Tagnone River, a triangular terrace of close to thirty-six hectares (90 acres) rises more than forty meters (130 ft.) above the floodplain. The site was especially suited for settlement, both because it holds a naturally fortified position with a view of the sea, and because of its resources, since it was able to support agriculture and cattle breeding. Meanwhile, the lagoon areas parallel to the coast guaranteed fishing in the great ponds of Urbino and Diane, in addition to salt from a pond of the same name, which has since been filled. Just as important were mineral deposits of lead, silver, and above all copper and iron that surfaced in the mountain valleys that lay behind. The exploitation of these ores was facilitated by the availability of water and wood from the forests, which still must have been quite thick and impenetrable even during the period of Romanization, if one believes the story that a group of colonists became lost there.

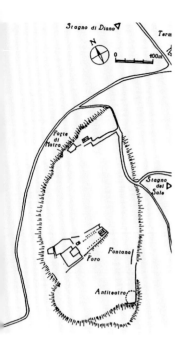

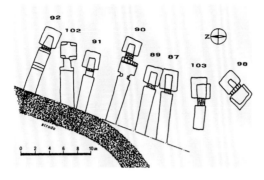

Above, plan of Aleria with the ruins of the ancient city, which was built on a triangular terrace overlooking the plain

At right, plan of the Casabianda necropolis, with chamber tombs aligned along road axes that were paved with cobblestones

On the preceding page, Attic red-figured *rhyton* by the Brygos Painter, shaped as a protome of a mule, from the early decades of the fifth century B.C., Tomb 91 in Aleria. Aleria, Museo Archeologico

Beyond these considerations, the island's geographic location was especially fortuitous with respect to navigation routes toward the coasts of Liguria and France, which were favored by dominant winds that blow from the northeast and southeast and by the prevailing currents. According to Herodotus (1.163), the inhabitants of Phokaia, an Ionic city of Asia Minor, traveled these routes. They were the first of the Greeks to make long sea voyages with their quick ships, which were pulled by fifty oarsmen (*pente-conteroi*). They explored the Adriatic, Tyrrhenian, and Iberian Seas as far as Tartessus, beyond the Pillars of Hercules.

In full agreement with the reports of Herodotus, archaeological research has certified that the Phokaians had already begun plying these Mediterranean routes in the last thirty years of the seventh century B.C., pushing as far as the distant markets of the Iberian Peninsula. Around 600 B.C. they founded Massalia (Marseilles), the first Phokaian colony in the West, located at the entrance of the Gaulish and Ligurian territories.

We also have it from the Greek historian (1.165) that about 565 B.C. the inhabitants of Phokaia, in response to the oracle at Delphi, chose the plateau at the mouth of the

Tavignano as the most suitable place to erect a colony on Corsica. It would be named Aleria (*Alalia* in Greek), and people from their mother city flowed there in a succession of waves. Twenty years later, at the advice of the Massaliots, almost half of the remaining inhabitants of Phokaia took shelter there, fleeing a siege by the troops of Arpagus, a general in the Persian navy of King Cyrus.

During the five years that followed this last transfer, the Phokaians dedicated themselves to piracy against their neighbors on every side, particularly besetting commercial interests that had been established for some time between the Carthaginians and the Etruscans of the Riviera cities.

Taking into consideration that these interests were not limited to the Tyrrhenian Sea but extended to the Ligurian Sea and southern France, where excavations of built-up areas and shipwrecks have turned up a stream of objects, from metals to pottery and wine vessels, it is easy to understand how acts of "piracy" by the new arrivals to Aleria could not long be tolerated. Thus began a sort of alliance between the powerful North African state of Carthage and the Etruscans, especially Caere. This coalition led to a naval battle with the Phokaians of Aleria, who may have been backed by those of Massalia, around 540 B.C.

The Etruscan-Punic coalition amassed a fleet of 120 ships that had been supplied equally by the two allies, with an additional 60 armed *penteconteroi* from the Greeks. The battle took place in the "Sardonian Sea," meaning, possibly, the stretch of water between Aleria and the northeast coast of Sardinia. (In antiquity, the term "Sardonian" generically stood for either the western Mediterranean or the sea around Sardinia.)

The contest ended in favor of the Phokaians, but according to Herodotus's narrative, they brought back a "Cadmean victory," that is, a victory in which the winners suffer huge damages. The city of Aleria was saved for the moment, but of the sixty ships that were deployed in battle, only twenty returned to port, and in such poor condition that they could no longer guarantee the city's security.

Thanks to a new response from the oracle at Delphi, it was decided that the inhabitants, including women and children, would embark on the surviving ships with all their transportable goods and sail toward Campania, where, after having passed Poseidonia, they founded a new colony at Velia (*Elea*).

The battle on the "Sardonian Sea" was an event of prime importance in the history of the Mediterranean. The Carthaginians conquered Sardinia, and Diodorus Siculus (5.13.3–4) relates that the Tyrrhenian coast of Corsica came under Etruscan dominion.

The Etruscans asserted their supremacy by dunning the native people in resin, wax, and honey, which were produced in abundance on the island, and by settling at the site of Aleria, which by then had been emptied of the most dynamic components of its population. There they "founded" a city that was given the Greek name *Níkaia*, which means "victory," clearly in memory of the naval event. We should not think of it as the founding of a new city but rather as the refounding of Aleria, on the part of Etruscans from Caere and, according to some scholars, others from Tarquinia. The new entity certainly bore the features of a proper colonial operation, with a deliberate plan to divide and exploit the territory. As a colonial enterprise, however, it was also open to ethnic groups other than Etruscans. Once again, Greeks were there in some numbers, as well as Carthaginians and native peoples.

In the oldest inhabited area of Aleria, which lies beneath buildings from the

Attic red-figured kylix by the workshop of the Penthesilea Painter, second quarter of the fifth century B.C., Tomb 98 in Aleria. Aleria, Museo Archeologico

Roman era, archaeological research has only been able to identify a few stretches of fortifications near an amphitheater and a fountain that once stood on the plateau at the beginning of the fifth century B.C. These structures, which include the remains of a rampart, were made with alternating rows of large river stones and unfired bricks.

Near the fortifications, a number of dwellings have also come to light. These were of modest size and had an irregular plan. Running along the sides of their river-stone foundations, we find holes at regular intervals of about two meters (6 ft.) for poles that must once have supported lattice walls. This technique was well known in Etruria.

The plateau has also revealed the wide-spread presence of iron dross. This was detritus from refining activities that, as in Populonia, must have taken place in an industrial quarter located just outside the residential area. In this quarter, near an imperial Roman fountain, a small furnace from the middle of the fourth century B.C. has been found. Inside it were pieces of coal, iron dross, and shells; the latter were layered in between the coal and the ore in order to lower the fusion temperature to around 1050 degrees Celsius (1900° F).

Both the plateau where the residential area stood and the plain around it show indications of ancient divisions by road axes that were astronomically aligned, in accordance with a planning model for the territory that suited colonial-type settlements. Such a land-division scheme, while possibly taking advantage of the lines laid out by the earlier Phokaian settlers, presupposes the use of surveying techniques. The Etruscans were in fact adept at these methods, as seen in the examples of Spina, Marzabotto, Pyrgi, and Capua.

Archaeological research has also pointed out that an axis that crosses the plateau toward Étang d'Urbino corresponds to a paved road of cobblestones more than two and a half meters (8 ft.) wide. A series of chamber tombs overlook this axis, which may be the oldest of those located thus far, and were part of the Casabianda necropolis. Other tombs are aligned along another axis that crosses it to the south. This once again shows a type of necropolis structure that was planned according to urban models, of which the most famous examples are those at the necropoleis of Orvieto and Caere.

The tombs, which were dug from compact Pliocene clay, could be accessed through a stairway, a hallway (*dromos*), or sometimes an antechamber with a door that had been sealed with bricks. The burial chamber had a mostly square plan and was equipped with three benches, one at the back and two on each side, where the deceased (normally two per tomb) were laid with their grave goods. The grave goods show a progressive increase over time in the number of materials from the central Tyrrhenian Sea, especially Etruscan materials. Significant epigraphic evidence accompanied these goods, to the point that some of the tombs are entirely similar to Etruscan ones on the mainland, architecture included. The symposium services are especially outstanding and initially included Attic pottery, which was followed by Etruscan pottery with an applied red-figure technique, together with Etruscan bronzes that were mostly produced in Vulci. Female burials stand out for their jewelry and toiletry items, while the burials of males, who were members of the colonial family groups with the role of "military leaders" in the community, included weapons, among which we find war spoils from as far away as Provence.

The rise of this urban entity must have projected the island's interests forcefully into the northern Mediterranean. The new arrivals could have relied both on the emporium settlement of Genoa and on a number of landing places on the Ligurian and French Midi coasts that were managed and frequented by the Etruscans. In this regard, the discovery at Pech Maho, a coastal *oppidum* of Languedoc, of a lead sheet with a text inscribed in Etruscan on one side and a Greek text on the other is significant. It confirms that commercial contacts between Aleria and the cities of southern France had been established by the early decades of the fifth century B.C.

Above all, however, it is in the upper Tyrrhenian Sea that the Corsican Etruscan presence can be seen. Aleria seems not to have suffered from the crises that struck the Etruscan coastal cities after the Battle of Cumae. In this respect, it was like Populonia, which by exploiting its mineral resources kept up its industrial activity throughout the fifth and fourth centuries B.C. and maintained its security through a system of fortresses on topographical salients that included the island of Elba. Aleria, too, continued to import a certain variety of Attic pottery that was quite rare in Etruria but was found in Populonia. These facts, which are certainly not coincidental, reveal a definite community of interests between Corsica and Populonia. Strabo recalls that the island was quite visible from the Populonia's acropolises, and Aleria, Elba, and Populonia all used a typical kind of pottery that was worked by hand and decorated

Etruscan *skyphos* with a depiction of a swan in applied red-figure technique, fourth to third centuries B.C., the Ferrara T 585 Group in Tomb 31 at Aleria. Aleria, Museo Archeologico

with motifs that were inscribed with a comb. Their ties are also supported by the discovery of a vase in Populonia bearing an inscription that names an individual who was a native of Corsica (*Kursica*), and by the circulation of Populonian coins on the two islands that lay opposite the city.

Corsica's city, therefore, seems to have played a fundamental role in the economic interests of the mineral district of Populonia. This justifies the origins of a certain tradition that was reported by Servius in his commentary on the *Aeneid* (10.172), according to which the people of Corsica founded Populonia, or the Volterrans stole Populonia from the Corsicans.

The Etruscan phase on Corsica began at Aleria, and it also ended there. In 259 B.C., the city fell to L. Cornelius Scipio, who used it as his base of operations for conquering the entire island. This undertaking would keep the Roman army occupied for a century and would cost the lives of half the population before the city became the capital of the province of Corsica.

The Etruscans in Sardinia

| PAOLO BERNARDINI

"Tyrrhenia received its name from Tyrrhenus . . . who came to these lands from Lydia, and from his wife Sardò came the name of . . . the island Agryóphelps, which is now called Sardò." The extremely ancient relations between the land of Etruria and the island of Sardinia emerge in this footnote from Plato's *Timaeus* (fr. 25b Greene). In addition, the Tyrrhenians were, as Strabo says (5.2.7), the ancient inhabitants of the island whom Iolaos encountered when he led the sons of Herakles to Sardinia to found a colony there. Later Ptolemy (3.3.6) would record the name of a Sardinian people, the

Aisaronesioi, who settled on the eastern coast of the island and who, it seems, were of Etruscan origin. In the Platonic note, Tyrrhenian Sardò is called "the island with veins of silver." The name, which describes the metalliferous wealth of Sardinian territory in an epic tone, is well placed within a context of two cultures, the Nuraghic culture of the island and the proto-Etruscan Villanovan, which had been heavily involved in metalworking and the metal trade since the early stages of the Iron Age, between the ninth and eighth centuries B.C. In these years, materials of Tyrrhenian provenance, such as razors, swords, fibulae, and certain types of axes, began to circulate on the island and Nuraghic materials, such as figured bronzes like miniature quivers, buttons, boats with animal protomes, vases in sheet bronze, and a typical pottery shape—a pitcher with a slanted neck—appeared in abundance on the Tyrrhenian's other shore.

The most famous context for the latter, and probably one of the most ancient, is a famous tomb in a necropolis at Vulci, in which the deceased is accompanied by

Miniature basket and stool,
ninth century B.C., from the
Tomb of the Sardinian
Bronzes in the Cavalupo
necropolis in Vulci
(Viterbo). Rome, Museo
di Villa Giulia

three bronze objects of Sardinian make: a
figurine of a warrior-athlete, a miniature
basket, and a ceremonial bell in the shape
of a stool or throne. It was the central and
northern part of the island and the northern regions of Etruria, the mineral-rich
Etruria of Populonia and Vetulonia, that
dominated the relationship during this
ancient stage. There is evidence of high-
level political and commercial relations
that united Sardinian and Tyrrhenian
groups of nobility and proto-aristocrats
through treaties and alliances. These elites
were engaged in a common trade circuit
that was tied to working and selling metals.

New merchants, Greeks and
Phoenicians, appeared on the Mediterranean in the eighth century B.C., lured
there by the western market's metal
resources. They must have been fully cog-
nizant of the community of motives and
interests that was in play between the two
shores of the Tyrrhenian; this awareness on
the part of the Greeks may have led to the
preservation of the image of the *Tyrrhenoi*
in Sardinian land in the ancient sources.

Sardò Argyróphelps immediately recalls
another western mythological Eldorado:
the land of Tartessus, with whose silver the
Phoenicians filled the hulls of their ships,
and which fascinated the Greeks. Tartessus,
like the Tyrrhenian island with its veins of
silver, would become another legendary land
where silver ran abundantly in the waters
of its rivers and spouted from its fountains:
Tartessos and its *pagas argurorizous*, described
by Stesichorus in Strabo (3.2.11). The circulation of a number of Tyrrhenian objects in
Sardinia illuminates aspects of a cultural
convergence in modes of behavior and personal image, at least within certain groups,
showing that their common interests went

The Phoenician settlement of Sulci at Sant'Antioco (Cagliari), from between the eighth and seventh centuries B.C., as it was being excavated. Note the section of pavement made of tufa chips that has been preserved within the perimeter walls of a rectangular room.

beyond metallurgical and mineral resources. This was the case with the notable diffusion of fibulae, which implied a high regard for types of clothing that differed from traditional styles. On the opposite shore, the spread of Nuraghic pitchers in Etruria was linked to a commercialization of their contents (wine), which must have had a certain prestige (some have imagined an ancestor of Sardinian *mirto* liqueur). It is not by chance that these containers are consistently found among the grave goods of a certain social class. With the arrival of the seventh century B.C., although we continue to see Sardinian objects of prestige in the rich tombs of Vetulonia, the overall picture appears to have changed. Etruscan materials from southern Etrurian cities, especially Caere (Cerveteri), became prevalent in the circulation of Sardinia's native cities.

At this point, certain types of luxury goods from the Orientalizing period began to reach Sardinia, such as silver and bronze pitchers with Phoenician palmettes, great bronze basins with lotus-flower handles, and fluted gold cups, which caused a flurry of imitations and modifications in native workshops. Historically, records indicate an important change in the seventh century B.C., when trade with the Etruscans gradually became concentrated in the island's Phoenician coastal cities. Less than a hundred years after their founding, they had become thriving and well-organized cities that were well positioned to turn the Tyrrhenian trade routes to their advantage and to marginalize the local indigenous communities.

The crux of this change can best be comprehended by looking at the encounters and relations that naturally occur between urban entities, such as the Mediterranean Phoenician cities and the Etruscan poleis. Sardinian society showed considerable delay

The sacred area in Santa Cristina (Paulilatino), dedicated to the worship of water, with a perimeter enclosure and, *at center*, an entrance to the monumental stairway that leads to the "well" temple underground.

and awkwardness at aligning itself with the formulas of nearby Western urbanism. It is no accident that the settlements of villages and nuraghi (truncated-cone structures typical of the island) never migrated toward city formulas, or that the Sardinians never acquired writing, the main tool for organiz-

ing city communities, during the late Orientalizing and Archaic periods.

The Phoenician colonies of southwestern Sardinia give witness to the high intensity of relations between the Phoenicians and Etruscans during the second half of the seventh and the first fifty years of the sixth centuries B.C., especially in the abundant evidence in Bitia, Tharros, and Othoca. During that period, ceramic works from Etruscan workshops reached the island in considerable quantities. These included works in bucchero and Etruscan-Corinthian vases, from the Etruscan shops that repeated the models and decorative motifs of prestigious Greek works from Corinth.

Etruscan imports can be divided into two basic categories: works destined for the use and consumption of wine and works destined for the storage and use of ointments and perfumes. Cups (*kylikes*), chalices, cups with raised handles (*kantharoi*), and bucchero pitchers (*oinochoai, olpai*), together with Etruscan-Corinthian cups, belong to the first category; Etruscan ointment jars and vases that imitate Corinthian works (*aryballoi, alabastra*) belong to the second.

We can guess that widespread consumption of wine was responsible for this first group of handmade goods. It is more difficult to say whether they also indicate that the symposium model, which Etruria had adopted in such a profound and rooted way from the Greek world, was adopted within the Phoenician cultural environment according to the same ceremonial, ideological, and social parameters. Today it is difficult to maintain that the Phoenicians did so. Even if the Phoenicians of Sardinia were steady patrons of Etruscan drinking services (and the situation of Carthage, despite differences in its selection of imported goods, is similar), Etruscan wine still had no market on the island, as witnessed by the extreme rarity of Etruscan wine amphorae that have been found to date. The Phoenicians had produced their own wine for a long time and had even exported it to Etruria since the

eighth century B.C. Etruscan wine services must have been used—as precious objects, and linked to the custom of wine drinking—to integrate at least partially the models of libations that had been taken from the Near East in ancient times. These models had been brought to the West by the Phoenicians themselves, and they had merged to some degree with the ideology of the Greek and Etruscan symposium, at least insofar as they tied in with banquets and the luxurious leisure (*otia*) of the king. Again, the absence of Tyrrhenian wine

amphorae suggests that the Phoenicians were the main administrators of the commercial relationship between the cities of Etruria and Phoenician Sardinia. This trade centered on goods that unfortunately left no archaeological traces (cloth, fabric, slaves, wood, minerals, etc.). However, it

The site of the Phoenician settlement of Tharros at Cabras (Cagliari). This image, taken from Capo San Marco, a spit of land off the peninsula of Sinis, shows a narrow isthmus connecting to the hill of San Giovanni, which was the site of the Archaic settlement. The necropolis of the colony was located on both the isthmus and the hill of San Marco.

At *right*, Tomb 48 at the Phoenician necropolis of Bitia, Domus de Maria, seventh century B.C. Among the objects inside the grave, a pit tomb for cremated remains, is an Etruscan-produced bucchero jug.

Below, Tomb 234 as it was being excavated at the seventh-century Phoenician necropolis of Bitia, Domus de Maria. The grave goods were composed of an urn that contained the cremated remains of the deceased, together with ritual vases and iron weapons.

also involved Phoenician ships unloading local vases at Etruscan ports, together with an abundant and parallel series of Greek pottery that circulated in Sardinia in the same period and closely resembled Tyrrhenian products: Corinthian and Laconic cups and ointment containers that were produced in eastern Greece (especially wine cups).

This steady commercial contact implies a steadiness of associations and encounters that, in a number of documented cases, became everyday closeness and community life. Etruscan merchants and artisans must have circulated throughout the island, established their residences and personal lives, and finally died and been buried there. Thus, Etruscan objects can be found in a number of tombs in the Phoenician necropoleis of Sardinia, which hewed closely to the funerary customs of their land of origin. Thus we can identify a tomb of a citizen of Etruscan descent by its characteristic contents: a typical series of small amphorae in

At *left*, Etruscan-Corinthian ointment containers and a cup from the middle of the sixth century B.C., from the Phoenician necropolis of Bitia, Domus de Maria. Cagliari, Museo Archeologico

Below, bucchero jug, cup, and *kantharos*, from the middle of the sixth century B.C., from the Phoenician necropolis of Tharros, Cabras (Cagliari). Oristano, Antiquarium Arborense

bucchero, and above all, a group of tiny *pyxides* on stands.

An inscription incised on a work in ivory that reproduces a crouching lion, found in the Roman sanctuary of Sant'Omobono, seems to speak of an Etruscan merchant who frequented Sardinia. The object, which can be dated to about 530 B.C., preserves the name of one *araz silquetenas spurianas*. According to one reading—although there is no general consensus on this point—a certain *Spurinna*, who may have been Tarquinian, assumed an ethnicity, *silquetenas*, that derived from his frequent stays in the Phoenician city of Sulci in Sardinia. Regardless of whether this interpretation is substantially correct, the object nevertheless belonged to a series of *tesserae hospitales*, a sort of document that verified a relationship of mutual hospitality between two partners or contracting parties. Another ivory depicting a boar, found in Carthage, belongs to this genre as well. It records a similar relationship of hospitality between a

Carthaginian and his counterpart in Etruscan lands. In this case the inscription reads *mi puniel karthazie eslf[...]na*, signifying a Carthaginian who declares his origins in Etruscan: "I am Punic, of Carthaginian citizenship."

In Sardinia once more, an Etruscan engraver or scribe wrote on a slab of sandstone at the end of the seventh century B.C. Unfortunately very little of the inscription has survived: *[...]vana s[...]*. It is a dedication

Above, sixth-century pit tomb as it was being excavated at the Phoenician necropolis in Mount Sirai, Carbonia. *In the background*, note the typical pitcher with a "mushroom" rim that contained oil and perfumes to be used during funeral ceremonies.

Below, Etruscan-Corinthian ointment containers from the beginning of the sixth century B.C., from the Phoenician necropolis of Tharros, Cabras (Cagliari). Oristano, Antiquarium Arborense

On the facing page, the lower coastal quarter of the city of Tharros, Cabras (Cagliari), which was occupied during the Roman era by the Forum and Capitolium

(*[mi mulu]vana s[puriesi]*?) connected to an important building that may have been in a sanctuary environment where foreign merchants were in attendance. The inscription came from Oristano and may refer to the Phoenician area of that region, where the Othoca necropolis shows a number of Etruscan imports and possibly the burial of Etruscan residents.

The years following the middle of the sixth century B.C. saw radical transformations in the relationship between Sardinia and the Tyrrhenian area. During this period, the allied Carthaginians and Etruscans faced the Phokaian pirates of Aleria, and more importantly, this was the period when the Carthaginian fleet conquered Sardinia. Aleria was threatened in 540 B.C., the conventional date when Etruscan-Corinthian works ceased to be produced for export. However, this date does not explain the sudden decline in the relationship between the island and the Etruscans. Although commerce continued, as is demonstrated by the

feeble circulation of Attic pottery (mostly Little Master cups—*kylikes*—brought from Etruria), the quantity of traffic between 530 and 500 B.C. was truly meager with respect to the past. The reason for this change was that Carthage conquered the island mili-

tarily between 540 and 510 B.C.; it sought particularly to destroy the economic and political system of the Phoenician poleis in Sardinia, and therefore the merchant and trade network, in order to replace it with their own objectives and strategies. Among these initiatives, emerging at the beginning of the fifth century B.C., was a commercial alliance between Athens and Carthage at a time when the great Greek cities began to adopt a decisive Mediterranean policy. The understanding between these new partners led to an openness of the Sardinian cities, which were controlled by Carthage, toward works from Athenian workshops. However, it is overstating the case to say that relations with Etruria ceased altogether, since Etruscan materials, such as ivory works from Nora and Tharros, continued to circulate sporadically on the island through the first half of the century. The era of Tyrrhenian *Sardò* was by now a faraway memory. The Etruscan influences recognized in Punic glyptic art during that same century do not essentially change this picture.

With the coming of the fourth century B.C., Sardinia and the Tyrrhenian area (and

by extension, the central-Italic area) fell under the unstoppable influence of Rome. In 386 B.C. the latter founded a colony on the island, the *Pheronia polis*, near the mouth of the Posada River, as Ptolemy mentions (3.3.4).

This event may belong within the context of the close relationships that existed between Rome and Caere, which received the *civitas sine suffragio* from this powerful alliance in 353 B.C. or thereabouts. A city fundamental to supporting Rome's commercial goals, Caere can be credited with a small number of examples of Etruscan red-figure pottery that circulated in Punic Sardinian cities in the late fourth century, such as Genucilia plates. Two "cartouche"-type pitchers from Mount Sirai and Tharros are also Etruscan.

Among the heap of central-Italic works that poured onto the island beginning with the third century B.C., there is no trace of an Etruscan imprint, except in the name of certain Sardinian *civitates*: In addition to the previously mentioned *Aisaronesioi*, the name *Patulcenses* (*CIL* 10.7852) may be traced back to a *gens* of Etruscan origin.

The Etruscans in Sicily

| ROSA MARIA ALBANESE PROCELLI

Geographic location is certainly one of the factors that most influences a region's history. Sicily's central location and triangular shape provided it with a number of projections into the Mediterranean, and consequently a variety of contacts with the ethnic groups that populated the sea. The northwest tip naturally projects toward sea routes between the Tyrrhenian world and North Africa (this was, not coincidentally, the Phoenician-Punic pole of the island). Similarly, in the central area the Aeolian archipelago took on a fundamental importance in the control over the lower Tyrrhenian and transit through the Strait of Messina, toward which the eastern coasts of the island gravitate. Consequently, a number of conflicts between Greek and Etruscans crystallized right around Lipari, as described by historical sources (Diodorus Siculus 5.9.4–5; Strabo 6.2.10; Pausanius 10.11.3–4; 10.16.7; Callimachus fr. 93) and reflected in the legend that the brothers Tyrrhenus and Liparus became enemies (Servius Auctus *Ad Aeneidum* 1.52).

Within an extremely complex picture of Mediterranean trade, the history of relations between Tyrrhenian peoples and Sicily has received a lot of scholarly attention in the last thirty years, opening new perspectives for inquiry. Although archaeological evidence allows us to divide the span of commercial contact into periods and furnishes quantitative elements for economic history, it is still difficult to identify which Etruscan cities were implicated in exchanges with various areas of Sicily and when.

The spread of imported goods from southern Etruria in Sicily was not homogeneous. The demand for goods of various kinds was of course not uniform, but the inconsistency of archaeological knowledge also contributes to the spotty record. Distribution maps for materials allow us to hypothesize two different sea routes. One began in northwest Sicily along a route to Carthage and included the southern coast, as indicated by finds in Selinunte; the other, through the Strait, reached the eastern coasts of the island.

The Eighth Century B.C.

One of the most debated problems for this period concerns the historical credibility of a well-known passage by Ephorus (in Strabo 6.2.2), which says that there were Tyrrhenian pirates in the waters of eastern Sicily before the Greeks founded their colonies. Although piracy and Etruscans were often linked as a kind of propaganda theme in Greek historiography, the sources may in fact have been describing a real situation. The notion of piracy had two separate connotations during Archaic times: one was political and military: piracy as a form of naval control that was organized in strategic areas; the other was economic: piracy as a form of transaction.

The history of contacts and trade between Sicily and the mid-Tyrrhenian area, where the important mineral districts of Tuscany and Lazio are located, began much earlier than the colonization of the island by the Greeks. Traffic in raw or partly worked metals (of which the cargo of copper and lead ingots from a shipwreck in Giglio, from the beginning of the sixth century B.C., is direct evidence) is indirectly indicated during the first half of the eighth century by the

importation of finished objects produced in central Italy (such as cannon-shaped axes in the deposit at Polizzello and flat axes from that deposit and the ones at Mount San Mauro and Pantalica).

Isolated Italic fibulae in the shape of leeches or boats, from the eighth and beginning of the seventh centuries B.C., respectively, which were discovered in Sicily (Pantalica, Mendolito, Giarratana, Paternò, Megara Hyblaea, Syracuse, Mineo-Olivo, and Mozia), are signs of people from the Tyrrhenian area: These items formed part of their typical costumes. It is perhaps no coincidence that up to now these have been found in sites where Villanovan (a small amphora from Mozia) and Etruscan materials from the proto-Archaic period are on record (Megara Hyblaea and Syracuse).

The Seventh Century B.C.

The legendary tale of the Corinthian Demaratos, who settled in Tarquinia, is emblematic of commercial practices during this period. According to Dionysios of Halikarnassos (3.46.3), Demaratos carried out his commerce in western waters, "carrying a Greek cargo to the Tyrrhenians and a Tyrrhenian cargo to Greece."

Regarding demographic mobility within this period, the figure of the artisan Aristonothos is also revealing. Around 675 B.C. he signed a krater that has an affinity with Siceliot works. It portrays a sea battle on one side and the blinding of Polyphemus on the other, allowing us a clear glimpse of the Etruscan preoccupation with naval supremacy and their conflict with the Greek colonies.

The most ancient imports of Etruscan goods to southern Sicily date to the first half of the seventh century. Other than a

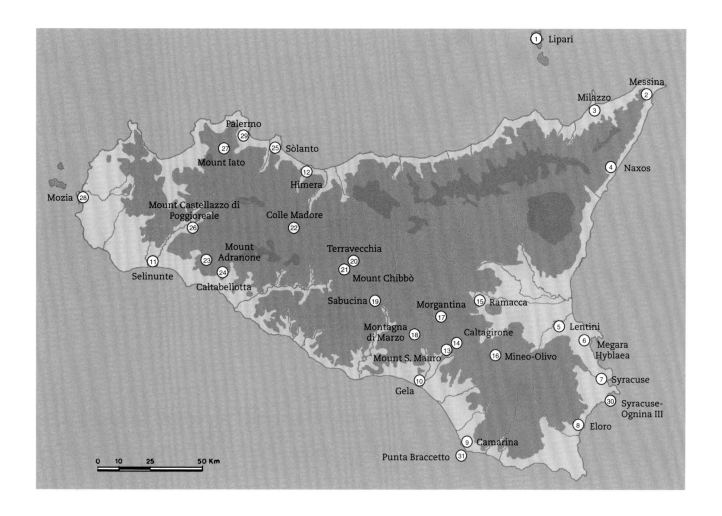

Map showing the distribution of imported Etruscan materials in Sicily.

a) commercial amphorae; b) bucchero; c) heron plates; d) Etruscan-Corinthian pottery; e) basins with beaded rims; f) so-called Rhodian *oinochoai*; g) *olpai* with handles in the shape of a lion cub; h) oinochoai with palmette handles

1. Lipari (a, b). 2. Messina (a, b). 3. Milazzo (a). 4. Naxos (a, b). 5. Lentini (b). 6. Megara Hyblaea (a, b, d, e). 7. Syracuse (a, b, c, d, e). 8. Eloro (c). 9. Camarina (a, b). 10. Gela (a, b, c, d, e). 11. Selinunte (a, b, e). 12. Himera (a, b). 13. Mount S. Mauro (a, b). 14. Caltagirone (e). 15. Ramacca (a, b). 16. Mineo-Olivo (e). 17. Morgantina (e). 18. Montagna di Marzo (e, h). 19. Sabucina (e). 20. Terravecchia (e). 21. Mount Chibbò (e). 22. Colle Madore (a, b). 23. Mount Adranone (g). 24. Caltabellotta (f). 25. Sòltanto (b).26. Mount Castellazzo di Poggioreale (b). 27. Mount Iato (b). 28. Mozia (b, d). 29. Palermo (b, d).

Shipwrecks: 30. Syracuse-Ognina III (a). 31. Punta Braccetto (a).

Bucchero *kantharos*, end of the seventh to first quarter of the sixth century B.C., an isolated example from the necropolis on Via Crispi in Gela. Gela, Museo Archeologico

sottile. Among the oldest pieces of bucchero tableware are two *kantharoi* with incised decorations from the inhabited area of Megara Hyblaea and the sacred area of Naxos. These were made with an especially refined technique and were connected to production from the area of Veii and Caere during the years between 640 and 630 B.C.

Works in bucchero with incised decorations of small fans, from the seventh century B.C., may also be from the Caeretan area, though other workshops in southern Etruria—Vulci, for example—cannot be ruled out. These works have been reported at colonial sites on the eastern coast (Lentini, Megara Hyblaea, and Messina), as well as Himera, which was a stopping point for traffic between Etruria and North Africa.

The systematic analysis of bucchero imports in a colony such as Megara Hyblaea has demonstrated that an extensively excavated inhabited area can yield various shapes of vases (cups and pitchers with round or three-lobed mouths) and not just *kantharoi*, though the *kantharoi* outnumber the others about three to one.

Beginning with the final quarter of the seventh century B.C., the volume and quality of trade to Sicily increased, including not only fine pottery but commercial amphorae as well. Both Caere and Vulci seem to have also played a privileged role in these exchanges.

Identifying the workshops that produced bronze basins with beaded rims, which reached Sicily from the Tyrrhenian area from the beginning of the seventh to the first quarter of the fifth century B.C., seems to be more problematic. Of the forty-two specimens known to date, most come from colonial sites: Gela, Megara Hyblaea, Selinunte, and Syracuse. In the necropoleis of this last colony, these objects were used for the entire seventh century (Fusco tombs 219, 439, 505, 712; Viale Ermocrate) and into the second quarter of the sixth century (Fusco Tomb 2). This period coincides with the highest quantity of Etruscan imports to eastern Sicily.

The Sixth Century B.C.

It was between the end of the seventh century B.C. and the first half of the century that followed that the transitional bucchero *kantharos* (type Rasmussen 3e) became a preferred product among imports of fine pottery. It represents a kind of index fossil for Etruscan trade in the Mediterranean during this period. Its shape was standardized, making it difficult to identify its city of origin without the support of petrographic analysis.

Kantharoi of this shape were well distributed throughout the Greek colonies (Camarina, Eloro, Gela, Himera, Lentini, Lipari, Messina, Megara Hyblaea, Naxos, and Selinunte). Up to this point only a few units are known at Punic sites (Marsala, Mozia, Palermo, and Sòltanto). They are also rarely found in inland cities (Mount San Mauro, Ramacca, Colle Madore, Mount Castellazzo di Poggioreale, and Mount Iato).

The colonial Greeks showed a strong preference for using this vase in their funerary ceremonies, which means that these works are found primarily in funerary contexts. Today more than ninety *kantharoi* from the necropoleis of Syracuse are known; a number of tombs (Fusco 24, 372; Giardino Spagna 1, 44) show four or five examples each. Fusco Tomb 551 particularly stands out, both for the quantity and quality of its grave goods and for the manner in which the deceased was buried: The body was cremated and placed in a bronze cauldron, surrounded by twenty or so bucchero *kantharoi*.

Certain exceptional forms can be found among the grave goods. In Fusco Tomb 309 there is a miniature *kyathos* of a type (Rasmussen 1e) that was related to Caeretan production; it is also seen in isolated examples in Lipari and Megara Hyblaea. Between the necropoleis of Gela (Via Crispi), Megara Hyblaea (the western necropolis), and Syracuse (Santa Lucia), a total of five large *kantharoi* have been found with handles that have a small bridge in the middle (type Rasmussen 3d); in Etruria these appear to be typical of the Vulcian area. The gray material that makes up one of the two examples from Gela (inv. 8698) does not rule out an Etruscan, or at least foreign, origin. Local workshops may also have attempted imitations, as in a *kantharos* from Syracuse of a beige material with ribbon-shaped handles that were coarsely modeled.

Bucchero vases were also used as offerings in sacred places. These were generally *kantharoi*, such as those found at Gela, Megara Hyblaea, Syracuse, and Selinunte. In some cases there were also chalices and *kyathoi*, such as at the sanctuary of Malophoros in this last colony.

The predominance of the *kantharos* in these imports was due to the fact that it was considered the wine vase *par excellence*. Thus they complemented Etruscan wine amphorae, which were produced in southern Etruria beginning with the final quarter of the seventh century B.C. and also exported to Sicily until the first half of the sixth century, along a trade circuit similar to that of the bucchero works.

At *right*, Etruscan commercial amphorae, end of the seventh to first half of the sixth century B.C., from Tomb 27 and Tomb 252 in the eastern necropolis (Pestavecchia) in Himera. Himera, Museo Archeologico

Below, bronze basin with a beaded rim, final quarter of the sixth century B.C., from Tomb West 326 in Sabucina. Caltanissetta, Museo Archeologico

On the facing page, burials of infants in Punic commercial amphorae (Tomb 131), first half of the sixth century B.C., from the eastern necropolis (Pestavecchia) of Himera

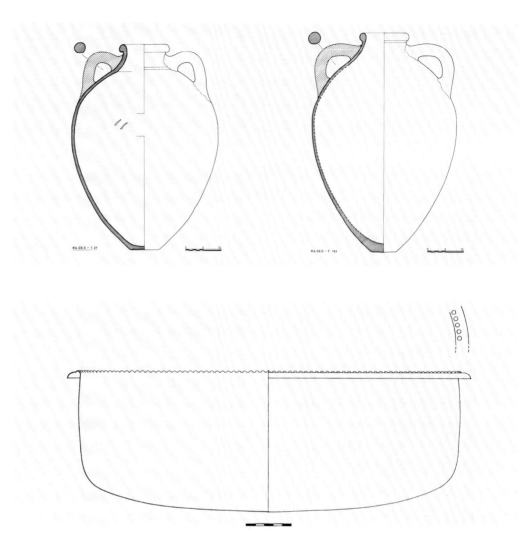

Identifying the cities in southern Etruria and Etruscan Campania where commercial amphorae were produced seems to remain problematic. A number of works have been located in Vulci and Caere. Amphorae with flat bases (types Py 1/2-Gras EMA) and pointed bases (types Py 3A/B-Gras EMC) have been ascribed to the first city, while Caere mostly produced the pointed variety.

The amphorae on record in Sicily between the last quarter of the seventh and the first half of the sixth centuries B.C. mostly belong to types Py 1/2-Gras EMA (Camarina, Himera, Lipari, Megara Hyblaea, Messina, Milazzo, Naxos, and Selinunte) and Py 3A/B-Gras EMC (Camarina, Himera, Megara Hyblaea, Naxos, and Selinunte). So far, these types are little known in Punic cities (Mozia or Palermo) or in indigenous sites inland. The latter were either centers occupied by the Greeks (such as Mount San Mauro) or areas

gravitating around colonial areas (such as Colle Madore for Himera, or Ramacca for Lentini). This situation mirrors the distribution of bucchero in the inland areas of the island.

But who transported these goods between Sicily and Etruria? The presence of a lone Etruscan amphora (type Py 3B-Gras EMC) among twenty-one Greek amphorae in the remaining cargo of a shipwreck at Punta Braccetto, from the middle of the sixth century B.C., seems to indicate that the Greeks managed the commerce. In addition, the Etruscan wine trade represented a fairly low percentage of the whole compared with Greek foodstuffs, at least based on partial data that can be inferred from colonial necropoleis of the sixth century. Of amphorae that were reutilized for the burial of infants, those of Etruscan origin make up only about four percent at Camarina and six percent in Himera and Naxos.

Regarding other Etruscan works, so-called Etruscan-Corinthian painted wares found little demand with a Siceliot clientele that was largely used to Greek products.

During the first half of the sixth century B.C., we find very few forms other than perfume containers (*aryballoi* at Megara Hyblaea, Palermo, Selinunte, and Syracuse; *alabastra* in Gela, Mozia, and Selinunte). There was one olpe at Syracuse and a footed cup from the Human Mask group (which was active in Vulci and Caere) in Palermo.

Imports of luxury metal tableware connected to wine consumption continued during the sixth century B.C. The only closed shape known was from midwestern Sicily. This so-called Rhodian-type *oinochoe* (a class linked to the Tarquinian environment) was uncovered in an inhabited area dating

to the first half of the sixth century in the indigenous city of San Benedetto, near Caltabellotta in the Selinunte area.

The Fifth Century B.C.

After the middle of the sixth century B.C., with the end of bucchero pottery exports, Etruscan imports noticeably diminished, although they did not cease entirely.

A few Etruscan amphorae reached Camarina, Himera, Colle Madore, and Lipari during the fifth century B.C. They were of the *fondo tagliato* or "cut base" variety (type Py 4-Gras EMD), which suggests they were produced in Caere and Veii.

Beginning with the last quarter of the sixth century B.C., the distribution of basins with beaded rims was concentrated within inland sites of central Sicily (Caltagirone, Montagna di Marzo, Mount Chibbò, Mineo, Morgantina, Sabucina, and Terravecchia di Cuti), especially the hinterland of Gela. Native acculturated elites created a demand for these items as they celebrated their social prestige with convivial ceremonies inspired by Greek models. Three examples from tomb contexts in Sabucina from the last quarter of the sixth century indicate that these basins—either by themselves or together with other bronze containers (small amphorae and strainers)—were part of services with vases of various makes linked to wine drinking. A tomb from the beginning of the fifth century yielded a basin with a beaded rim that bore the incised name of a native woman, *Duspseta*.

Other Etruscan bronze vases also belong to wine services found in settings from the second quarter of the fifth century B.C. An *oinochoe* with a handle that ended in a palmette (the 9 Weber shape) came from Tomb

East 31 in Montagna di Marzo, where two warriors are buried. An olpe with a handle shaped as a lion's body (the III-BEtrb Weber shape), probably produced in Vulci, was from Tomb South 3 in Mount Adranone.

Between the second half of the sixth and the beginning of the fifth centuries B.C., architectural coroplastics gradually appear in cities on the Tyrrhenian side. In Himera and Lipari a series of antefixae paralleled developments seen in the Tyrrhenian area, from Campania to Etruria. These artworks were especially significant because they were destined for public buildings, and they presume the circulation of artisans as well as molds. Such contacts and exchanges obvi-

ously demonstrate a level of ethnic mobility, although it is difficult to infer the identities of these individuals through archaeological evidence. Epigraphic records offer a very few indications. Two figures with Etruscan names, one *Romis* son of *Kailios* and a woman named *Turranà*, are mentioned at the beginning of the fifth century B.C. on two lead laminae from the Malophoros sanctuary in Selinunte. The presence of these two individuals, who were of a different social status, is not surprising in a colony where Etruscan imports are well documented back to the seventh century.

On the following pages,
Tanella di Pitagora,
Cortona (Arezzo)

Bibliography

Abbreviations

AION ArchStAnt	*Annali dell'Istituto universitario Orientale di Napoli, Dipartimento di studi del mondo classico e del Mediterraneo antico, Sezione di archeologia e storia antica*
CIL	*Corpus Inscriptionum Latinarum*
MEFR	*Mélanges d'archéologie et d'histoire de l'École Française de Rome*
MEFRA	*Mélanges de l'École Française de Rome, Antiquité*
Quad AEI	*Quaderni di Archeologia Etrusco-Italica*
RömMitt	*Mitteilungen des Deutschen Archäologischen Institutes. Römische Abteilung*
TLE	M. Pallottino, *Testimonia linguae etruscae* (Florence, 1954).
TLE2	M. Pallottino, *Testimonia linguae etruscae,* 2nd ed. (Florence, 1968)

Etruscan Civilization, by Giovannangelo Camporeale

Barocchi, P., ed., *L'Accademia Etrusca*, exh. cat. (Florence, Palazzo Casali, 1985).

Bartoloni, G. et al., eds., *Principi etruschi tra Mediterraneo ed Europa* (Venice, 2000).

Borsi, F., ed., *Fortuna degli Etruschi*, exh. cat. (Florence, Sotteranei dello Spedale degli Innocenti, 1985).

Camporeale, G., *Gli Etruschi. Storia e civiltà* (Turin, 2000).

———, ed., *L'Etruria mineraria*, exh. cat. (Portoferraio, Fontezza della Linguella, 1985).

Carandini, A., ed., *La romanizzazione dell'Etruria. Il territorio di Vulci*, exh. cat. (Orbetello, Polveriera Guzman, 1985).

Carratelli, G. Pugliese, ed., *Rasenna* (Milan, 1986).

Cipriani, G., *Il mito etrusco nel rinascimento fiorentino* (Florence, 1980).

Colonna, G., ed., *Santuari d'Etruria*, exh. cat. (Arezzo, Museo Civico, 1985).

Cristofani, M., *L'arte degli Etruschi. Produzione e consumo* (Turin, 1978).

———, *Saggi di storia etrusca arcaica* (Rome, 1987).

———, *Gli Etruschi del mare* (Milan, 1989).

———, *Etruschi e altre genti nell'Italia preromana. Mobilità in età arcaica* (Rome, 1996).

———, ed., *Gli Etruschi. Una nuova immagine* (Florence, 1984).

———, ed., *Civiltà degli Etruschi*, exh. cat. (Florence, Museo Archeologico, 1985).

Gli Etruschi e l'Europa, exh. cat. (Paris, Grand Palais, 1992).

Harari, M., *Gli Etruschi del Po* (Pavia, 2000).

Maetzke, G. et al., eds., *Atti del secondo congresso internazionale etrusco* (Rome, 1989).

Maggiani, A., ed., *Artigianato artistico. L'Etruria settentrionale interna in età ellenistica*, exh. cat. (Volterra, Museo Guarnacci, 1985).

Mansueli, G. A., *L'ultima Etruria* (Bologna, 1988).

Martelli, M., and M. Cristofani, eds., *Caratteri dell'ellenismo nelle urne etrusche* (Florence, 1977).

Pallottino, M., *Etruscologia* (Milan, 1984).

————, *Storia della prima Italia* (Milan, 1984).

Prayon, F., *Die Etrusker* (Munich, 1996).

Sordi, M., *Prospettive di storia etrusca* (Como, 1995).

Stopponi, S., ed., *Case e palazzi d'Etruria*, exh. cat. (Siena, Spedale di Santa Maria della Scala, 1985).

Torelli, M., *Storia degli Etruschi* (Rome and Bari, 1981).

————, *L'arte degli Etruschi* (Rome and Bari, 1985).

————, ed., *Gli Etruschi* (Milan, 2000).

**The Etruscans in the Mediterranean, by
Giovannangelo Camporeale**

Almagro-Gorbea, M., *Gli Etruschi e l'Europa*, exh. cat. (Paris, Grand Palais, 1992), pp. 174–79.

Bouloumié, B., *Gli Etruschi e l'Europa,* exh. cat (Paris, Grand Palais, 1992), pp. 168–73.

Bouloumié, B., and C. Lagrand, *Revue Archéologique de la Narbonnaise* 10 (1977), pp. 1–31.

Colonna, G., *I grandi santuari della Grecia e l'Occidente*, A. Mastrocinque, ed. (Trent, 1993), pp. 43–76.

Cristofani, M., *Gli Etruschi del mare* (Milan, 1989).

Gilotta, F., *Miscellanea etrusco-italica* 2, M. Cristofani, ed. (Rome, 1997), pp. 113–28.

Gras, M., *Trafics tyrrhéniens archaïques* (Rome, 1985), pp. 651–701.

Hase, F. W. v., *Kleine Schriften aus dem Vorgeschichtlichen Seminar Marburg* 5 (1979), pp. 62–69.

————, "Die Aufnahme fremder Kultureinflüsse in Etrurien und das Problem des Retardierens in der etruskischen Kunst," *Schriften des Deutschen Archäologen-Verbandes* 5 (Mannheim, 1981), pp. 9–24.

————, *Jahrbuch des Römisch-Germanischen Zentralmuseums Mainz* 36 (1990), pp. 327–410.

Herrmann, H. V., *Annuario della Scuola Archeologica Italiana ... di Atene* 61 (1983 [1984]), pp. 271–94.

Kilian, K., *Hamburger Beiträge zur Archäologie* 3 (1973), pp. 1–39.

Kunze, E., *Studies Presented to D. Robinson* 1 (St. Louis, 1951), pp. 736–46.

Kyrieleis, H., *Athenische Mitteilungen* 101 (1986), pp. 127–36.

Macintosh, J., *Hesperia* 43 (1974), pp. 34–45.

Martelli, M., *Prospettiva* 53–56 (1988–89), pp. 21–22.

Moustaka, A., *Archäologischer Anzeiger* (1985), pp. 353–64.

Naso, A., *Studies in Honour of Ellen MacNamara* (London, 2000), pp. 193ff.

Philipp, H., "Bronzeschmuck aus Olympia," *Olympische Forschungen* 13 (Berlin, 1981), pp. 286–95.

Remesal, J., and O. Musso, eds., *La presencia de material etrusco en la península Ibérica* (Barcelona, 1991).

Strøm, I., *Proceedings of the Danish Institute at Athens* 3 (2000), pp. 67–95.

Thuillier, J. P., *MEFRA* 97 (1985), pp. 639–46.

Treister, M. J., *Die Welt der Etrusker*, H. Heres and M. Kunze, eds. (Berlin, 1990), pp. 165–69.

————, *Studi Etruschi* 57 (1991), pp. 71–79.

Weber, T., *Archäologischer Anzeiger* (1990), pp. 436–48.

The Etruscans in Europe, by Giovannangelo Camporeale

Boucher, S., *MEFR* 80 (1968), pp. 143–65.

————, *Recherches sur les bronzes figurés de Gaule pré-romaine et romaine* (Rome, 1976).

————, *Revue Archéologique* (1973), pp. 79–96.

Bouloumié, B., *Gallia* 31 (1973), pp. 1–35.

————, *Les oinochoés en bronze du type "Schnabelkanne" en Italie* (Rome, 1973).

————, *Gallia* 34 (1976), pp. 1–30.

————, *Gallia* 35 (1977), pp. 3–38.

————, *Latomus* 37 (1978), pp. 3–24.

————, *Il commercio etrusco arcaico* (Rome, 1985), pp. 167–78.

Bouloumié, B., and C. Lagrand, *Revue Archéologique de Narbonnaise* 10 (1977), pp. 1–31.

I Celti (Milan, 1991).

Colonna, G., "La preistoria," *Archeologica in Piemonte*, I. L. Mercando and L. Venturino Gambari, eds. (Turin, 1998), pp. 261–66.

Gli Etruschi e l'Europa, exh. cat. (Paris, Grand Palais, 1992).

Foresti, L. Aigner, ed., *Etrusker nördlich von Etrurien* (Vienna, 1992).

Frey, O. H., *Mostra dell'Etruria Padana e della città di Spina* 2 (Bologna, 1960), pp. 147–52.

————, *Piceni popolo d'Europa*, G. Colonna, ed. (Rome, 1999), pp. 18–23.

Gran-Aymerich, J., *Les phocéens vus de Lyon et d'ailleurs* (Paris, 2000), pp. 27–81.

Hase, F. W. v., *Atti del secondo congresso internazionale etrusco*, G. Maetzke, ed. (Rome, 1989), pp. 1031–61.

————, *Römisch-Germanische Forschungen* 59 (2000), pp. 177–95.

Martelli, M., *Aparchai. Nuove ricerche e studi . . . in onore di Paolo Enrico Arias* (Pisa, 1982), pp. 185–90.

Rolley, C., *Ocnus* 3, pp. 169–78.

Sestieri, A. M. Bietti, *Archeologia Classica* 1 (1998), pp. 1–67.

Simon, K., *Arbeits und Forschungsberichte zur sächsischen Bodendenkmalpflege* 41 (1999), pp. 61–96.

Taffanel, O., and J. Taffanel, *Revue Archéologique de Narbonnaise* 3 (1970), pp. 21–31.

Treister, M. J., *Studi Etruschi* 57 (1991), pp. 71–79.

Verger, S., *Studi Etruschi* 64 (1998 [2001]), pp. 265–316.

The Etruscans in Veneto, by Loredana Capuis

Capuis, L., *I Veneti. Società e cultura di un popolo dell'Italia preromana* (Milan, 1993).

Chieco Bianchi, A. M., "I Veneti," *Italia omnium terrarum alumna*, G. Pugliese Carratelli, ed. (Milan, 1988), pp. 3–98.

Gli Etruschi a nord del Po, exh. cat. (Mantua, Palazzo Ducale, Galleria dell'Estivale, 1986).

Fologari, G., and A. L. Prosdocimi, *I Veneti antichi. Lingua e cultura* (Padua, 1988).

Protostoria e storia del 'Venetorum angulus.' Atti del ventesimo convegno di studi etruschi ed itali, Portogruaro ecc. 1996 (Pisa, 1999).

Il Veneto nell'antichità. Preistoria e protostoria. (Verona, 1984), esp. pp. 617–873.

The Etruscans in the Lepontine and Raetian Regions, by Luciana Aigner Foresti

Aigner-Foresti, L., ed., *Etrusker nördlich von Etrurien*, Sitzungsberichte der Österreichischen Akademie der Wissenschaften Wien 589 (Vienna, 1992).

Archeologia in Lombardia (Milan, 1982).

Campanile, E., ed., *I Celti in Italia* (Pisa, 1981).

Celti ed Etruschi nell'Italia centro-settentrionale dal V secolo all romanizzazione. Atti del colloquio internazionale (Bologna, 1985).

Ciurletti, G., and F. Marzatico, eds., *I Reti* (Trent, 1999).

Como fra Etruschi e Celti. La città preromana e il suo ruolo commerciale, exh. cat. (Como, Società Archeologica Comense, 1986).

Dal Ri, L., "Influssi etrusco-italici nella regione veneto-alpina," *Gli Etruschi a nord del Po*, I. R. De Marinis, ed. (Mantua, 1987), pp. 160–79.

De Marinis, R., "Le tombe di guerriero di Sesto Calende e le spade e i pugnali hallstattiani scoperti nell'Italia nord-occidentale," *Archaeologia. Scritti in onore di Aldo Neppi Modona* (Florence, 1975), pp. 213–69.

————, "La protostoria," *Archeologia in Lombardia* (Milan, 1982), pp. 83–106.

————, "Protostoria degli insediamenti urbani in Lombardia," *Archeologia urbana in Lombardia* (Modena, 1984), pp. 22–23.

————, "I commerci dell'Etruria con i paesi a nord del Po dal IX al VI secolo," *Gli Etruschi a nord del Po*, I. R. De Marinis, ed. (Mantua, 1987), pp. 52–81.

————, "Le popolazione alpine di stirpe retica," *Italia omnium terrarum alumna*, G. Pugliese Carratelli, ed. (Milan, 1988), pp. 101–30.

————, "Liguri e Celto-Liguri," *Italia omnium terrarum alumna*, G. Pugliese Carratelli, ed. (Milan, 1988), pp. 159–259.

————, and S. Biaggio Simona, eds., *I Leponti tra mito e realtà*, 2 vols. (Locarno, 2000).

Lunz, R. *Studien zur End-Bronzezeit und älteren Einsenzeit im Südalpenraum* (Florence, 1981).

Maggiani, A., and A. L. Prosdocimi, "Leponzio-Ligure," *Studi Etruschi* 44 (1976), pp. 258–66.

Mercando, L., and M. Venturino Gambari, eds., *Soprintendenza archeologica del Piemonte, Archeologia in Piemonte* I: *La preistoria* (Turin, 1988).

Pauli, L., "Studien zur Golasecca Kultur," *RömMitt Ergänzungsheft* 19 (Heidelberg, 1971).

Primas, M., "La necropoli della Ca' Morta nei suoi rapporti culturali con le valli alpine," *Società archeologica comense, Età del ferro a Como. Nuove scoperte alla Ca' Morta (Scavi 1975–76)*, Mostra in onore di Ferrante Rittatore Vonwiller (Como, 1978), pp. 43–63.

Prosdocimi, A. L., "Cultura etrusca transpadana," *Gli Etruschi a nord del Po*, I. R. De Marinis, ed. (Mantua, 1987), pp. 114–15.

Rix, H., "Il problema del retico. Varietà e continuità nella storia linguistica del Veneto," *Atti del Convegno della Società Italiana di Glottologia* (Venice and Padua, 1996), pp. 25–48.

————, *Rätisch und Etruskisch* (Innsbruck, 1998).

Vonwiller, F. R., "La civiltà del Ferro in Lombardia, Piemonte, Liguria," *Popoli e Civiltà dell'Italia antica* 4 (Rome, 1975), pp. 225–345.

The Etruscans in Liguria, by Adriano Maggiani

Bonamici, M., "Contributo all rotte arcaiche nell'alto Tirreno," *Studi Etruschi* 61 (1995), pp. 3–43.

Gervasini, L., and A. Maggiani, "La stele di Lerici e l'oplismos dei Liguri in età arcaica," *Studi Etruschi* 62 (1996), pp. 27–62.

Lamboglia, N., "La necropoli di Chiavari. Studio preliminare," *Rivista di Studi Liguri* 26 (1960), pp. 91–220.

Maggiani, A., "Problemi del popolamento tra Arno e Magra dalla fine della età del bronzo alla conquista romana," *Studia di antichità offerti a G. Maetzke* (Rome, 1984), pp. 333–53.

Melli, P., *Restauri in Liguria* (Genoa, 1978).

————, "Il recupero della tomba di Rapallo. Nuovi dati sul popolamento del Tigullio tra la fine del VII e l'inizio del VI secolo a.C.," *Rivista di Studi Liguri* 62, with bibliography (1996), pp. 95–114.

Paribeni, R., *Ausonia* 5 (1910), pp. 13–55.

The Etruscans on the Po Plain, by Giuseppe Sassatelli

Colonna, G., and C. Morigi Govi, "L'anforetta con iscrizione etrusca da Bologna," *Studi Etruschi* 49 (1981), pp. 67–93.

La formazione della città in Emilia Romagna: Prime esperienze urbane attraverso le nuove scoperte archeologiche, exh. cat. (Bologna, 11th Biennale d'arte antica, 1987).

Malnati, L., "Le instituzioni politiche e religiose a Spina e nell'Etruria padana," *Spina. Storia di una città tra Greci ed Etruschi*, exh. cat. (Ferrara, Castello Estense, 1993), pp. 145–77.

————, and V. Manfredi, *Gli Etruschi in Val Padana* (Milan, 1991).

————, and A. Violante, "Il sistema urbano di IV e III secolo in Emilia Romagna tra Etruschi e Celti," *L'Europe celtique du Ve au IIIe siècle avant J. C., Actes du 2e Symposium International, Hautvillers 1992* (Sceaux, 1995), pp. 97–120.

Mansueli, G. A., and R. Scarani, *L'Emilia prima dei Romani* (Milan, 1961).

Sassatelli, G., "Bologna etrusca: nuovi dati e recenti acquisizioni," *Atti e Memorie della Deputazione di Storia Patria per le Province di Romagna*, n.s. 36 (1986), pp. 9–56.

————, "Felsina e l'Etruria Padana. Vita società e cultura della città etrusca," *Storia Illustrata di Bologna* (San Marino, 1987), pp. 1–20.

————, "La situazione in Etruria Padana," *Crise et transformation des sociétés archaiques de l'Italie antique au V siècle av. J.C., Table Ronde, Rome 1987* (Rome, 1990), pp. 51–100.

————, "La funzione economica e produttiva: merci, scambi, artigianato," *Spina. Storia di una città tra Greci ed Etruschi*, exh. cat. (Ferrara, Castello Estense, 1993), pp. 179–217.

————, "Problemi del popolamento nell'Etruria padana con particolare riguardo a Bologna," *La presenza etrusca nella Campania meridionale*, Atti del Convegno, Salerno-Pontecagnano 1990 (Florence, 1994), pp. 497–508.

————, "Verucchio, centro etrusco 'di frontiera,'" *Ocnus. Quaderni della Scuola di Specializzazione in Archeologia (Bologna)* 4 (1996), pp. 249–71.

————, "Gli Etruschi a Bologna e nella pianura padana. Alle origini della nostra storia," *Saecularia* 9, 14 (1998), pp. 11–16.

————, and C. Morigi Govi, "Felsina etrusca," *Bologna 1. Da Felsina a Bononia: Dalle origini al XII secolo. Atlante delle Città Italiane-Emilia Romagna* (Bologna, 1996), pp. 11–28.

Storia dell'Emilia Romagna 1. Dalla preistoria all'età delle signorie (Imola, 1975).

Taglioni, C., *L'abitato etrusco di Bologna* (Bologna, 1999).

Vitali, D., *Tombe e necropoli galliche di Bologna e territorio* (Bologna, 1992).

The Etruscans in Umbria, by Paolo Bruschetti

Bruschetti, P., "La necropoli di Todi e la ricerca archeologica," *Gens Antiquissima Italiae. Antichità dall'Umbria a New York*, exh. cat. (New York, Gray Art Gallery; Perugia, 1991), pp. 335–37.

————, and A. E. Feruglio, *Todi Orvieto* (Perugia, 1998).

Gaggiotti, M., D. Manconi, L. Mercando, and M. Verzar, *Umbria. Marche*, Guide Archeologiche Laterza (Rome and Bari, 1993).

Gens Antiquissima Italiae. Antichità dall'Umbria a Leningrado, exh. cat. (St. Petersburg, Hermitage Museum, 1990).

Ponzi, L. Bonomi, "Gli Umbri: territorio, cultura e società," *Gens Antiquissima Italiae. Antichità dall'Umbria a New York*, exh. cat. (New York, Gray Art Gallery; Perugia, 1991), pp. 51–62.

———, *La necropoli plestina di Colfiorito di Foligno* (Perugia, 1997).

Roncalli, F., "Gli Umbri," *Italia omnium terrarum alumna*, G. Pugliese Carratelli, ed. (Milan, 1988), pp. 373–407.

The Etruscans in Picenum, by Maurizio Landolfi

Baldelli, G., "Numana-Sirolo," *La ceramica attica figurata nelle Marche*, G. Baldelli, M. Landolfi, and D. G. Lollini, eds. (Castelferretti, 1986), p. 100, n. 2.

Boucher, S., "Problémes concernant une anse étrusque," *Italian Iron Age Artifacts in the British Museum: Papers of the Sixth British Museum Classical Colloquium* (London, 1986), pp. 107–16.

Camporeale, G., "Recensione a B. B. Shefton, Die 'rodischen' Bronzekannen," *Archeologia Classica* 33 (1981), pp. 400–405.

———, "Un gruppo di vasi chiusini di facies orientalizzante," *Studi Etruschi* 59 (1993), pp. 29–37.

Colonna, G., "Il Santuario di Cupra fra Etruschi, Greci, Umbri, e Picenti," *Picus*, suppl. 2 (1993), pp. 3–31.

———, ed., *Piceni popolo d'Europa* (Rome, 1999).

Devoto, G., "Interpretazioni umbre IV. Il nome 'Naharko' e gli antefatti dell'umbro di Gubbio," *Studi Etruschi* 33 (1965), pp. 369–77.

Geiger, A., *Treibverzierte Bronzerundschilde der italischen Eisenzeit aus Italien und Griechenland*, Prähistorische Bronzefunde, Abteilung 3, 1 (Stuttgart, 1994).

Menke, M., "Borsdorf-Filottrano-Waldalgesheim," *Germania* 69, 2 (1991), pp. 392–93.

Naso, Alessandro, *I Piceni. Storia e Archeologia delle Marche in epoca preromana* (Milan, 2000).

Peroni, R., "Villanoviano a Fermo?" *La Civiltà Picena nelle Marche. Studi in onore di G. Annibaldi* (Ripatransone, 1992), pp. 13–18.

Strøm, J., *Problems Concerning the Development of the Etruscan Orientalizing Style* (Odense, 1971).

The Etruscans in Lazio, by Alessandro Naso

Colonna, G., "I Latini e gli altri popoli del Lazio," *Italia omnium terrarum alumna*, G. Pugliese Carratelli, ed. (Milan, 1988), pp. 409–528.

———, ed., *Civiltà del Lazio primitivo*, exh. cat. (Rome, Palazzo dell'Esposizioni, 1976).

Cristofani, M., *Saggi di storia etrusca arcaica* (Rome, 1987), pp. 39–49.

———, "Über die Anfänge der 'römischen Kunst.' Die Zeit der Tarquinier," *RömMitt* 99 (1992), pp. 123–38.

———, ed., *Etruria e Lazio arcaico, Atti dell'incontro di studio* (*Quad AEI* 15) (Rome, 1987).

———, ed., *La grande Roma dei Tarquini*, exh. cat. (Rome, Palazzo delle Esposizioni, 1990).

De Santis, A., "Contatti fra Etruria e Lazio antico alla fine dell'VIII secolo a.C. La tomba di guerriero di Osteria dell'Osa," *Settlement and Economy in Italy 1500 B.C. to A.D. 1500: Papers of the Fifth Conference of Italian Archaeology*, N. Christie, ed. (Oxford, 1995), pp. 365–75.

Gli Etruschi e Roma. Incontro di studio in onore di Massimo Pallottino (Rome, 1981).

Guaitoli, M., "Lavinium: nuovi dati dalle necropoli," *Archeologia Laziale* 12, 2 (Quad. AEI 24) (Rome, 1995), pp. 551–62.

"La formazione della città di Lazio," *Dialoghi di Archeologia*, n.s. 2 (1980).

La Rocca, E., "Linguaggio artistico e ideologia politica a Roma in età republicana," *Roma e l'Italia. Radices imperii* (Milan, 1990), pp. 287–495.

Roma medio-repubblicana. Aspetti culturali di Roma e del Lazio nei secoli IV e III a.C., exh. cat. (Rome, Assessorato Antichità, 1973).

Storia di Roma. 1. Roma in Italia, A. Momigliano and A. Schiavone, eds. (Turin, 1988), pp. 291–316.

The Etruscans in Campania, by Bruno D'Agostino

Carri da guerra e principi etruschi, exh. cat. (Viterbo, Palazzo dei Papi, 1997), pp. 25–32, 311–12.

Cerchiai, L., "Nuova tomba principesca da Pontecagnano," *Opus* 3 (1984), pp. 411–20.

———, "Una tomba principesca del periodo Orientalizzante Antico a Pontecagnano," *Studi Etruschi* 53 (1985), pp. 27–42.

———, "La situle de type Kurd découverte dans la tomb 4461 de Pontecagnano," *Le princes celtes et la Méditerranée* (Paris, 1988), pp. 103–8.

———, "Le officine etrusco-corinzie di Pontecagnano," *AION ArchStAnt* (Quad. 6) (Naples, 1990).

———, *I Campani* (Milan, 1995).

———, "Il caso della tomba detta di Brygos," *Ostraka* 6, 2 (1997), pp. 129–34.

———, "Le tombe 'a cubo' di età tardoarcaica della Campania settentrionale," *Nécropoles et pouvoire, Actes, Lyon 1995* (Lyons and Athens, 1998), pp. 117–24.

Cinquantaquattro, T., "Dinamiche insediative nell'Agro Picentino dalla Protostoria all'Età Ellenistica," *AION ArchStAnt* 14 (1992), pp. 245–58.

Coarelli, F., "Venus Iovia, Venus Libitina? Il santuario del fondo Patturelli a Capua," *L'incidenza dell'antico. Studi in memoria di E. Lepore* I (Naples, 1995), pp. 370–87.

Colonna, G., "Acqua Acetosa Laurentina, l'Ager Romanus Antiquus e i santuari del I Miglio," *Scienza dell'Antichità* 5, pp. 209–32.

———, "Le civiltà anelleniche," *Storia e civiltà della Campania. L'evo antico* (Naples, 1991), pp. 25–68.

Cuozzo, M. A., "Patterns of Organisation and Funerary Customs in the Cemetery of Pontecagnano (Salerno) during the Orientalising Period," *Journal of European Archaeology* 2, 2 (1994), pp. 263–98.

D'Agostino, Bruno, "Pontecagnano. Nascita di un potere di funzione stabile," *La mort, les morts dans les sociétés anciennes*, G. Gnoli and J. P. Vernant, eds. (Cambridge and Paris, 1982), pp. 203–21.

———, "Le genti della Campania antica," *Italia omnium terrarum alumna*, G. Pugliese Carratelli, ed. (Milan, 1988), pp. 531–89.

———, "Greci, Campani e Sanniti: città e campagna nella regione Campana," *La Campania fra il VI e il III secolo a.C., Atti Convegno Benevento 1981* (Galatina, 1992), pp. 73–83.

———, "La Campania e gli Etruschi," *Atti del trentatresimo convegno di studi sulla Magna Grecia, Taranto 1993* (Naples, 1996), pp. 431–48 (esp. 437ff.).

———, "I principi dell'Italia centro-tirrenica in epoca orientalizzante," *Le princes de la Protohistoire et l'émergence de l'Etat, Actes table ronde, Naples 1994* (Naples, 1999), pp. 81–88.

D'Agostino, Bruno, and L. Cerchiai, "Aspetti della funzione politica di Apollo in area tirrenica," *I culti della Campania antica. Atti Convegno Valenza, Naples 1995* (Rome, 1998), pp. 119–26.

D'Henry, G., "La presenza attica nella Valle Caudina," *Ostraka* 6, 2 (1997), pp. 415–31.

Friederiksen, M., *Campania*, H. Purcell, ed. (Oxford, 1984).

Gastaldi, P., "Struttura sociale e rapporti di scambio nel IX sec. a.C.," *La presenza etrusca nella Campania meridionale, Atti Salerno-Pontecagnano* (Bibl. Studi Etruschi 28) (Florence, 1994), pp. 49–60.

———, "Pontecagnano II.4 La necropoli del Pagliarone," *AION ArchStAnt* (Quad. 10) (Naples, 1998).

Giangiulio, M., "Epéios et Philoctète en Italie," *Cahiers du Centre Jean Bérard* 16, J. de la Genière, ed. (Naples, 1991), pp. 37–53.

Greco, G., "Ritrovamenti museali. Poseidonia e Cuma," *Deliciae Fictiles* 2, Patricia S. Lulof and E. M. Moormann, eds. (Amsterdam, 1997), pp. 83–94.

Johannowsky, W., "Aggiornamenti sulla prima fase di Capua," *AION ArchStAnt*, n.s. 3 (1996), pp. 59–66.

Jovino, M. Bonghi, "Aspetti dell'Etruria Campana. Sistemi di copertura fittili degli edifici capuani," *La presenza etrusca nella Campania meridionale, Atti Salerno-Pontecagnano* (Bibl. Studi Etruschi 28) (Florence, 1994), pp. 485–96.

Koch, H., *Dachterrakotten aus Campanien* (Berlin, 1912).

Mertens-Horn, M., "Die archaischen Baufriese aus Metapont," *RömMitt* 99 (1992), pp. 1–122.

Murray, O., "Nestor's Cup and the Origin of the Greek Symposion," *Apoikia. Scritti in onore di G. Buchner* (*AION ArchStAnt*, n.s. 1) (1994), pp. 47–54.

Musti, D., "Epéios et Philoctète en Italie," *Cahiers du Centre Jean Bérard* 16, J. de la Genière, ed. (Naples, 1991), pp. 21–35.

Rescigno, C., *Tetti campani. Età arcaica* (Rome, 1998).

The Etruscans in Lucania, by Angelo Bottini

Bottini, Angelo, *Principi guerrieri della Daunia del VII secolo* (Bari, 1982).

———, "Il candelabro etrusco di Ruvo del Monte," *Bollettino d'Arte* 75, 59 (1990), pp. 1–14.

———, and E. Setari, "Una metropolis della Lucania antica," *Ostraka* 5, 2 (1996), pp. 205–14.

———, and M. Tagliente, "Osservazioni sulle importazioni etrusche in area lucana," *Magna Grecia, Etruschi, Fenici, Atti del trentatresimo convegno di studi sulla Magna Grecia, Taranto 1993* (Taranto, 1994), pp. 487–528.

D'Ercole, M. C., "Observations sur quelques ambres sculptées archaïques d'Italie méridionale," *Revue Archéologique* (1995), pp. 265–89.

Due donne dell'Italia antica: corredi da Spina e da Forentum, exh. cat. (Comacchio, 1993).

Greci, Enotri, Lucani nella Basilicata meridionale, exh. cat. (Policoro, Museo Nazionale della Siritide, 1996).

The Etruscans in Apulia, by Ettore M. De Juliis

Ciancio, A., "Un gruppo di vasi apuli a figure nere del V secolo a.C.," *Bollettino d'Arte* 80, 93–94 (1994–95), pp. 71–86.

De Juliis, Ettore M., "Importazioni e influenze etrusche in Puglia," *Magna Grecia, Etruschi e Fenici. Atti del trentatresimo convegno di studi sulla Magna Grecia, Taranto 1993* (Taranto, 1994), pp. 529–60.

Mazzei, M., "Appunti preliminari sulle antefisse fittili 'etrusco-campane' nella Daunia preromana," *Taras* 1, 1 (1981), pp. 17–33.

Tagliente, M., "Mondo etrusco-campano e mondo indigeno dell'Italia meridionale," *Magna Grecia. Politica, Società, Economia* (Milan, 1987), pp. 135–50.

Todisco, L., "Nuovi dati e osservazioni sulla 'Tomba delle Danzatrici' di Ruvo," *Atti e Memorie della Società Magna Grecia*, ser. 3, 3 (1994–95), pp. 119–42.

The Etruscans in Calabria, by Claudio Sabbione

Accademia dei Lincei, ed., *Notizie degli scavi di Antichità* (1988), pp. 35, 229, 239.

Cristofani, M., "I buccheri di Reggio," *Aparchai. Nuove ricerche e studi sulla Magna Grecia e Sicilia antica in onore di Paolo Enrico Arias* 1 (Pisa, 1982), pp. 121–22.

Guzzo, P. G., *La Parola del Passato* 28 (1973), p. 303.

Martelli, M., *Il commercio etrusco arcaico* (Rome, 1985), pp. 216, 222, 228.

Parise Badoni, F., *Ceramica campane a figure nere* (Florence, 1968), pp. 26–34.

Sabbione, C., *Atti del venticinquesimo convegno di studi sulla Magna Grecia, Taranto 1985* (Taranto, 1986), p. 232.

———, *Santuari della Magna Grecia in Calabria* (Naples, 1996), p. 15.

Spadea, R., *Bollettino d'Arte* 79, 88 (1994), pp. 22–24.

The Etruscans on Corsica, by Luigi Donati

Colonna, G., "Nuove prospettive sulla storia etrusca tra Alalia e Cuma," *Atti secondo Congresso Internazionale Etrusco, Firenze 1985* (Rome, 1989), pp. 361–74.

Cristofani, M., *Etruschi e altre genti dell'Italia preromana, La 'lettera' di Pech Maho, Aleria e i traffici del V secolo a.C.* (Rome, 1996), pp. 83–96.

Gras, M., *Trafics tyrrhéniens archaïques* (Rome, 1985).

Jehasse, J., and L. Jehasse, "La nécropole préromaine d'Aléria," *Gallia*, suppl. 25 (Paris, 1973).

———, "Les importations attiques à Aleria et leur significations," *Grecs et Ibères au IV siècle av. J.C.* (Paris, 1989), pp. 377–84.

Martelli, M, and M. Cristofani, "Aléria et l'Etrurie à travers les nouvelles données des fouilles de Populonia," *Archeologia Corsa* 6–7 (1981–82), pp. 5–10.

Le rotte nel Mar Tirreno. Populonia e l'emporio di Aleria in Corsica (Piombino, 2001).

The Etruscans in Sardinia, by Paolo Bernardini

Bernardini, Paolo, R. D'Oriano, and P. G. Spanu, eds., *Phoinikes b Shrdn = I Fenici in Sardegna. Nuove Acquisizioni*, exh. cat. (Oristano, Antiquarium Arborense, 1997).

———, and C. Tronchetti, "La Sardegna, gli Etruschi e i Greci," *La Civiltà Nuragica* (Milan, 1990), pp. 264–82.

Gras, M., *Trafics Tyrrhèniens Archaiques* (Rome, 1985), esp. pp. 113–252.

Moscati, S., P. Bartoloni, and S. F. Bondì, "La penetrazione fenice e punica in Sardegna. Trent'anni dopo," *Memorie dell'Accademia dei Lincei*, ser. 9, 9, 1 (Rome, 1997).

Tronchetti, C., *I Sardi. Traffici, Relazioni, Ideologie nella Sardegna arcaica* (Milan, 1988).

———, "La Sardegna e gli Etruschi," *Mediterranean Archaeology* 1 (1988), pp. 66–82.

Zucca, R., *I rapporti di scambio tra Etruschi e Sardi. Atti del secondo congresso internazionale etrusco* (Rome, 1989), pp. 1073–82.

The Etruscans in Sicily, by Rosa Maria Albanese Procelli

Ampolo, C., "Greci d'Occidente, Etruschi, Cartaginesi: circolazione di beni e di uomini," *Atti del trentatresimo convegno di studi sulla Magna Grecia, Taranto 1993* (Taranto, 1994), pp. 223–52.

Camporeale, Giovannangelo, "La vocazione marittima degli Etruschi," *Gli Etruschi e l'Europa* (Paris and Milan, 1992), pp. 44–53.

Colonna, G., "La Sicilia e il Tirreno nel V e IV secolo," *Kokalos* 26–27, 1 (1980–81), pp. 157–83.

Il commercio etrusco arcaico. Atti dell'Incontro di Studio, 5–7 dicembre 1983 (Rome, 1985).

Gras, M., *Grafics tyrrhéniens archaïques* (Rome, 1985).

———, *La Méditerranée archaïque* (Paris, 1995).

———, "I commerci marittimi," *Nuove Effemeridi* 56, 2 (1999), pp. 38ff.

Hase, F. W. v., "Il bucchero etrusco a Cartagine," *Produzione artigianale ed esportazione nel mondo antico. Il bucchero etrusco*, M. Bonghi Jovino, ed. (Milan, 1993), pp. 187–94.

Rasmussen, T. B., *Bucchero Pottery from Southern Etruria* (Cambridge, 1979).

Torelli, M., "L'incontro con gli etruschi," *I Greci in Occidente*, G. Pugliese Carratelli, ed. (Milan, 1996), pp. 567–76.

Weber, T., *Bronzekannen* (Frankfurt am Main, 1983).

For discoveries of Etruscan materials after 1985:

Allegro, N., et al., "Himera 1989–1993: ricerche dell'Istituto di Archeologia nell'area della città," *Kokalos* 39–40, 2, 2 (1993–94), pp. 1119–33.

Brea, L. Bernabò, and M. Cavalier, *Meligunìs Lipára 7* (Palermo, 1994).

———, M. Cavalier, and F. Villard, *Meligunìs Lipára 9* (Palermo, 1998).

Di Stefano, G., "Il relitto di Punta Braccetto (Camarina), gli emporia e i relitti di età arcaica lungo la costa meridionale della Sicilia," *Kokalos* 39–40, 2, 2 (1993–94), pp. 111–33.

———, and R. Panvini, "Contributo alla conoscenza di un centro indigeno ellenizzato presso Caltabellotta (Agrigento)," *Quaderni Messina* 2 (1986–87), pp. 105–9.

Di terra in terra, exh. cat. (Palermo, Museo Archeologico regionale di Palermo, 1991).

Greco, C., "Note di topografia soluntina: saggi di scavo sul promontorio di Sòlanto," *Kokalos* 39–40, 2, 2 (1993–94), pp. 1165–76.

Kaenel, Ch. Dehl v., *Die archaische Keramik aus dem Malophoros-Heiligtum in Selinunt* (Berlin, 1995).

Lentini, M. C., "Naxos nel quadro dei rapporti tra Egeo e Tirreno: gli apporti delle esplorazioni più recenti," *Atti del ventiseisimo convegno di studi sulla Magna Grecia, Taranto 1986* (Taranto, 1987), pp. 415–32.

Palermo punica, exh. cat. (Palermo, Museo Archeologico Regionale Antonino Salinas, 1998).

Pelagatti, P., "Paolo Orsi, Biagio Pace e la necropoli orientale di Camarina," *Magna Grecia* 31, 4/6 (1996), pp. 9ff.

Spigo, G. Bacci, "Aspetti della ceramica arcaica dello Stretto," *Atti del ventiseisimo convegno di studi sulla Magna Grecia, Taranto 1986* (Taranto, 1987), pp. 247–74.

Tigano, G., "Archeologia a Milazzo: nuove acquisizioni," *Kokalos* 39–40, 2, 1 (1993–94), pp. 1059–85.

Vassallo, S., "Ricerche nella necropoli orientale di Himera in località Pestavecchia," *Kokalos* 39–40, 2, 2 (1993–94), pp. 1243–55.

———, "Il territorio di Himera in età arcaica," *Kokalos* 42 (1996), pp. 199–223.

Photography Credits

Archivio Fotografico Antiquarium Comunale, Rome, pp. 221, 230 (above), 231–32

Archivio Fotografico Musei Capitolini, Rome, pp. 45, 82

Azienda Promozione Turistica di Reggio Calabria, p. 269

Museo Archeologico dell'Alto Adige, Bolzano, and Foto Marco Samadelli, pp. 156 (above), 157 (below)

Musée Archéologique Jérôme Carcopino, Fort de Matra 20270, Aleria, pp. 274–79

Museo Archeologico Provinciale Sigismondo Castromediano di Lecce, pp. 262, 264

Museo Civico Archeologico di Bologna, pp. 1, 115, 169, 170, 178, 181 (right), 182, 187

Museo Civico di Foggia, pp. 263 (below), 266 (below)

Museo Guarnacci, Volterra, pp. 11, 83

Smith, Mark Eduard, pp. 12–15, 19–22, 24–25, 50, 66, 79, 101, 192–95, 199, 200–205, 208–11, 218 (below), 230 (below), 304–5

Soprintendenza Archeologica Beni Culturali ed Ambientali Sezione Archeologica, Palermo, pp. 298 (above), 299

Soprintendenza Archeologica del Piemonte, Turin, by permission of the Ministero per i Beni e le Attività Culturali, pp. 147, 152–55

Soprintendenza Archeologica della Basilicata, Potenza, by permission of the Ministero per i Beni e le Attività Culturali, pp. 252–59

Soprintendenza Archeologica della Calabria, Reggio Calabria, by permission of the Ministero per i Beni e le Attività Culturali, pp. 268–73

Soprintendenza Archeologica della Liguria, by permission of the Ministero per i Beni e le Attività Culturali, pp. 159–62, 165, 167

Soprintendenza Archeologica della Lombardia, Milan, by permission of the Ministero per i Beni e le Attività Culturali, pp. 148–51, 154 (above), 155 (above), 157 (above)

Soprintendenza Archeologica della Puglia, Taranto, by permission of the Ministero per i Beni e le Attività Culturali, pp. 260, 263 (above), 265 (above)

Soprintendenza Archeologica della Toscana, Florence, by permission of the Ministero per i Beni e le Attività Culturali, pp. 8–9, 28, 33, 35–37, 43 (left), 44, 46–47, 49, 52, 58, 60, 71–75, 85, 106–7, 110, 117

Soprintendenza Archeologica delle Provincie di Napoli e Caserta, by permission of the Ministero per i Beni e le Attività Culturali, pp. 233, 261, 265 (below), 266–67 (above)

Soprintendenza Archeologica per il Veneto, Padua, by permission of the Ministero per i Beni e le Attività Culturali, pp. 130–145

Soprintendenza Archeologica per l'Etruria Meridionale, Villa Giulia, Rome, by permission of the Ministero per i Beni e le Attività Culturali, pp. 2, 6, 26–27, 30–31, 39, 40–42, 43 (right), 51, 55–57, 59, 61, 65, 68–70, 76, 84, 220, 224–27, 282

Soprintendenza Archeologica per l'Umbria, Perugia, by permission of the Ministero per i Beni e le Attività Culturali, pp. 196–98, 205

Soprintendenza Archeologica per le Marche, Ancona, by permission of the Ministero per i Beni e le Attività Culturali, pp. 213 (right), 215–17, 218 (above)

Soprintendenza Archeologica per le Provincie di Cagliari e Oristano, Cagliari, by permission of the Ministero per i Beni e le Attività Culturali, pp. 281–91

Soprintendenza Archeologica per le Provincie di Sassari e Nuoro, Sassari, by permission of the Ministero per i Beni e le Attività Culturali, p. 280

Soprintendenza per i Beni Archeologici dell'Emilia Romagna, by permission of the Ministero per i Beni e le Attività Culturali, pp. 175–77, 179, 181 (left), 183–86, 188, 191

Soprintendenza per I Beni Culturali ed Ambientali, Caltanisetta, Sezione III/Beni Archeologici, by permission of the Assessorato Regionale dei Beni Culturali e Ambientali e P.I., pp. 292–93, 296, 298 (below), 301–3

The publishers should be excused if, because of all the independent authors contributing to this volume, we have omitted or erroneously cited a source.